twenty-first-century American students and the Russians they study, I am excited by the opportunities Lisa Paul's moving and inspiring story presents. Reading of the impassioned efforts of an American student, particularly one motivated by her personal faith, to help a Soviet dissident gain the medical assistance she so desperately needed, will help to bridge those gaps, as a far-away culture becomes infinitely closer and more comprehensible through the story of these two very human and deeply impressive women."

— Dr. Judith E. Kalb, Associate Professor of Russian and Comparative Literature, University of South Carolina; author of *Russia's Rome: Imperial Visions, Messianic Dreams, 1890-1940.*

Lisa Paul has written a powerful memoir about hope, courage, and faith—the faith that one person's actions can still make a difference in the world. Through her devotion to the Soviet era human rights activist, Inna Meiman, Paul challenged a totalitarian system and moved leaders of the U.S. government to action. I well remember meeting Inna Meiman and her husband Naum in Moscow in 1986. She was an extraordinary woman, firm in her convictions about human rights and human dignity, and paying a dreadful price for her beliefs. Lisa Paul, who began her friendship with Inna as a young college student from the American Midwest, carried Inna's case to the highest corridors of power and used the power of her own moral integrity to change history. The lessons of this book are urgently needed today.

— Dr. Alan Mittleman, Chair, Department of Jewish Thought, The Jewish Theological Seminary; author of *Hope in a Democratic Age*

"*Swimming in the Daylight* is a story about universal human rights values as portrayed in the plight and heroism of Inna Meiman, an internationally famed and revered Soviet *refusenik*, and Lisa Paul, who embodied the not-so-universal but eternal virtue and religious imperative of rescue. The threats to the abridgement of freedom in today's Russian Federation, throughout the former Soviet Union, and the world make this story of vital interest to the same readers who were among the millions of supporters of the Soviet Jewry Movement."

— Micah Naftalin, of blessed memory, former National Director and CEO of the Union of Councils for Jews in the Former Soviet Union

SWIMMING
IN THE DAYLIGHT

SWIMMING
IN THE DAYLIGHT

AN AMERICAN STUDENT,
A SOVIET-JEWISH DISSIDENT,
AND THE GIFT OF HOPE

LISA C. PAUL

Skyhorse Publishing

Skyhorse Publishing books may be purchased in bulk at special discounts for sales promotion, corporate gifts, fund-raising, or educational purposes. Special editions can also be created to specifications. For details, contact the Special Sales Department, Skyhorse Publishing, 307 West 36th Street, 11th Floor, New York, NY 10018 or info@skyhorsepublishing.com.

www.skyhorsepublishing.com

10 9 8 7 6 5 4 3 2 1

Library of Congress Cataloging-in-Publication Data

Paul, Lisa C.

 Swimming in the daylight : an American student, a Soviet-Jewish dissident, and the gift of hope / Lisa C. Paul.

    p. cm.

 ISBN 978-1-61608-203-1 (hardcover : alk. paper)

 1. Paul, Lisa C. 2. Meiman, Inna Kitrosskaya. 3. Meiman, Inna Kitrosskaya--Health. 4. Americans--Soviet Union--Biography. 5. College students--United States--Biography. 6. Jews--Soviet Union--Biography. 7. Dissidents--Soviet Union--Biography. 8. Refuseniks--Soviet Union--Biography. 9. Immigrants--United States--Biography. 10. Friendship--Case studies. I. Title.

 DK275.A1P38 2010

 947'.0049240092--dc22

 [B]

                              2010035787

Printed in the United States of America

To the Soviet dissidents and Jews of the 1970s–'80s
and all those who fought for their freedom.

And to Jamie, Catherine, and Ross—
the beat of my heart.

In loving memory of my parents,
Helen Hickey Paul and Jerry Paul.

Contents

Hope is the thing with feathers
That perches in the soul
And sings the tune
Without the words
And never stops at all.

—Emily Dickinson

PART I

MOSCOW

CHAPTER

1

The Barter System

> We all live with the objective
> of being happy; our lives are
> all different and yet the same.
> —Anne Frank

I bought a jar of Nescafé coffee for Andrei Sakharov. I really did. Not that I had any idea when I bought the jar in a foreigner-only store in Moscow that it would end up in his cup 250 miles away in Gorky, a city where Soviet authorities had banished him and his wife, Elena Bonner, four years earlier. Rather, as I stood in line waiting to pay for the Nescafé, all I knew was that it would pay for one Russian-language lesson with my teacher, Inna Kitrosskaya Meiman.

The day that I brought the two jars of Nescafé to Inna, she smiled and said in a hushed voice, "Oh, excellent, Leeza, I will send one to our friend in Gorky." *Could she actually be referring to the famous Soviet dissident Andrei Sakharov?* I wondered, taken aback. While I did not want her to think I was too naive to understand her reference, I had to ask if she actually meant Sakharov.

Inna, in a manner that seemed ordinary rather than peculiar—and clearly intended to keep "Big Brother" from listening—turned on the television behind her, cranked up the volume, and only then whispered, "Yes, that's exactly who I mean."

2

Swiftly and deliberately changing the subject, she said, "Let's begin your lesson." Returning both the television and her voice to a normal volume, she asked, "Did you prepare your assignment for today?"

I began taking Russian language lessons from Inna in September 1984, just a few weeks into my second year living in Moscow, where I worked as a nanny for an American family. This was at a time when the Cold War between the United States and the Soviet Union was as chilly as ever. Tense political disputes and confrontations between these two global superpowers and archenemies had raged since the end of World War II, against the backdrop of an ever-escalating nuclear arms race. In such a hostile climate, it was rare for an American college student to actually live in Moscow—even those, like me, who were studying the Russian language and about the Soviet Union. When the opportunity arose for me to work for Joan and Paul Smith in Moscow (Paul ran the Russian office for Caterpillar Tractor Company) as the nanny for their two young daughters, Laura and Kjirsten, I jumped at what I considered a chance of a lifetime.

The Soviet government did not allow American families living in Moscow to hire local Russians to watch their children. While there had been some progress since the pre–World War II days under Joseph Stalin, when Soviet citizens who engaged in unauthorized contacts with foreigners were actually arrested, imprisoned, and sometimes shot, Soviet officials' continued distrust of foreigners had not radically changed. The half dozen or so American families in Moscow who had nannies in the early '80s recruited them through contacts in the States. I heard about the job with the Smiths in my Russian-language class at the University of Minnesota, where Paul studied ten years before I.

As for meeting Inna, Michelle Lynch—my friend and also a nanny for an American family—gave me her telephone number. She studied with Inna the year before, during my first year in

Moscow. Michelle arranged for me to take her place as Inna's student when she returned to the States in June 1984.

There was no inherent risk to an American who engaged in contact with a Russian, as long as the purpose of that contact was legal and not anti-Soviet. The Russian, however, faced the definite risk of being watched, questioned, and threatened by the KGB (the Soviet national security agency) for such interactions. Therefore, Americans were necessarily discreet about their contact with Russians, and thus the information Michelle initially gave me about Inna was sparse. I knew that Inna had received her doctoral degree in English education from the Moscow Institute of Foreign Languages and taught there for many years until she was forced to quit her job soon after applying to emigrate from the Soviet Union in 1979. The government denied her a visa, and thus she became a *refusenik*, Russian slang for someone who had been refused permission by the Soviet government to emigrate. Michelle told me Inna had an operation in October 1983 to remove a tumor on the back of her neck and that she didn't believe Inna was receiving any additional medical treatment. When I met Inna in late August 1984, she was teaching Russian to a half dozen Americans, including journalists, the wife of an American diplomat, and teachers at the Anglo-American School (the school for children of Americans and other foreigners living in Moscow).

"Oh, yes, Leeza, I have been expecting your call," Inna said in a friendly, spirited voice when I contacted her about taking Russian lessons. She asked if I understood Russian and I replied *nemnoshko*— a little—not wanting to overstate my Russian-language ability and then disappoint her if she took me on as her student. Then Inna, speaking in English, suggested we should meet. "It is important for a teacher to know a student's ability before teaching an actual lesson," she explained.

We agreed to meet at eleven o'clock the following Saturday morning at Inna's apartment. She said she would be at the Osepenko

Street trolley stop waiting for me, a twenty-minute trolley ride from my apartment on Serpukhovsky Boulevard. She began to describe herself, then stopped and said, "Not to worry, Leeza. I will recognize you, an American."

I set out to meet Inna on a typical Saturday—my day off. When I woke up just before eight o'clock the girls were already happily watching a Bugs Bunny cartoon on a video sent by their uncle in the States. Laura, who was five years old, had long, fiery, light red hair and a cluster of freckles on each cheek. Kjirsten, older by a year and taller by an inch, had long, golden-wheat blonde hair and as many freckles as her sister. They were sitting together on a recliner like two peas in a pod, eating their Rice Krispies, shipped as part of the family's grocery order from Denmark.

After promising Joan and Paul that I would be back that evening to babysit the girls, I caught the number 32 trolley at 10:30. It took me directly north toward the center of the city and into the slender streets of one of Moscow's oldest districts, Zamoskvorechye, which means "behind the Moscow River."

At least a dozen people were standing on the sidewalk when the trolley approached the Osepenko Street stop. At first, I didn't see a "short woman with dark hair, wearing a black coat and white scarf," as Inna had described herself, but as I stepped down off the trolley into a slight drizzle, my eyes connected with the sparkling brown eyes of a middle-aged woman who smiled at me and spoke quietly in Russian: "Are you Leeza?"

"*Da*," I replied, saying the easiest word in the Russian language. "Yes."

"And I am Inna. It is very nice to meet you."

Inna was just an inch or two over five feet and stocky. Her black hair was sprinkled with gray and was short, brushed back off her forehead and in place behind her ears. The damp air created round, ruby-like circles on each side of her wide and square face. She looked pleasant, healthy.

"Please, follow me. My apartment is just around the corner from here," she said, turning away from me and walking north on Osepenko Street.

Short and to the point was the standard routine when meeting a Russian in public. The objective was to blend in and go about your business rather than calling undue attention to yourself, since you never knew whether anyone was watching.

We crossed a small bridge over a canal and then turned right. Had we continued walking north a few blocks, we would have come to the Moskvoretsky Bridge, which arches over the Moscow River and reaches into the east end of Red Square, which is anchored by St. Basil's Cathedral.

As we crossed the street at the middle of the block, Inna spoke for the first time since leaving the trolley stop. She quietly instructed me not to say anything until we were inside her apartment building. Two elderly women sitting on a bench next to the entrance stopped talking and took notice of us as we walked by. I looked straight ahead to avoid making eye contact with them.

Inside, we took an elevator to the fifth floor and then stepped out into a dim hallway. Her apartment was just to the right. She opened the door and made sure I had followed her in before shutting it behind us. Then she hung up her coat, took mine, and hung it on the hook next to hers. She gave me a pair of slippers as she put on a pair of her own, a gesture with which Russians greeted guests to their home. Just then a man with white wispy hair, who appeared to be much older than Inna, at least in his mid- to late sixties, walked into the hallway, which was illuminated only by the light of day coming in from an adjoining room.

"Naum, this is Leeza. She is Michelle's friend. And Leeza, this is my husband, Naum."

"A pleasure to meet you," he said in English, which he spoke in a choppy, unsure fashion. "How is our Michelle?" His bushy, arched eyebrows moved up into his forehead as he smiled.

"She is back in Texas and just found a job. She asked me to give you her very best greetings," I replied. Inna and Naum smiled fondly, as would grandparents hearing news about their grand-daughter. As we reminisced about Michelle, I was impressed by all they knew about her and by their obvious affection for her.

"Naum, Leeza is also a nanny for an American family," Inna said, changing the subject to me. "Are they diplomats?"

"No, I work for a businessman," I answered. This fact seemed of interest to them both.

"What does he do?" Inna asked.

"He runs the office for Caterpillar Tractor Company. He and his wife, Joan, are starting their fifth year here. They have two girls, Kjirsten and Laura."

We engaged in a few more pleasantries and then Naum reached for his coat, explaining he was going to the market. Naum shook my hand and said, "I look forward to seeing you again."

As he shut the door, Inna asked me in Russian, "Are you hungry? Let's have a bowl of soup. Come, follow me to the kitchen." I followed her a few feet through the hallway, which was narrowed on one side by floor-to-ceiling shelves packed with books, then a few more feet into the kitchen. A small and narrow room with a door leading out to a balcony, it was pungent with the smell of garlic and cabbage simmering in a soup stock on the stove.

"Would you like coffee or tea?"

"Coffee, please," I replied in Russian, aware she was assessing my ability to speak her language.

She took bowls and cups from the cupboard and set them on a small table. "Please bring the bread over from the counter and the sour cream from the refrigerator for the soup," Inna instructed. "Ah, my students like to bring me your American goodies," she explained as she noticed my eyes watching her scoop two spoonfuls from a jar of Nescafé into a cup. "I have been spoiled by the taste of this coffee. It is so much better than ours."

After we both sat down, she commented that I seemed to be very comfortable with my conversational Russian and asked how many years I had been studying the language.

I told her I had studied a year in college and then attended a summer Russian-language school in Middlebury, Vermont, before I came to Moscow in the fall of 1983.

"And your Russian accent is also good," she observed. I often received that compliment from Russians, even when I first arrived in Moscow. Perhaps it was because the melodic sound of the Russian language has always appealed to me. I feel an intuitive cadence whenever I speak it.

"Do you have any Russian ancestors?" Inna asked.

"No. My mom is one hundred percent Irish, and my dad is mostly German."

"Ah, interesting. Tell me more about yourself, Leeza, such as where you are from, about your family, why you came to Moscow."

I told her about my hometown, Appleton, Wisconsin, and about my two sisters and two brothers. Then she asked how old my parents were and if they worked.

"My father is fifty-five and works as a maintenance mechanic at a technical college and my mother will be fifty-four in October. She works as a teacher's aide at a high school," I replied.

Inna told me that all of her family lived in Moscow—her son, Lev Kitrossky, his wife, Marina, and their two young children; her two brothers; and a sister and her husband and their two children. She was very interested to know the reason I wanted to live in Russia, which was often the subject of fascination for many Russians who I met in Moscow; Inna was no exception.

I briefly told her the events that had taken place in my life the last three years, beginning with a class my sophomore year of college that sparked my interest to learn all I could about the Soviet Union, and about my studies and travels to Leningrad, Vilnius,

Kiev, and Moscow that followed. I explained that I learned about the nanny job in my Russian-language class a year and a half earlier.

"And here I am," I smiled.

"You have been busy," she exclaimed, then paused for a moment. "So, you have not graduated from college?" she asked.

"I still have at least one year to go," I replied, "But obviously I can learn more about the Soviet Union living here than I can in a classroom in Minneapolis. Plus, it's an adventure."

Inna smiled. "Many of my students say they come here for the adventure. This is so funny to me. That is, you Americans consider Moscow an adventure. You can go anywhere in the world—Paris, Italy, Africa. Ah, yes, for you an adventure," she paused, and then reflected, "with a happy ending. You get to go home."

Inna cleared the bowls from the table, offered more coffee, and then took on the more formal tone of a teacher.

"What are your expectations of our lessons?" she asked.

I paused for a moment and then said, "I want to improve my reading and writing skills. I'd like to test into at least third-year Russian when I return and maybe even fourth."

"So you are a serious student," Inna observed. I nodded in agreement. Then she handed me a Russian-language textbook and asked me to read a couple of paragraphs aloud. "Go ahead, don't be nervous," she said.

I stumbled midway through the second paragraph, looked up at Inna, and said in English, "I don't feel confident reading out loud."

"But you are doing quite well," she said encouragingly. "Please continue."

After I read a few more minutes and she had sufficient time to evaluate me, she said, "Now, let's talk about the lessons." She described her format as follows: begin with reviewing homework, then on to a new lesson and assignment, and end with a discussion of topics of interest. She asked me to come prepared each week.

"This is not always true of my American students, because they are so busy and have so many distractions here," she explained. "But you know it is better for both of us if you review the assigned materials. That way we will not waste our time."

I assured her I would prepare for each lesson. Then I asked her about her fees.

"There are many things money cannot buy for me here. I feel I can ask you because you are young and may not find my request an imposition," she said. "If and as you are able, I would like you to bring me a bottle of olive oil, which is sold in the *Beriozka* stores that only you can shop in, Leeza, with your American dollars. It is better for my health to cook with olive oil instead of lard. You can also bring me jars of Nescafé from the *Beriozka*. This you may consider a frivolous request, but as I told you, I have become accustomed to this coffee."

I considered her proposal for a moment, then told her it wouldn't be a problem for me to bring those items for her. Our barter system agreed upon, we made plans to begin the next Monday afternoon at two o'clock.

The Courier

Imagine how much good we could accomplish,
how much the cause of peace would be served,
if more individuals and families from our
respective countries could come to know
each other in a personal way.
—President Ronald Reagan,
Geneva Summit, 1985

I lived two lives in Moscow that were completely separate from each other—my "American life" and my "Russian life." Like all foreigners in Moscow, the Smiths lived in a designated apartment building that was fenced off from the Russian apartments around it. You could only enter the gate after being approved by a Russian militiaman, who guarded the entrance twenty-four hours a day, seven days a week. The official Soviet explanation was that the militiaman was there to protect foreigners who resided in the building from crime— a statement that contradicted the Soviet propaganda that no crime existed in the Soviet workers' paradise. Everyone knew, however, that the real reason for the fence and guard was to deter Russians from visiting anyone who lived there, as all guests were required to give their name so a record could be made and reported to the appropriate Soviet authorities.

This was part of the general Soviet policy to restrict its citizens from accessing information from the West. Soviet citizens were not allowed to subscribe to Western publications or radio broadcasts from the West. Thus, programming such as that provided by Voice of America and Radio Free Europe/Radio Liberty were jammed. Foreign mail was also routinely opened, read, and sometimes not delivered. International telephone calls were guaranteed to be monitored.

My "American life" with the Smiths was comfortable and enjoyable. Their apartment had been remodeled by Caterpillar and contained modern furniture and appliances (washer, dryer, and dishwasher)—all typical in an American apartment but not in the neighboring Russian flats. The Smiths' residence, actually two Russian apartments combined, was still small by American standards. Even so, I had my own bedroom. My diet consisted of packaged, canned, and preserved American food shipped in from Denmark, supplemented by fresh dairy, produce, and meat that Joan was able to buy at the *Beriozka* along with whatever might be available at the local bread store or market.

Best of all, the Smiths treated me like an older sister in the family rather than an employee. I considered myself lucky to work for and live with them. My original plan when I arrived in the beginning of October 1983 was to stay until June or July of 1984. It was Paul's fourth—and supposedly final—year working for Caterpillar in Moscow. However, in the spring of 1984, Caterpillar asked Paul to stay in Moscow for one more year. I had an ideal situation— a modern apartment in the middle of Moscow where I lived with a great American family and plenty of free time to pursue my own interests—so I told Joan I wanted to stay on with them. They were all happy to have me stay and, with that, I decided to remain in Moscow for another year.

While my nanny duties were never onerous, the amount of free time I had during my second year was greater than during my first since Joan and Paul were, to put it mildly, burned out. During their four years in Moscow, many Americans and others from the West with whom they had become friends had come and gone. Their energy to meet people and socialize during their fifth and final year was low, and they were often content to stay home and be with the girls.

My "Russian life" was busy. I spent a lot of time with Daphne— my one friend from the previous year who was still in Moscow. From Amsterdam, Daphne worked as a nanny for a diplomat in the Dutch Embassy. I had introduced her to a group of Russians— Andrei, Volodya, "Uvol" (a pseudonym for "Yuri"), and Natasha, whom I met the year before through my American nanny friend Elizabeth. She was given Andrei's name and number by a professor of hers, who met him when lecturing at Moscow University in the late 1970s.

Andrei was in his mid- to late forties and worked with computers. He always wore a suit coat and tie with pants that never matched the fabric or color of the jacket. His chin and jaw were covered with a beard that crept up chaotically onto his cheeks. He was divorced and lived with his daughter, Anya, who was seventeen. Volodya was in his late twenties, lived with his mother, and was a sickly type. He often complained of cold, allergy, or flu symptoms and discussed in detail the homeopathic "family" remedy he used to treat a specific ailment. Natasha and Uvol, married, were both artists. Uvol had a large build and was close to six and a half feet tall. His face was big and wide and often covered with an ear-to-ear grin. He had a full head of hair, although it was just beginning to recede from his forehead. Natasha, a foot and a half shorter than Uvol, was strikingly attractive. She usually wore her long, full hair loose instead of clipped back and opted for bangs that fell just above her eyelashes. Her Russian nationality was complemented with dark features that would best be described as Middle Eastern. Both Uvol and Natasha were outgoing and good-natured. Natasha's dream was to be a fashion designer, and she often showed me designs of modern, Western-looking apparel that she had sketched.

Daphne and I saw this group every couple of weeks, initially at Andrei's apartment. Andrei had the standard three-room Russian apartment: the first room was the kitchen; the second a bedroom, which was Anya's; and the third was a room that functioned as a living room, dining room, and at the far end, separated by a bookshelf, Andrei's bedroom. A large piano occupied part of the "living room," and an ornate glass chandelier hung from the center of the ceiling, which gave the room a Victorian feel. The walls were covered by paintings, large and small, most done by Andrei's friends. A typical night at Andrei's consisted of eating, drinking (usually vodka, wine, or Soviet champagne), talking, laughing, and drinking some more.

I met several new Russians at the beginning of my second year, courtesy of some of my American friends who, like Michelle and Elizabeth, had returned to the States in the summer of 1984. Because I worked for an American businessman, my mail was routed to the U.S. Commercial Office via the American Embassy in Helsinki, Finland, and then delivered in the diplomatic pouch to Moscow, bypassing Soviet censorship. I became an international mail carrier of sorts—receiving a letter from the States addressed to me with a letter to a Russian inside the envelope, and then calling the Russian addressee from a pay phone to arrange delivery (Americans assumed the telephones in our apartments were bugged by the KGB). Next, I would deliver the letter to the Russian's apartment, stay for a while to chat, and arrange another meeting to pick up the return letter to send back to the States.

I traveled around the city with ease—by bus, trolley, and, most often, metro. The Dobryninskaya metro station, which was just two stops southeast of the more centrally located Kievskaya station, was about a half-mile walk from my apartment. It was not unusual for the travel time to my destination to take an hour or more, for it included walking to a metro station, taking the metro, often having to transfer to another line to get to my stop, and then walking from there to the Russian's apartment. Even though I would occasionally take a taxi home after these visits, I usually opted for taking the less expensive metro, which was clean and safe, even late at night.

In my role as an international courier, I began to form my own friendships with the Russian addressees. This became especially true of Galya and Vera, who were friends with my American friends Karen and Elizabeth. They had met the year before while walking from a metro station to a soccer game. They asked directions from Galya and Vera, who were initially reluctant to talk to them. They later explained that they had never before spoken to an American. The four quickly hit it off and decided to sit together at the game, and then agreed to meet again and became friends.

At least a few times a month I visited Galya and Vera at Galya's apartment, which she shared with her mother, Victoria, and their large standard poodle, Godfrey. Both Galya and Vera were easygoing and of gentle spirit, and so at ease with each other that you might think they were sisters. They looked like they had been cut from the same cloth—each in her early twenties, of petite height and slim frame. They differed, however, in their facial features. Galya's long and narrow nose dominated her slender face, and her poufy, brownish hair fell just above her shoulders. Vera's face was oval and her cheeks plump. Her short, black hairstyle could be construed as a tribute to any member of the Beatles at the peak of their career in the 1960s.

They were both talented artists. Galya had worked in an art studio, but the paint fumes aggravated her asthma and caused her difficulty breathing. She had recently been deemed "disabled" by the government and was granted a monthly pension. As a hobby, she and Vera painted wooden eggs with traditional Russian Orthodox religious scenes. Both women were taking classes (in a room with less fumes or better ventilation than the art studio) to learn how to restore paintings and murals in old churches and buildings.

My nights with Galya and Vera were usually low-key. At first, it was difficult to communicate because neither of them spoke English, and my Russian was far from fluent. But I relied on my Russian dictionary, worked my way through words I didn't know, and improved my conversational skills with each visit.

I was also spending time with Igor, or "Gary," as he preferred to be called. When Elizabeth gave me his telephone number, she told me he was a black marketer but assured me he would never ask to buy anything from me. At that time, the black market economy was thriving in Moscow. The trading on the market was usually done by young Russian men who hung out at tourist attractions—such as Red Square or the Bolshoi Theater—and bought Levis, Nikes, cigarettes, and Walkmans from foreigners with Soviet rubles. Having acquired these items, they would sell them to Russians for a huge markup, since the demand for such goods was high and the supply low. Western currency was also traded on the black market. Instead of obtaining the official rate of one ruble for one dollar, a black marketer would pay at least five rubles for a dollar, the logic being that items bought with dollars—such as electronics, books, liquor, and clothing at the *Beriozka* stores—would have greater value when sold to Muscovites for rubles.

Gary was a handsome nineteen-year-old with black hair cut in such a way that he would have looked completely at home on the cover of a J. Crew catalog. He dressed "American," as he liked to say—that is, he always wore Levis and usually a white or blue oxford shirt, the fruits of his own trading on the black market. He was very candid about his "work" on the black market the first time I met him and made it clear he would not mix his business with our friendship. That was fine with me, as it was illegal for a foreigner in Moscow to buy or sell items on the black market. He spoke English well enough for us to carry on a decent conversation. He always noticed when I used a slang word, asked me what it meant, and usually carried a piece of paper and pen with him so he could write it down.

One evening we went to a popular Russian restaurant that served pizza, which might have been the only restaurant in Moscow at the time that did so. Gary was very frustrated because there was a long line to get in. As we waited, he told me how he would design the restaurant if it were his. Then he talked about the food he would serve and the rock music he would play. He told me it was his dream to have his own restaurant someday but doubted it would ever be possible because he lived in a place that was, as he said, "the opposite of capitalism."

A full hour later we sat down at the end of a table for six. There was a young couple seated next to us who had finished their dinner and were smoking, drinking wine, and talking. When I commented to Gary that he had become quiet, he looked around and then back at me and said, "It is a Stalin tradition to listen."

I asked him to tell me a little about his business, explaining I had heard many different quotes on how much a carton of Marlboro cigarettes could sell for on the black market and asking him how much he charged.

"I pay twenty-four rubles for carton and sell carton to Russian for forty [at that time equivalent to about fifty U.S. dollars]," he said. "One pack of American cigarettes is very good bribe. You know, bribes are how Russians get things done, how we survive in this godforsaken place."

The waitress brought us our bottle of wine, and we each took a sip.

"It tastes a little watered down," I observed.

"I know, I live here," Gary answered sarcastically. Then he explained, "In this country, we skim off the top. Our waitress opened bottle in kitchen, poured wine out, poured glass of water into bottle, and then gave to us. By the end of the night, she will take bottles home and sell them for whatever she needs, medication or clothes."

When we finished our meal and the check came, I offered to help pay. This offended Gary. "The man must pay," he insisted. He paid the bill, and we left.

One night, near the end of October, I was invited to Andrei's and was told that Volodya, Natasha, and Uvol would also be there. When Natasha and Uvol arrived an hour later, Natasha looked upset and as if she had been crying. She immediately told us a *babushka*, grandmother, who was not related to either of them but lived in one of the two rooms of their apartment, had died the day before. Natasha burst into tears and explained that she had come to know and like the babushka even though it was inconvenient to share their small apartment with her. Then, through her tears, she explained that at least now they could claim the apartment as their own. She paused for a moment, as if imagining it, and then smiled, but only for a moment, saying that she was going to miss the old babushka, and that brought on more tears. The sudden change in her mood and expressions made us all fall into fits of laugher, and brought on extra teasing from Uvol and Andrei.

It was Uvol and Natasha's passionate love for each other that broke up her first marriage. Sergei, her first husband, did quite well by Soviet standards. They lived in a three-bedroom apartment with a spacious and well-decorated kitchen. When she married Uvol, she and her son, Kostya, moved into Uvol's humble room in the apartment he shared with the babushka.

That explained why I had not been to their apartment previously. It also explained why Natasha did not want to waste any time after the babushka died to invite us all over for a party to celebrate their "inheritance."

The festivities were held in the babushka's room, which was empty except for a collection of furniture in the middle: a small wooden table, a few chairs, and one light stand with a single bulb and no shade. The walls were covered with newspaper, which Uvol explained was put on the wall before a layer of wallpaper, and her room had never made it to the wallpapering stage. Despite the drab decor, the mood was jovial. An abundant supply of wine, champagne, and vodka—which we drank in no particular order—livened things up even more. Natasha, who reveled in her role as hostess, had prepared quite a feast—the classic *stolichny* salad—chopped boiled eggs, potato cubes, carrots, and pickles, sprinkled with dill and mixed generously with mayonnaise—homemade pastries, kolbasa, and bread.

I wandered over into the room that Natasha, Uvol, and Kostya shared before the babushka died. It was an average-sized room, eight feet wide by twelve feet long, but a very small habitat for two adults and one child. There was a small refrigerator and desk by the entrance to the room, and, farther in, a couch that doubled as Kostya's bed. The back third of the room was blocked off by a wood frame partially covered with a blanket; behind it was just enough room for Natasha and Uvol's bed. Natasha came into the room and told me that she was planning to turn the babushka's room into Kostya's room. She also wanted to redecorate the entire apartment, starting with the kitchen—new curtains, a shelf, and yellow paint. Then she said that it would still not be as nice as the one she had with her ex-husband—but it would be all hers!

Natasha and I returned to the babushka's room just as Uvol hooked up a record player that looked like one I had as a child. It was set in a small, suitcase-like box that opened up with a turntable on the bottom. Uvol, a big fan of jazz, had a collection of American jazz classics, including Louis Armstrong's rendition of "What a Wonderful World," which was his favorite song. To this day, I think of him whenever I hear it. He also had an Eagles album and, throughout the night, we listened repeatedly to such songs as "Take it Easy," "Tequila Sunrise," and "Best of My Love."

Andrei offered Uvol and Natasha a toast, beginning by solemnly mentioning the deceased babushka, a tribute to her for bringing us together that evening. This caused Natasha to cry. When she composed herself, she took over the toast from Andrei—a bold move since Russian men were typically the designated toast-givers. She made it clear that the toast should only be in honor of the babushka, then raised her glass and asked us all to wish the babushka eternal peace.

That evening was the beginning of many more at Natasha and Uvol's. Within a couple of weeks, Kostya had moved into the babushka's room. Natasha told me he tried to come back into their room a couple of times his first night alone because he was afraid.

In November, Natasha had to petition the regional housing board to prevent the babushka's room from being taken by another occupant. As the review on her petition approached, she grew nervous, hoping that she could convince them that her family needed the extra space and wondering if her 100-ruble bribe would be enough. It was. This, of course, was cause for another party, which was held in Natasha and Uvol's room, which had remained the same as always.

"Natasha, it must be great to have the apartment all to yourselves," I commented.

"Yes, we wonder how we survived before," she acknowledged. Then she whispered to me, "But I have two thousand rubles saved, and someday I want a three-bedroom apartment near the center of the city."

CHAPTER

I Wish I Had Your Worries

> Whatever you may say,
> the body depends on the soul.
> —Nikolai Gogol

Each weekday morning I was up with the girls by seven o'clock helping Joan with the morning routine—getting the girls dressed, fed, and out the door on time with their backpacks and lunch. Then I would commute to my job at the U.S. Embassy with another American who lived on the floor below and who drove his car to work. The Smiths gave me the green light to get a part-time job during my second year as long as it did not interfere with my obligations to them. In September, I started working Monday through Friday, 9:00 AM to 1:00 PM, as an administrative assistant in the consular office. I helped process applications from Soviet citizens applying for visas to travel to the United States as tourists or for business. The job was not exactly demanding, given the Soviet government's tight restrictions on permitting its citizens to travel abroad. The section in the office that processed emigration visas was even slower. Jewish emigration, especially, had slowed dramatically at that time—the Soviets had permitted fewer than 1,000 Jews to leave each year since 1980, compared to allowing more than 50,000 in 1979.

Amid my busy schedule, Mondays with Inna became the place where I slowed down and caught my breath each week. She was always in a pleasant mood and always seemed genuinely interested in how I was and what I had been doing since the last lesson. In those early weeks, I was a diligent student and came prepared for my lessons. The lessons followed the format Inna established when we first met at her apartment: She began by teaching me a rule of Russian grammar, then I read aloud for five minutes or so, and we ended with my favorite part—conversation in Russian about ourselves, our families, and what was happening in the world.

In no time at all, however, my meetings with Inna came to be about so much more than conjugating a Russian verb or learning the plural form of a noun. From the first time I met her, I was captivated by what she had to say and how she said it. It all seemed so important to me. I made a practice of writing down her expressions and stories. I'd write the first two or three letters of a word she said on the palm of my hand under the table so as not to impose any intrusion on the casual nature of our conversations. Then, once in the stairwell of her building, these simple letters would help trigger a sentence or two that I'd write down on a piece of paper, and this sentence would assist me in writing the full expression or story in my journal that night.

In the beginning, our discussions were about ordinary things.

"Leez, do you eat Russian or American here?"

"American," I answered.

"Oh, you eat out of tins," Inna smiled. She'd obviously had enough American students to know that we stocked our cupboards with food shipped in from the States or Europe.

One afternoon, as I was putting on a pair of slippers, Inna gasped in amazement. "How do you Americans keep your white socks so white?" she kidded me. Then she earnestly asked, "Do each of you have your own washing machine in your apartment?"

"Yes, and a dryer," I answered, as Inna shook her head in amazement.

"You know, we could never dress our children in such light colors. How could we keep them clean, washing only by hand?"

"Isn't this fruit beautiful?" Inna exclaimed another afternoon as she cut me a piece of pineapple. "This is only the second or third time I have seen a pineapple in my life."

"Did an American friend bring it for you?"

"No. Believe it or not, I bought it at the local market today. At first there was no line, because people were not sure what it was, but word spread that it was a tropical fruit. Within minutes a long line formed, and they quickly sold out. I bought one for my son and another for my sister, Olga."

She offered me a piece, but I hesitated to accept it. I asked her if she would prefer to share it with Naum. "Oh, no, Leeza, you are here now with me, so let's enjoy it together."

"I wonder what it would be like not to constantly worry about food," Inna remarked. "What would Russians do with so much free time on their hands? In the villages, the people simply live off of what they themselves grow. The store may have dairy and bread products, but in the winter, even those cannot be depended on. Life in the villages is difficult. A village woman in her forties looks as if she is in her sixties, yet she probably won't live to be that old."

I learned about Inna's passion for literature during one discussion we had about American and Russian writers. She had several books by one of her favorite poets, Emily Dickinson. She was also a fan of John Cheever. We discussed twentieth-century Russian writers Anna Akhmatova and Boris Pasternak.

"Do you know Pasternak was awarded the Nobel Prize in Literature for his book *Doctor Zhivago*? But our government did not allow him to accept it, banned the book, and refused to publish it here. I, myself, do not see the danger of this book. The story is about the Russian Revolution, of course, but it is also a romantic story. Our government considers it dangerous, because it is a realistic story about the Revolution—the fighting and deaths and suffering—not one, like official Soviet literature, that only glorifies it. "

"I recently watched the movie on the VCR in my apartment," I told Inna.

"You are so lucky! We cannot see that film or many others," she said. Then her eyes lit up as she added, "Ah, but we can read. Of course, I am not referring to the books sold in our stores. I am referring to those we pass among ourselves in an underground system referred to as *samizdat*. Do you know this word, Leez? It combines two words, 'self' and 'publish.'"

As soon as the third or fourth lesson, I arrived unprepared, having not been quite able to find time to study. I tried to wing it, but couldn't really pull it off, so I confessed, "I'm sorry Inna, but I haven't had any time to myself, and when I did, I was too tired to study. I even feel too tired to speak Russian today. Maybe it would be better if I just came back next Monday."

"You do not have to leave. We can review this material next week. Let's just talk."

She asked me questions about my childhood and my education. I told her I went to a Catholic grade school and then to a public junior high and high school.

"Oh, yes, Irish Catholic, because of your mom," she commented, remembering that my mother was of Irish descent.

"My parents are Jewish, so, of course, so am I, although I do not consider myself a religious person. But my son, Lev, is. He started to study Hebrew after our requests for visas to emigrate were denied. As a result, he became very interested in Judaism and he and his wife are religious."

She asked me what the biggest problem my family had when I was growing up. I thought for a while, and finally answered, "Money, or rather lack of."

"Really? Money seems to be such a problem for Americans."

"My dad was a printer for a small print shop," I explained. "He also worked a couple of nights a week as a bartender, and, with both incomes, he made just enough to cover the basic bills: utilities, the mortgage, car payments."

I told her about a trip our family took the summer before I started third grade. My parents rented a camper and hitched it up to our station wagon, and we drove to Washington, D.C. The first night, my brothers and sisters and I slept in the back of the wagon, while my dad drove as far as he could before stopping to sleep at a rest stop for a few hours.

"We stopped in Pennsylvania and stayed a few days with a friend of my dad's from the Navy. When we finally got to D.C., we camped about thirty minutes outside the city and drove in each day to see the sights. When I was older, I learned that my parents had not saved money for this trip. They simply cashed my dad's paycheck on the Friday we left and let the bills wait until we returned."

"Did you have a house?"

"Yes. We have a two-story, four-bedroom house. My parents live there now with my younger brother, Tom. They have a nice-sized backyard, with a big apple tree with a tree house in it."

"What was your biggest problem growing up?" I asked Inna.

"Food and shelter. I was born in 1932. My brothers, sister, and parents had a single room in an apartment that we shared with five other families, maybe as many as forty people, so you can imagine how crowded the little space that we had was. My sister and I shared one bed. My brothers were next to us in another bed, and my parents slept at the far end of the room behind a curtain. A table was designated in the kitchen for each family, and there was a scheduled time for my mother to cook on two burners on the stove. There was only one bathroom in the apartment, and Saturday morning was our scheduled time to use it for bathing. Each family had their own washbasin hanging on the wall, and my father would take it down, put it in the tub, fill it with water, and then give us each our turn.

"Once, my brother came home from school with a bad report card and my father yelled at him. My brother was so upset that he locked himself in the bathroom and refused to come out. This created a great problem because no one was able to access the bathroom. Finally, after a couple of hours and after my father promised not to punish him, my brother opened the door. He should have been more afraid of what the other families were going to do to him after having been locked out of the bathroom for all that time.

"During World War II, all Muscovites were given the opportunity to be evacuated from the city. My father was an engineer at the Steel Research Institute, and all the workers from there, with their families, were sent to the city of Orsk in the Ural Mountains. They all worked in a steel production plant in the Urals that supported the Soviet war effort. It took us several days by freight train to get there. My mother put me in charge of making the tea whenever there was hot water. Once, as I was pouring the water, the cover fell off the pot and bounced out the door of the train. This was a great tragedy, because it was impossible to keep the water from sloshing out of the pot without the lid. My mother was very angry, and I cried about it for some time.

"When we returned to Moscow after the war, we discovered that our apartment was still standing but with several windows broken from the bombings. The glass was shattered in our room, but other than that, things were just how we left them. The building next to ours wasn't so lucky. It was completely destroyed.

"It was very difficult to find food during that time, certainly more so than before the war. Everything was rationed. In 1950, when I was a student at the Institute, I left in the morning with two pieces of bread for the entire day. And Leeza, I considered myself lucky!"

I never felt the need to solicit personal information from Inna, because I believed it was her place to decide what to tell me and when. I never questioned her, for example, about what Michelle told me—that she was refused a visa to emigrate and that she had been ill the year before. However, as our friendship grew, our conversations evolved into Inna telling me more about her own situation.

One day, we were talking about her son, Lev. "I am very proud of him," she said. "He graduated from Moscow University with a degree in theoretical chemistry in 1979. That same year he and I and his wife, Marina, decided to apply to immigrate to Israel, but we were refused visas. So we became refuseniks, meaning we were refused visas to leave, and then treated by the authorities as if we do not exist.

"After we applied to leave the Soviet Union, I was asked to resign my position at the Institute of Foreign Languages, where I had taught English for over twenty years. Perhaps more devastating to me than being fired was that an English language textbook I wrote, and that was published in 1978, was removed from the Institute and is no longer used." She reached behind her and took a blue textbook off a shelf. "See," she showed me proudly. "*Modern English for Advanced Learners*. I worked extremely hard on this book and am very proud of it."

I learned about her illness in that same manner. During one lesson, I commented that she looked tired, and she agreed she was. She then told me that a tumor on the back of her neck, which had been operated on and removed the year before, had recently reappeared. She explained how she first discovered the tumor: "One day, sitting right here at this table, I reached back to scratch the back of my neck and felt a lump. That was just last fall, less than two years after Naum and I were married. At first I thought nothing of it, but a few days later I noticed that the lump was still there, and so that is when my struggle with this tumor began. I went to the doctor, and he told me that I had a tumor in an unusual and sensitive place, very near to my spine. The tumor has been operated on twice, each time with the idea that removing the tumor will stop its growth.

"I am entitled to a monthly disability check and, since I taught for many years, I also receive a pension. When I was a teacher, I made 320 rubles a month, which was good money for me and my son. Now I receive 120 rubles in pension each month. I have to stand in line for a full day to collect it, and although I sometimes can manage to do so, I am not always able. In order to receive my disability check, I must go to the doctor twice a year to prove that I am disabled and qualify.

"My last checkup I was treated very politely and did not have to wait to see my doctors. They examined me and did a few tests. While I waited by myself in a room, I overheard my doctors, who did not know I was could hear them, discussing my case. They were very fatalistic. One doctor said that I did not have long to live.

"But when they spoke to me, they were optimistic. They suggested that I try to get a certain medicine for my pain. Then one doctor smiled and said, 'Come back in a year.'

"'If I am still alive,' I replied.

"'What are you saying?' one doctor asked. Then another tried to assure me, 'Of course you will be alive.'

"'But I overheard you discussing my case, and you were not at all optimistic.'

"'Oh, we were talking in general,' one doctor tried to explain.

"Before I left the clinic, I went to the counter in the lobby and asked one of my doctors to give me permission to work from my home. You see, you are not allowed to work if you are on pension unless you get special permission. The doctor looked at me in disbelief, not knowing how to react to my honesty. 'If I am collecting this money because of my illness,' I told him, 'I want you to know that when I am well enough, I will teach English lessons in my home.' The room became quiet. The people could not believe their ears. Many of them were probably working without permission and were surprised that I admitted it. But we, that is Naum and I, are under constant observation by the authorities, and I must not give them any reason to punish us."

Inna also liked to talk about "her village," Navolok, where she owned a small *izba*—cottage. She explained it was located an overnight train ride west of Moscow, halfway to Riga, Latvia. She bought the *izba*, sight unseen, for 800 rubles from friends who had emigrated to the West a few years earlier. Her friends talked so fondly about it and the nearby forest that when they offered it to her before they left, she did not hesitate to buy it. Inna spent the summer months there—some of the time with just Naum, and often with her son and his family, her sister Olga and her family, and her brothers.

"Village people are very patriotic. They believe in this country and would die fighting to save it. Those who are older remember World War II as if it was yesterday. If they complain about things, it is with a complacent smile because they feel that they are better off now than during the war.

"Each spring, when I get ready to go to my village, I must always plan how many bottles of vodka to bring, because vodka is how things get done there. If I need a load of wood, two bottles; if my roof needs to be patched, one, and so on."

"But Inna, don't they have vodka in the villages?"

"Of course, but it might not always be in supply, or the shop where it is sold might be closed. Russians do not like to wait for their vodka, so in this way, having vodka to barter with is always helpful.

"Unfortunately, there is really too much drinking in the village. It is often the topic of conversation: who drank how much and when, as if consuming a large amount is courageous or heroic. The theory is one bottle of vodka will cheer you a little, two bottles will make you very happy, and after drinking three, you won't have a care in the world.

"The single source of information for those who live in the countryside is what they see or hear on Soviet television or the radio. Rarely do they have any actual exposure to the rest of the world. I was talking to one village woman about the United States and she said, 'Reagan is such a scoundrel, all he wants is war.'

"I asked her, 'And, if there is a war?'

"She answered without hesitation, 'Of course, only the Soviet Union will survive.'

"Another time a woman knocked on my door and said she wanted to tell me something. She insisted I walk with her in the nearby forest so that no one would overhear us. So we walked, and walked, and finally when we were deep in the forest and quite secluded, she spoke in a whisper. Oh, now I can't remember what she spoke about, but it certainly did not seem to me that she needed to take such precautions for our privacy.

"The last time I was there, I overheard two women talking. One told the other, 'It has been almost twenty years since we liberated Czechoslovakia, and they still haven't shown us any appreciation.'"

Inna also enjoyed telling me stories about Anuta, the woman known as the village hag. "She interferes in everybody's business, and the villagers think she is very nasty and dislike her. But my cottage is next to hers, so I befriended her. It took me some time and effort to get to know Anuta, but when I did, I discovered that underneath it all she is a very lonely person and has had a sad life. Her two daughters died when they were young, and then her husband left her many years ago. We were sitting in her cottage one day, near the wood-heating stove, and Anuta told me, 'I am like a lone piece of coal in the stove. The others have left me behind and I am unable to burn by myself. I am neither alive nor dead.'

"You know, maybe if her life had not been so tragic, she might have been a nicer person. And she is very smart. For every topic or incident that comes up, she can respond with a Russian proverb.

"Once a man arrived in the village from Moscow, and he stopped and talked with Anuta. He asked her what she thought about the Soviet authorities. She replied, 'I like them as much as you do.' I asked her why she did not tell him the truth.

"'The truth? What truth?' Anuta answered. 'I don't know the truth.'

"'Just the truth,' I insisted.

"'Ah, thirty-seven years ago we had a man here who told the truth, and we have not seen him since.'

"This fear of telling the truth is certainly not unique to the village," Inna continued. "And it is not unique to the things we say. It influences every aspect of our behavior.

"Our government does not tell the truth, here or abroad. This I know because sometimes we are able to get Radio Liberty from the West on our radio, and one of my students often brings Naum and me the *International Herald Tribune* newspaper. And though sometimes the news is outdated, I am always astonished by our government's statements about the problem of dissidents or refuseniks here: 'We have no problem of Jewish emigration,' 'We have no dissidents.' 'Everyone who wishes to leave may.' It is as if I am here living in an unreality, as if I do not exist."

One day, while sitting in Inna's kitchen, I noticed an American-looking Tupperware container.

"Inna, what is that on your counter?"

"I am not quite sure," she laughed. "My friend, Teeny, whose husband is an American diplomat here, brought it for me the other day and told me that it is a lettuce-leaf dryer. It was so nice that she thought of me, but what can I do with a lettuce-leaf dryer?" Inna explained that she did not regularly buy lettuce because it was available only seasonally and, even then, for a short time and at an expensive price.

"You Americans are spoiled by such things," Inna chuckled. "Such a luxury—a machine to dry lettuce!"

"That reminds me of one of my favorite stories. My grandmother told it to me when I was young. The story took place during the time of one of the *pogroms* against the Jews. These were periods before the Communist Revolution in 1917 when Jewish people were attacked by mobs and their property was destroyed. You know, Leez, it has never been easy to be Jewish in this country.

"Well, as the story goes, one day, during the worst of the pogroms, Haim, a Jewish schoolboy, was sitting in class with many worries on his mind. His teacher, who was holding a rose, noticed he was daydreaming and asked, 'Haim, how many petals does this rose have?'

"Haim looked at the rose and at his teacher, and answered, 'I don't know.' But the teacher was persistent, 'Look closely, how many petals?' Haim looked at the rose again and at the teacher and finally replied, 'I wish I had your worries,' meaning that he wished he only had to worry about how many petals were on that rose. So, you see, Leez," Inna said teasingly, "while Americans can worry about how you are going to dry your lettuce, we Russians are not even able to buy it, so I wish I had your worries."

This, I learned, was Inna's trademark story, and she would often say she wished she had my worries, not in a way to evoke pity from me but rather to illustrate the profound differences between her world and mine.

Irina Grivnina

> It is people like these who are
> making a change for the better
> in the moral visage of the world.
> —Andrei Sakharov

At the end of one Monday lesson in November, Inna told me that a friend was coming to her apartment that Wednesday night and invited me to join them. She did not offer any more details, but I was flattered she invited me to a "non-lesson event" and told her I would be happy to come.

"Can you be here at seven?"

"I'll check with Joan, but I think that will be fine," I replied.

I arrived at Inna's apartment as planned. She met me at the door and, as usual, took my coat, gave me a pair of slippers, and then walked me into the study (the room to the side of the hallway where we usually had our lesson). Instead of the usual quiet, however, there was a radio on with the volume a little high—the intended purpose of which, I soon learned, was to muffle our conversation.

Inna's friend was sitting at a chair by the table. She looked like a shadow of a person—like photographs I had seen in high school of Holocaust survivors. She was ghostly pale and could not have weighed more than 100 pounds. The skin on her face was smooth and without wrinkles. I couldn't even guess her age because, ï b b

depending on her expression, she either looked young or very old and exhausted. Inna later told me she was thirty-nine.

I was careful not to squeeze the bones of her hand as I shook it.

"Leeza, please meet Irina Grivnina," Inna said in Russian.

Irina smiled at me, "A pleasure to meet you." I responded in kind.

Inna told me Irina spoke English very well and then asked me to tell her why I came to Moscow, where I was from in the United States, about my college studies, and so on. I did, briefly, but was much more interested in learning about Irina than continuing on about my life. So, I shifted the conversation to her and asked where she worked. She responded that she didn't work and then became quiet. Inna looked at Irina and Irina nodded her head as if in agreement and then Inna explained the reason why. Irina had returned to Moscow the summer of 1983 from internal exile—1,500 miles away in the Soviet republic of Kazakhstan in Central Asia.

As I wondered what crime the frail woman in front of me could have possibly committed, Inna told me that Irina had been a member of a small group of people who formed a commission in 1977 to document and expose the Soviet government's forced treatment of Soviet dissidents in psychiatric hospitals. The commission made a record of individuals whom the Soviet government charged with political crimes, declared mentally unfit, and then forced by court order to undergo psychiatric treatment. Inna explained, "So, in this barbaric and inhuman way, the government makes a mockery out of a person—a writer, scientist, or academic who has openly fought for human rights—and destroys them with painful injections of psychotropic drugs."

The official name of the group was the Moscow Working Commission to Investigate the Use of Psychiatry for Political Purposes.[1] "Leez, can you imagine such a commission in your own country?"

[1] The Commission was created on January 5, 1977, as part of the Moscow Helsinki Group, by Petr Grigorenko. The members of the Committee were Viacheslav Bakhmin, Irina Grivnina, Irina Kaplun, Aleksandr Podrabinek, Felix Serebrov, and Leonard Ternovsky. Others who participated in its work were Dr. Aleksandr Voloshanovich and Dr. Anatoly Koryagin.

Inna asked me. "Our government had absolutely no tolerance for this group. It no longer exists because all of the members have been sent to labor camps or prison or have been forced to leave the country. One of the members on the Commission, Anatoly Koryagin, who is himself a psychiatrist, was sentenced to a maximum term of seven years in prison and then even more years in exile." His crime, she explained, was that he openly expressed his opinion that dissidents who had been sent to the psychiatric hospitals were sane.

As a side note, a few years later I read in *The New York Times* that Koryagin received permission to emigrate to Switzerland in April 1987. The article quoted him as saying the following in court before he was sentenced in 1981: "Regardless of the sentence imposed on me, and I know it will be harsh, I will never accept the situation that exists in our country, where mentally healthy people are imprisoned in psychiatric hospitals for trying to think independently." The article also noted he was in poor physical condition after a long confinement in a Soviet labor camp. In notes he managed to smuggle out of the camp, which were reported in an earlier *Times* article (December 1986), he stated that he had been put in solitary confinement for three years, had been on a hunger strike for two years, and stayed in a punishment cell for six months. The government's opinion of him as the worst of criminals was reflected in another smuggled note in which he reported what the head official of the camp said to him: "You are not going to have any canteen privileges or visits with your family. You have caused so much harm to the Soviet Government that it would have been better if you had shot ten people. You are going to drop dead here."

Irina explained in a very soft and matter-of-fact voice, "You can survive in the psychiatric hospital—I mean, keep your mind—only if you say what they want to hear. If you cooperate with them, you will escape the injections. The other possibility to survive—if you have strong support from the West, like Grigorenko or Bukovsky."

She paused and then concluded calmly and convincingly, "Most people, after such an experience, can never be the same, and many are not ever well again."

Inna told me that Irina was arrested in 1980 for taking part in writing articles and editing "Information Bulletins" of the Commission. The bulletins documented the abuse that took place in psychiatric hospitals. Her crime was "slandering the Soviet State." She was kept in a KGB prison for thirteen months during the pretrial investigation and the trial.

She was sentenced to internal exile in Kazakhstan and lived there with her daughter, Masha. Her husband visited them as often as he could and, after one of his visits, Irina discovered she was pregnant. "The Soviet officials tried to force me to have an abortion. But I refused," she said firmly. "Around that same time, my friends got in contact with Joan Baez, and informed her of my situation. She wrote a letter to the Soviet officials and it was also signed by Mrs. Jimmy Carter, Mrs. Martin Luther King, and Mme. Mitterrand. Their activity helped me enormously. The local officials became very afraid to take any action against me. So we had a very quiet time until my exile ended in the summer of 1983 and we returned to Moscow, where my second daughter Jana was born a month later."

At a volume I could barely hear, Irina explained that now she must concentrate on trying to get her family out of the country. I wanted to ask her what she was doing about that but could not because the topic was too dangerous for us to be talking.

In October 1985 OVIR—an acronym for the Soviet emigration authorities—stripped Irina, her husband, and children of their Soviet citizenship and gave them all of two weeks to leave the Soviet Union. They were welcomed by the Netherlands, where a group had been active in pressuring the Soviet government for her release during her years of exile, and she and her family settled in Amsterdam.

What difference, if any, had the handful of members of the Commission made? They were able to expose the Soviet government's punitive use of psychiatry to prestigious medical and psychiatric organizations throughout the world and, therefore, create pressure on the Soviet government and hold it somewhat accountable (had this group not done so, there would have been absolutely *no* accountability in this regard). For example, I subsequently learned that this exposure caused the Soviet government to withdraw from an international psychiatric association a year before I met Irina, rather than suffer the embarrassment of being expelled because of the documented abuse it had been provided by the Commission.

I never asked Inna why she wanted me to meet Irina, but I thanked her for introducing us as I left her apartment that night.

I had only that one encounter with Irina, which lasted no more than an hour, but her impact on me was like an expression I read on a greeting card: "Some people come into our lives and quickly go. Others stay for a while and leave footprints on our hearts and we are never the same." Irina was one of those people to me. Her raw might in fighting injustice and her pure sense of freedom allowed her to surmount the confinement imposed on her by her own government, and that conviction has left a lasting impression on me. She will always be someone I think of when I get to a seemingly-insurmountable impasse in my life, or a situation that frightens me, and ask myself what it is that I feel unable to do? What is it, really, that I am afraid of?

CHAPTER

All Because of a Book

It was a bright cold day in April,
and the clocks were striking thirteen.
—George Orwell, from *1984*

The first time I traveled to the Soviet Union was in April 1982 as a student at St. Cloud State University. As we stepped off the plane and onto the tarmac at Leningrad airport, a fellow classmate proclaimed, "We are now in the land that's the exact opposite of everything we are and everything we know," and he was exactly right.

I was raised in a country founded on the importance of the individual, self-reliance, and freedom of expression, whereas the Soviet Union enforced doctrines of totalitarianism and mass conformity and had an omniscient censorship system that repressed expressions of ideas contrary to official dogma and propaganda. I was raised in a democracy in which the people had voted in twenty-one presidential elections from 1900 through 1984, but during that same time only five autocratic leaders had come to power in the Soviet Union. I was raised with religion and was taught to respect others whose faith differed from mine, while the Soviet Union was founded on the basis that there was no god, there was only the Communist Party, which had *zero* tolerance for those who believed in anything else. Unlike the fundamental presumption of "innocent until proven guilty," which is paramount in the U.S. criminal justice system, the

Soviet system was based on the fundamental presumption of guilt. Needless to say, there were some things in Moscow I was unable to fully comprehend due to the simple fact that I was born and raised an American.

Meeting Irina was one of those experiences. My next visit to Galya's was another.

It was about an hour-long journey from my apartment to Galya's. It had been a tiresome week and I started daydreaming as I rode the metro. Had the plan for the night been more adventurous or ambitious, I might have backed out and hung out with the girls at home. But I was anticipating a typical, quiet night at Galya's, filled with lighthearted conversation.

I was quickly disabused of that notion when Galya opened the door to greet me. She looked as if someone had died.

"Is something wrong, Galya?" I asked as I stepped into her apartment and took off my coat.

"Come in the kitchen and sit down, and I will explain," Galya said in a voice quieter than usual.

After we sat down at a small table in the kitchen. Galya pulled her chair close to mine and began to talk, her worried face just a few inches from mine.

She said that her mother worked at the Institute of Scientific Information for Social Sciences of the USSR Academy of Sciences, which was responsible for reviewing written material by authors in the West—in other words, the institute of censorship. Some who worked there were assigned to prepare summaries of books or articles written by a specific author. The summaries were read by appropriate government officials who would then decide whether and to what extent the book should be made available in the Soviet Union.

"My mom is an authority on the author George Orwell, and she has read all his books," Galya began to explain. "After work today, she decided to bring home a book about his writings called *George*

Orwell and the Writings of 1984 so that she could read it this evening. Although it is forbidden to take a book from the Institute, it is common practice to do so, and usually not a problem because the book is returned before anyone notices that it is missing.

"My mother stopped at our neighborhood bread store on the way home from work today. As soon as she got home, she realized she had left a bag with the book in it at the store. She immediately rushed back and asked everyone who worked there if they had seen her bag. No one knew a thing about it. So now the book is gone, and my mother will face great trouble unless she is able to replace it."

"What kind of trouble?" I asked naively, not fully appreciating the gravity of their situation.

"At the very least, my mother will be fired from her job when the book is discovered missing. Without a job, the authorities could kick us out of our apartment and out of Moscow altogether. Even worse, my mom could be arrested and sent to jail."

"All because of a book?" I asked again.

"Of course, it is impossible for us to get the book here because our government forbids anyone to have any writings by George Orwell. And even if we find the identical book, we then need to find a way to get it marked and stamped at the Institution so that it looks like the original."

Now the nature of the problem was starting to penetrate through my dense American skull. Their only option, Galya explained, was to find someone in the West who could buy the book and then get it to them in Moscow. This was long before the Internet made books instantly available to a global market. Moreover, Soviet officials censored mail arriving from abroad, so just having the book sent from the States directly to Galya's address was also not an option. Galya and Vera did not know many foreigners but were desperate to try to find anyone who could help. Since I was going to be in Austria over the December holiday, I assured Galya that I would look for the book there.

I mentioned Galya's mom's situation to Inna at my next lesson and my opinion that the "Institute of Scientific Information" sounded like it came right out of George Orwell's *1984*. "Do you really think Orwell is describing the Soviet Union?" I asked, with some skepticism. That led to a lengthy narrative by Inna about the similarities between *1984* and her life as a Soviet citizen in what just happened to be the year 1984. "Perhaps. In some ways, it is a gross exaggeration," Inna answered. "However, there are many state-ments in the book that are quite true about our government and how the Kremlin controls our lives. There may not be a 'Ministry of Love' here, but the Kremlin very effectively engages in 'thought control.'

"Thought control causes us to act in two completely different ways. We say one thing in public but inside feel the exact opposite. Stalin was a master of this. For example, he went to Mikhail Bulgakov's play *The Days of the Turbins* at least eighteen times, even though he publicly denounced that work and made life very difficult for Bulgakov.

"Certainly our government attempts to control what we think by deciding what we can and cannot read." Then she said quietly, "But that doesn't stop all of us. A small group of very brave people here circulate books and articles that the government forbids—both from the West and from our own writers. This system, as I have told you, is called samizdat. There is no simple way to reproduce documents so people retype page by page or use carbon copy. But the system does work, and Naum and I are able to read many books because of it. We could be arrested and sent to prison if we were caught with these books, so even in my apartment, I am not free to read what I want and often turn my head to make sure no one is watching me. Isn't that like having a television screen monitoring me just like Big Brother in *1984*?

"In April of last year, the KGB searched our apartment for five hours. Half of our books were taken; none of them were samizdat. Then, a few days later, they came back and took Naum to interrogate him. They warned him they had evidence to bring charges against him and then let him go.

"Let me tell you about a funny thing that happened while the KGB was searching our apartment. There was a knock on my apartment door. I opened it to find a friend of mine who was returning a samizdat book to us that was written by Solzhenitsyn. You are familiar with our great writer, Solzhenitsyn, right, Leeza?"

"Yes," I answered, having had read *A Day in the Life of Ivan Denisovich*, which describes an ordinary day for a prisoner in a Soviet labor camp.

"Can you imagine—there was my friend right before me with an illegal book in her hands and, right behind me, the KGB officers were searching through my bookshelves for such a book? I quietly, yet emphatically, told my friend that I was busy at the moment and quickly shut the door right in her face."

While I was willing to accept the comparison Inna made between life in the Soviet Union and Orwell's "thought control," I pointed out to her that people were actually shot for going against the system in *1984*. "That doesn't happen here, does it?" I asked.

"No, you are right. People here who think differently or challenge the system may not be shot. But they may be sent to a labor camp in Siberia or a psychiatric hospital, or stripped of their citizenship and expelled from the country. Every day I talk to people who have a friend or a family member in the camps, not because the person committed a vicious crime but simply because he fought for a human right or expressed an alternate political belief.

"You must also know that Russians do not display their real feelings or character in public. We cannot afford to. We lead our public lives in a way that is completely opposite of how we feel or what we believe on the inside. I know a man who is KGB and works in a department for propaganda against religion. But he himself is Jewish, Leeza, and behind the closed doors of his apartment, he practices his faith.

"Several Soviet laws make it easy for the government to control or ruin our lives. If you are creating some sort of trouble, the district KGB office can see to it that you are dismissed from your job and keep you from getting another. The government can then label you a parasite on society if you do not have a job and forbid you from living in the city. So if the KGB wants you out of Moscow, it will happen simply by having you fired from your job. Therefore, you must always weigh the consequences of your actions.

"Here is another example. Each spring, when I am preparing to go to my village for the summer, I try without success to find another teacher among my old friends to tutor some of my American students. 'Oh, it must be very interesting, but American students, that is too dangerous for me,' is what they say to me. This fear controls their decision. I am not judging them, because I was controlled by that same fear for many years.

"Just a few months ago, I went to the market to buy flowers and saw an old friend. She did not seem to recognize me. I thought it was because of my illness, for I have physically changed since she had last seen me. I was so happy to see her. As I approached her, I said, 'It's me, Inna Kitrosskaya! Don't you recognize me?'

"She looked at me and sternly replied, 'Yes, Inna, I know exactly who you are,' and then walked away from me. She was afraid to be seen with me. I am not sure what she has heard about my life now, but she does at least know that I have applied to leave and am now a refusenik, so for her to associate with me is to put herself at risk.

"During all the years I taught at the Institute, I constantly considered what I could and could not say to my students. We were required to discuss current events with our students, although 'discuss' is not the right word. There was no exchange of ideas. My students merely repeated what was fed to them in *Pravda*, Truth, the official Soviet newspaper, and I would passively agree. During that time, I was a single parent, trying to raise my son. His father and I were divorced when he was a young boy. I could not tell my students what I really thought, what I really knew. It was not worth risking my job.

"Sometimes it happened that there was a school function, and one of the students could not attend because of a religious obligation. Of course, it is forbidden for our students to have any religious beliefs. If the teacher were a decent person, he would have a private talk with the student and tell him that it was okay for him to miss school this time, but caution him not to tell anyone his reason for being absent.

"One time, I remember, a brave child, or maybe one who simply did not know any better, stood up in my class and announced that he could not attend a school event because he had to go to a church meeting. This created a great scandal. The principal called his parents to the school and told them, 'I cannot have such a child in my school. I am a communist.' The student was expelled from the school, and that was it.

"There are other ways the school administrators can control their staff. Out of one thousand teachers, only fifty may actually get permission to travel abroad. I taught at the Institute of Foreign Languages, where all the teachers at the Institute specialized in a foreign language and had interest in traveling abroad, but the same people were chosen to go over and over again. When they returned, they were required to give a speech to the staff about their trip.

"One of the teachers in my department, the English department, went to England. When she returned, she gave a paper and presentation called 'Impressions of England.' She was very critical about the evils of capitalism: 'There are so many poor people; the air is so dirty.' She continued as if she had not enjoyed a single moment of the trip. But in private she said only good things, such as 'England is such a beautiful country, the people are so friendly, the stores have so many things.'"

"Were you ever able to travel abroad?" I asked.

"No. I was refused the first time I applied. They never gave me a reason. I suppose that they did not have to. I was very disappointed. Then I decided not to apply again, not to give them another chance to say no."

Inna became quite serious, pausing for a moment. Then she turned to me, "Everything else aside, try to imagine what it would be like if you were not allowed to go anywhere outside of your country. Imagine if someone told you, 'You cannot see the rest of the world.' The difference between your government and mine is as simple as that."

No, I couldn't possibly imagine what she described. My government's view of my travel plans never even crossed my mind when I made the decision to move to Moscow, even though I was going to a country that, in 1982, President Reagan declared the "Evil Empire."

I decided it was the perfect time to invite her to my apartment to watch the movie *Doctor Zhivago*. I explained that the Smiths were going on a weekend vacation to Helsinki at the end of November and that I had gotten Joan's permission to invite her and a couple of her friends to come over to watch the movie.

"So you can spend an evening in an American apartment right here in the middle of Moscow," I said.

Inna was very happy to be invited and said she would surely bring a couple of friends. I assumed that, like Inna, her friends would not be concerned if they were asked to give their identity to the militiaman.

On Sunday night I met Inna and three of her friends at the entrance to my building and escorted them past the militiaman who looked at all of us very seriously but recognized me. I politely said,

"*Dobryi vecher.*" Good evening. He nodded his head up and down and did not stop any of us from proceeding.

I took their coats and welcomed them to take off their shoes when we got into my apartment. They commented on the modern furniture and two Oriental rugs in the living room. Then one of Inna's friends wondered if the Russians who lived in the surrounding buildings had been chosen specially. Another remarked, "How can they live there, in the shadow of such luxury?"

I expected they would be thrilled and mesmerized by the movie. The opposite proved to be true. They critiqued it throughout: "Julie Christie as Larisa? She does not even look like one of our Russian girls." During one of the scenes in Siberia, in the dead of winter, one of Inna's friends pointed out a vase on the table and said, "Do they really expect us to believe that there would be any flowers in Siberia in the winter?"

But there were also poignant moments. The scene when Doctor Zhivago rode on the train to the Urals evoked childhood memories for each of them. They talked about how uncomfortable that trip was and how they were constantly hungry. One remarked, "Every time the train stopped, we made a small fire between two bricks to cook on."

"What did you eat?" another asked.

"Potatoes."

"Of course," Inna agreed, "for us it has always been potatoes."

It was after ten o'clock at night when they finally left. I walked the group outside, through the gate and past the militiaman. Inna's friends were going to take the metro home, so I offered to walk with her in the opposite direction, across the boulevard, to the trolley stop.

While we were waiting for the trolley, she told me some upsetting news.

"I was going to tell you tomorrow at our lesson, but I will tell you now. I saw my doctor last week, and the tests showed that my tumor is growing again. I am going to have an operation in January."

I would have never guessed from her cheery mood that night that she had been preoccupied with any sort of worry.

"My tumor is in a very delicate spot, very close to my spine and brain. So we must contain the size. It will be my third operation, actually, so at least I will know what to expect."

"I'm so sorry, Inna," I said, the reality of her illness hitting me as briskly as the winter air against my face. "When are you going to the hospital?"

"January 3. I will be in the hospital for about a week and then hope to recuperate at home."

I told her that I wouldn't be in Moscow at that time because I was traveling to Austria over the holidays. "Let me know if there is anything I can bring back for you from Vienna."

As we walked in the cold night air, I pulled my collar up around my neck and stood by Inna for a minute, not sure what else to say. As the number 32 trolley approached, I asked her if she would like to take a break in our lessons until after her surgery.

"No, Leez, I want to keep teaching for as long as I am able," she replied without hesitation. "Thank you for this evening. It was very nice." Then she said, *"Dogovorilis,"* a common Russian farewell expression that means "As we agreed."

"Dogovorilis, Inna."

She turned and stepped up into the trolley. I watched through the window as she took a seat, and then I waved to her and smiled as the trolley drove away.

We Must Have Change

Every seed knows its time.
—Russian Proverb

I wanted to see Gary before going to Vienna. I had not seen him for a few weeks and was glad to have the chance to before the New Year. We met at our usual place, the last train car on the north line at the Kievskaya station. He also had a friend with him, Misha, and I had my American friend along, Teresa Conboy, who was a nanny for an American family. Gary and I quietly made introductions and then we took a cab to Gary's apartment.

We were quiet as we rode in the cab, as we got out, as we walked up to his building, and as we walked into his apartment. I was not sure if anyone else was home, because he escorted us directly to the end of the hall and into his room, which was unlike anything I had ever been in before. It was dark, cluttered, and cave-like. At the far end of the room, the wall was painted to look like a red brick wall, and on it, in large, black, capital English letters were the words "WE MUST HAVE CHANGE." Below these words was a large American flag. He had a collection of World War II paraphernalia, which he said he found on excavation digs he took in high school near battle sites in the Ukraine. A German SS hat with bullet holes was on one shelf, along with several grenades, a pair of boots, and other artillery artifacts.

We talked about my upcoming trip, and he was visibly envious that I had such an opportunity to travel. Then he told me, "Many black marketers do not want to leave this country. They want to dress like Americans and have American things. But I want to leave here. I want your way of life, not your things."

"So what makes you different from the others?"

Gary told me he discovered the truth about the Soviet Union when he was fifteen. He explained it happened as he watched French workers building the Cosmos Hotel for the 1980 Moscow Olympics. "I saw their faces, and they were happy. I looked at Russians walking by, they were all unhappy." It was then that he started trading on the black market with a friend, and the interactions he had with foreigners caused him to see his life differently. "We are not allowed to think freely in school," he admitted. He reached from underneath his T-shirt and showed me a necklace with a crucifix. "Wearing this, very dangerous. If authorities see it," he stopped and made an off-with-his-head gesture with his hand across his neck. Then Gary told me that he would soon be drafted to fight in the war in Afghanistan: "If I survive the war, I must stay here five years because I will know military secrets. Five years impossible for me."

Gary was the only Russian I knew who was at the age to be drafted in a war that had begun much like the Soviet invasion into Czechoslovakia in 1968. While the Afghans established a communist government through a military coup in 1978, it was never stable because of strong internal opposition by anticommunist *mujahedeen* forces. Not wanting a communist country on its border to fail, the Soviets invaded Afghanistan in 1979. However, unlike the Soviet army's success in Czechoslovakia, it was unable to immediately crush the *mujahedeen* in Afghanistan and became involved in a war that would last nearly ten years.

"We know from guys in Afghanistan that it is hell, guys getting killed, no food, not good supplies. They get sick and die from diseases. I do not go there."

"How can you possibly avoid it?"

Gary explained that he and his mother were saving 1,000 rubles so that they could bribe a doctor to admit him into a psychiatric hospital. "I will pretend I am crazy, earn my paper that I am crazy, and no army."

"How long will you be in the hospital?"

"Maybe a month or two."

As Teresa and I rode home in a cab together we were both speechless and in a state of disbelief. I replayed what Irina Grivnina had said about the debilitating injections given in psychiatric hospitals. I couldn't help but feel that Gary being in any hospital, no matter the alternative, would be a terrible situation. I couldn't help comparing him to my younger brother, Tom, as Gary was just a year younger than he. Even though Tom was unsure of what he wanted to do with his life, the road ahead of him was full of possibilities of his own choosing. I thought how great it would be if Gary could live in the United States. Then it occurred to me that if I married Gary he could, as the spouse of an American, get a visa to leave the Soviet Union.

I whispered the crazy idea to Teresa, telling her lightheartedly that if she married Misha and I married Gary, we could all live happily ever after. She whispered back that she had been thinking about the same thing and then she put her finger over her mouth, indicating we shouldn't talk about it in ear range of the cab driver. "Let's talk tomorrow."

That night while falling asleep, I realized there would only be problems involved in marrying Gary. The Soviet government had never set the precedent of easing its strict emigration policy merely because one if its citizens was in love, or purported to be in love, with an American. I had heard of several "divided spouse cases" where the American spouse was forced to return to the States alone and, once there, waged the fight for his or her spouse's visa to leave the Soviet Union, which was rarely granted.

What really worried me was that such action by me would not be good for the Smiths and could potentially result in the Soviets expelling them from Moscow. My first priority and responsibility in Moscow was to them, and I felt a great sense of loyalty to them not only because I was their employee but also because I felt like a part of their family.

And I was not in love with Gary. *Maybe it would be an easier decision to make if I were*, I thought, *or maybe not*. But as my mom always said, "Where there is a will, there is a way," so all the obstacles and concerns did not immediately deter me.

Teresa and I met at the American Embassy snack bar the next day and quietly discussed the subject. She said all she had been thinking about was Misha and Gary, but had the same concerns I had about actually going forward with a sham marriage. We agreed that it was probably not a good idea, but it was still unsettling to me.

My next lesson with Inna was the last one before my trip and before her surgery. We began, as usual, with the formal part of the lesson, but it was soon apparent to Inna that my thoughts were somewhere else.

"Leeza, you look as if you have something on your mind today. Is everything all right?"

At first I told her everything was fine. I had never confided in her about a personal problem, and that afternoon did not seem like the right time for me to start—she had enough on her mind with her upcoming surgery. But she prodded me again, and I could not resist her kindness and concern.

I told her about Gary, without admitting that it was I who was thinking of marrying him. I suppose I felt a little embarrassed and nervous about what she would think. "One of my friends, an American nanny, is considering marrying a Russian," I explained.

"Is she in love with him?" Inna asked.

"No. She wants to do it because he will be drafted into the army if he doesn't find a way to leave here. She would do it to give him freedom. He is a good guy and is not expecting this from her or asking it of her." I paused because I was going to cry. "Inna, it just seems so hopeless here sometimes," I said with tears in my eyes.

"I should be the last person to advise you not to marry one of our boys," Inna said, acknowledging that she knew I was talking about myself. "But you mustn't do such a thing unless you are certain about it. It will affect your life, not only here, but when you return to America."

"It's just that everything in my life seems so insignificant compared to the possibility of giving someone else a chance to leave here and be free," I responded, feeling relieved she had seen through my charade and I could talk about it directly with her.

I told her I was most concerned about how taking such an action could cause problems for the Smiths and maybe even Caterpillar's office in Moscow, so it wasn't just about putting my own visa in jeopardy.

"Certainly, Leez, you must think about it very carefully before you make your decision."

Soon after this conversation, I received a letter from my mom with surprising news. She wrote that she was planning to come to Moscow to visit me during her Easter vacation. I was completely shocked. We had never discussed even the idea of her visiting me in Moscow, which she acknowledged in the letter. She only considered the idea, she explained, after she told a new neighbor that her daughter lived in Moscow, and he asked if she was going to visit me.

All during my childhood, my mom had talked about her dream of going to Ireland after her children were raised and my parents could afford such a trip. In anticipation of my question about sidestepping that dream for a trip to Moscow, she wrote, "Lisa, I can go to Ireland any time, but how often will I be able to visit my daughter in Moscow?"

As for my dad, his travels in the Navy—mostly in the Mediterranean—had fulfilled any desire he had to travel overseas. And, as a practical matter, they could not both afford to come, so he was content to stay behind and let my mom make the trip by herself.

While I was excited about my mom's potential visit, I doubted it would even be possible. The Soviets funneled all American visitors through its one and only official travel agency, Intourist, in order to keep tabs on them and to maximize the amount of American dollars brought into the country, which had much more value on the international market than the Soviet ruble. I wasn't sure that as a nanny for an American businessman, I could sponsor my mom's visa and bypass the Intourist route. I would have to talk to Paul and Joan about it and see if they thought it was possible.

Thinking about how great it would be to see my mom made me realize how much I missed her and everything else back home. I decided that returning to college and finishing my degree was my priority, and I couldn't imagine living with Gary or being responsible for him while I did so. It would be best, I realized, for me to return home by myself and not with a Russian husband. I could always find a way back to Moscow and marry Gary, on my own terms, if that was I something I ultimately decided to do.

And yet, while I felt I made the right decision about Gary, I did not feel entirely good about it.

7

From Russia with Love

'Cause remember you have neither lived,
Nor have breathed, if you have never loved.
—Vladimir Vysotsky

There was still one event that stood between me and my vacation to Austria—my friend Daphne's departure from Moscow. Daphne and I had shared some great adventures, including a trip on the Trans-Siberian railway to the city of Irkutsk in March of 1984 and a trip to the capital cities of three Soviet republics known as the Caucuses—Azerbaijan, Georgia, and Armenia—in November, 1984. We also took many excursions in and around Moscow, such as to the village of Peredelkino to see Boris Pasternak's grave among other things. In September 1984, I introduced her to Volodya, with whom she soon became involved in a romantic relationship.

The Saturday night before she left Moscow was the last of our many nights with Andrei, Volodya, Natasha, and Uvol. We were all at Natasha and Uvol's for Daphne's farewell party. There was an abundance of toasts in Daphne's honor, followed by shots of vodka. Many weeks earlier, Daphne had posed so that Natasha could paint her portrait. The highlight of the night was Natasha's presentation of the portrait to Daphne, who had not seen it before. It was a strikingly close and beautiful resemblance.

We gathered together on the night of December 21 at the Belorrusky train station in Moscow to wish Daphne good-bye—a good-bye that turned out to be one of the most emotional experiences of my then twenty-two years.

Although we all shared a common affection for Daphne, our reactions to her departure were varied. For Volodya, he was saying good-bye to the woman he loved, with no guarantee that they would ever meet again. Andrei was hardened by so many good-byes that he was the least emotional of the group. Uvol and Natasha were new to seeing a foreign friend leave, and this caused overwhelming sadness to wash over them. None were sympathetic to my sadness because, as Natasha stated, "I will never see her again, and you will always have the chance." So I tried to hide the heartache I felt at losing a good friend and focused on supporting those around me.

As the whistle blew, a puff of black smoke flowed through large snowflakes, and a steward yelled, "*Poyekhali.*" We're leaving. We each took our turn hugging and kissing Daphne good-bye. Then she turned away with tears flowing down her face, and walked a few feet over to the train with a carry-on bag over her shoulder and stepped up though the doorway.

Within seconds she appeared in a window and waved to us as the train slowly started chugging from the station. Volodya ran and pressed his hand on the glass. When their hands connected on each side of the window, Daphne covered her mouth with her other hand, tears still flowing down her face.

Volodya began walking with the train and then he ran, as far as he could, to the last possible inch of concrete at the end of the platform. Finally he stopped and bent over as if completely deflated. Andrei walked to him and leaned over, putting his hand on Volodya's shoulder. Eventually Andrei turned Volodya around and walked with him toward the rest of us.

I put my arms around Natasha's shoulders and held her in my embrace. I felt the vibrating of her stomach against mine as she sobbed. Uvol was standing nearby and came over and embraced us both, and then we were joined by Andrei and Volodya. We stood there for a moment, quietly, and then walked together through the station and went our separate ways home.

I finally cried as I started walking home from the metro near my apartment building. My tears felt triumphant rather than painful, though. Despite the obstacles, we had all managed to become good friends and bridge our cultural differences—Dutch, American, and Russian—and that aspect of Daphne's departure felt exhilarating to me.

As I went to bed that night, I experienced a deep pang of loss knowing that Daphne was already so far away from Moscow. I took my journal out of my dresser drawer and wanted to write about the experience at the train station, but I was unable to capture it in words. Then I remembered what Daphne said once when we were on an excursion. I told her that I wished I'd had my camera to capture a moment for posterity. She said, "You will remember it anyway. Some experiences are meant to be lived through and written on your soul."

George Orwell and the Writings of 1984

Surprise is the greatest gift which life can grant us.
—Boris Pasternak

I returned from Austria on January 7, 1985. The Smiths were still in the States on vacation, so I had the rest of the afternoon and night to myself. I had worried about Inna every day of my trip and, anxious to know how she was, I dropped my suitcase off at the apartment, ran outside to a pay phone across the boulevard, and called Naum.

"Hello," Naum answered in Russian.

"Hello, Naum, this is Leeza," I responded in Russian, then asked, "How is Inna?"

"Oh, Leeza, hello," he said, speaking now in English, "she is fine, but still in *gospital*."

"When will she be able to go home?" I asked.

"We do not know. The doctors . . . ah . . . tell us maybe a week."

My Soviet visa did not give me unrestricted permission to go wherever I pleased. Hospitals were among the many places that were off limits to foreigners, except for prearranged tours of only the best. Knowing it would not be possible for me to visit Inna, I asked Naum if there was anything I could bring to him for her.

"Thank you, no, Leeza."

"Please tell her I called and that I hope she feels better soon."

"I will. She will be happy to hear that you are back."

My next call was to Galya. I told her I was unable to find the book about Orwell in Vienna. She reported to me that there had been no progress on her end either. I said I would write to my mom and ask her to do all she could to get the book and mail it to me as soon as possible. I regretted that I had not done that in the first place, especially because of the time involved in corresponding with her by letter. While it was possible to reserve a fifteen-minute time slot with a Soviet operator to call overseas, I could not risk talking about the book during such a conversation because all international calls were likely listened to by the KGB.

While I could receive letters "care of Paul Smith" through his U.S. commercial office address, neither the Smiths nor I could receive packages. That was a privilege only for American diplomats living in Moscow. An American friend of mine, Jesse, who worked at the construction site of the new American Embassy and had diplomatic status, offered his address to me so I could receive packages from my family.

I mailed a letter to my mom the next day, writing "URGENT! URGENT!" in red marker at the top of the page and explained that a Russian friend needed the book as soon as possible or she would get in a lot of trouble at her job—maybe fired, maybe even arrested. I included all relevant information about the book, including that it was published in 1975 by the University of Michigan Press. Finally, I made a passionate and direct plea that she do whatever was necessary, at whatever cost and as soon as possible, to locate it. I suggested her best route would be to call the college bookstore in Appleton, Conkey's, and, if necessary, have it shipped from the publisher.

I estimated—best-case scenario—it would take two weeks for my letter to get to Appleton, a few days for my mom to get the book, and two weeks for the book to get to Moscow. So even if everything went well, it would be over a month before I could expect it to arrive.

Just about a month later, while working at the consulate section, I received a routine call that the mail for our office was ready to be picked up. That meant that Sandy, the woman with whom I worked, was to go down to the mailroom in the basement and get the mail. I had told her all about the situation involving the book a week or so earlier, so she invited me to come with her to look for the package. Although I considered it too soon for the book to have made it to Moscow, I could not resist her invitation.

The mailroom was not a high-security area, but one did have to be a diplomat to enter. Sandy—a diplomat—explained to the American who ran the mailroom that I was helping her, and he allowed me in without any problem. As I walked with Sandy, I looked for the area designated for the construction department— the department through which Jesse received his mail. I slowed down as I approached that section, scanning all the packages with my eyes. Then I saw a small package . . . about the size of a book . . . wrapped in brown paper with a "Conkey's Bookstore" label on it and Jesse's address written in black marker in my mom's handwriting. "There it is!" I wanted to shout to Sandy. Instead I whispered "Sandy" in a low voice to get her attention, and when I had it, pointed to the package and made a gesture with my head and eyes for her to go and pick it up. I was thrilled as I watched her walk over, grab the package, as if it were her right to do so, and then put it in her mailbag for the consulate section.

Just like that, I had the book.

As soon as we got back to the office, I opened the package and was ecstatic to be holding *George Orwell and the Writings of 1984*! I had about ninety minutes left to work, but Sandy released me early to go deliver the book.

I took the first bus that came along in front of the embassy because Americans assumed the public pay telephones in and around the embassy were bugged. I rode a couple of miles before getting off at a random stop and walked a couple of blocks until I found a pay phone to call Galya.

Galya's mother, Victoria, answered.

"Hello, this is Leeza," I said in Russian.

"Hello, Leeza."

Although Victoria could read English fluently, she was unable to speak it, a common situation for those who learn a foreign language without an opportunity to practice conversation. So we communicated with each other in Russian. And while I often found Russian to be full of cumbersome and complicated words that were difficult to pronounce, I also appreciated that it could be amazingly efficient, as I was about to demonstrate.

With just two words, *ya poluchila*, I informed Victoria that I had received the book.

"*Prekrasno*! Excellent! Can you come tonight?"

"I'll be there at eight o'clock," I told her.

I felt extremely paranoid on the way to deliver the book to Victoria. I guarded the book close to my side in an inconspicuous shopping bag from a Russian store. As I waited for the train in the metro station, I hugged the book close against my chest as I imagined someone running by and pulling the bag away from me or being stopped by the militia and ordered to hand over the book. Fortunately, the metro ride passed without incident.

I jogged along the usual shortcut I took from the metro to Galya's apartment—down a slight hill and on a foot-worn path across a field. The moon was bright enough so that I could see where I was going and, in some spots, I had to run alongside the path in the snow to avoid sheer patches of ice. By the time I got to the sidewalk near Galya's apartment, I was breathing rapidly with lungs filled with cold air.

My heart was pounding with excitement as I rang the doorbell at Galya's. Victoria answered and immediately hugged me. Once in the apartment, I took the book from my bag and handed it to her, proclaiming in Russian, "Here it is!"

She held the book in her hands, looked at it, and said, "Yes, he
it is! It is exactly like the book I lost!" She cupped her hands over h
face, shook her head in disbelief, and breathed deeply, composin
herself. Then she hugged me, thanked me, and thanked me again
She told me Galya would be home within the hour and did not know
that I had called about the book or that I was there that evening.

Victoria told me to follow her to the kitchen, where the table
had been set with two wineglasses and a bottle of red wine. She put
the book down and lifted up the wine bottle as if grabbing an award
and then proudly showed me the label. "Look, this is a vintage bottle of wine from the republic of Georgia where I am from," she said,
smiling and looking incredibly happy. "I have been saving it for a
special occasion." She opened the bottle, poured each glass to the
top, handed me a glass, raised hers, and said, "In a world full of
troubles, kindness and helping one another are gifts. I thank your
mother for her helping hand."

As we sat down at the table, Victoria asked how my mom was
able to get the book. I tried to explain that it was delivered to a
bookstore in Appleton directly from the publisher via next-day air
delivery, but the combination of my limited Russian-language skills
and Victoria's total unfamiliarity with the concept of express delivery via an airplane left me unable to convey my point. So we moved
on in our conversation. She asked me questions about my mom,
which I was able to answer in Russian with ease. She had started to
tell me about her childhood in Georgia when our conversation was
interrupted by the sound of the apartment door opening.

Victoria handed me the book and instructed me to hide behind
the kitchen door.

"Hi, Mama, I'm home," Galya shouted.

"Hi, Galya," Victoria said, as she walked to greet her daughter
in the hallway. "We have a visitor tonight."

"Who?" asked Galya, very curious.

"Guess."

Galya guessed several names, to which her mother responded, "No, not him" or "No, not her, "*Luchshe, luchshe.*" Better, better.

Finally, I stepped out from behind the door and said with a big smile on my face, "Hi, Galya, it's me."

"Leeza, hi," Galya said with an appearance of surprise and curiosity. She looked at me and then at her mother and asked me, "Why are you here?"

I responded by bringing the book out from behind my back and handing it to her. She looked at it in disbelief. Then she hugged me and then her mom, who told her that it was exactly the right book. Then they both started to cry. "Oh, thank you very much! Thank you! Thank you!" Galya said to me. "Oh, Mama, everything is going to be all right!"

⁓◦⊙◦⁓

There was more good news coming my way, although it didn't appear so at first. I received a letter from my mom in January informing me about the status of her trip to Moscow. The first visa application she had submitted to the Soviet consulate in Chicago was returned to her because she mistakenly indicated my nationality as Soviet. She had resubmitted it, this time even recruiting a Russian language teacher at Lawrence University in Appleton to perform the unnecessary task of completing questions on the application in Russian, just to be as thorough as possible. She had submitted the application and was waiting for a response.

On my end, the Soviet Ministry of Trade rejected Paul's request to sponsor her trip because, as I expected, she was not related to him; therefore, he lacked status to do so. My attempt to sponsor her based on my status as a part-time, non-diplomat employee of the embassy was also rejected. I had no choice but to accept that it would be impossible for her to stay as my guest in Moscow. So I scheduled a time to call and talk to her about it.

The call went through as planned, and fortunately my mom was home. It was great to hear her voice, as it had been months since we

had last talked. We chatted briefly about how everyone was there, but each minute cost me almost $12, so I promptly directed the conversation to her trip to Moscow. She interrupted me as soon as I began to sell her my contingency plan of meeting in Ireland.

"Lisa, I am not at all interested in meeting you in Ireland. I want to come to Moscow."

"But, Mom . . . ," I said, about to give her all the reasons why it was impossible, but she interrupted me again.

"Listen to me," my mom insisted, her voice full of excitement. "At about eleven o'clock this morning I received my visa, by special UPS delivery, from the Soviet Consulate in Chicago. I can travel the dates over Easter that I had requested and stay with you at your apartment. Your dad and I could not believe it. Can you?"

"Really?" I asked, astonished. "How did it happen?"

"Your dad and I have no idea! We wondered what on earth UPS was delivering to me on a Sunday and never guessed it could be my visa," my mom exclaimed.

The Soviet government's issuance of my mom's visa taught me an important lesson about Soviet bureaucracy—the right hand did not always know what the left was doing. But the greater and more indelible lesson I learned, and not until long after her visit to Moscow, was that some things in life are just meant to be. The time my mom would spend with Inna in Moscow would mark the beginning of my call to take action for Inna's freedom. It would inspire me to suggest something to Inna that I otherwise would not have thought of, and that "something" would play out as the foundation of greater action I would take for Inna when I returned to the States.

The Dirty Dog

Many factors contributed to the collapse of
the Soviet Union—an antiquated economy,
a senseless political system incapable of
modernizing—and surely the publication of
The Gulag Archipelago was among them.
—David Remnick,
author of *Lenin's Tomb*

I called Naum at the end of January to check on Inna. He told me
that she was recuperating at a *dacha*, or small cottage, in Razdory,
a village just outside Moscow, and that she was feeling a little better
each day. The dacha belonged to Inna's friend, who used it primarily
in the summer and let Inna use it during the winter. Naum said that
Inna wanted to invite me to join her and some friends and family
there next Saturday. He assured me that it was located within the
twenty-seven-kilometer (sixteen-mile) radius around Moscow that
foreigners were allowed to travel without obtaining a special visa. I
gladly accepted and was very happy that I would have the chance to
see him and Inna.

That Saturday I took an early morning train from the Belorrusky
station, having last been there the night that Daphne left Moscow.
The station was full of Muscovites, many of them carrying cross-
country skis on their way out of the city for a day of winter recreation.
I felt conspicuous without a pair and apprehensive traveling by

myself to a place I had not been before. I found a seat near the window and kept to myself during the trip. The train made its way through the city, then by row after row of Lego-block-like apartment buildings at the edge of the city, and finally into the countryside. Naum was standing on the platform as the train pulled into Razdory. A black fur hat completely covered his head so there was no indication what color his hair was or if he had any at all. I could see his breath in the air, and his khaki trench coat was bundled around his neck with a dark brown scarf.

He greeted me with a kiss on the cheek after I stepped off the train. He appeared to be in a very pleasant mood and commented he felt good to be out of the city. I agreed and enjoyed walking quietly with him through a colony of small, bungalow-style cottages, all frosted white with snow and with the pungent smell of burning wood flowing out of their chimneys.

Less than ten minutes later, we turned onto a path that had been shoveled through snow a few feet deep. This led to a dacha painted green with white trim. It was the first Russian dwelling I had seen since my time in Moscow that resembled a private home in the States—a small, single-family, one-story house that sat on its own plot of land surrounded by a fence. The scene reminded me of times spent at my uncle's cottage in the middle of a winter wonderland in northern Wisconsin, and I felt so at home there.

I followed Naum up a few steps to the porch and then through the front door, which opened into a small living room where Inna was sitting up on a couch, her head propped on a pillow. Her face was ashen, and the hair around her face was out of its usual order. A few feet beyond the couch, a group of people were sitting at a dining table and turned to look at me. Naum introduced me to Inna's sister Olga, Olga's husband Shura, their two children, Ilusha, age eight, and Emilia, age five, and a young Russian couple who was there with their baby. Naum told me two American teachers from the Anglo-American school, who also studied Russian with Inna, were outside cross-country skiing.

After taking off my coat and boots, I went over and knelt down by Inna. Sitting so close to her, I could see how tired and sick she looked—an image that was extremely upsetting to me. I wasn't sure what to say, so I suggested she might be more comfortable resting in bed. She told me she had done so all morning and what she needed most was to be with her friends and family. "It is so nice to see you, Leeza," she said, her voice absent of its usual energy.

I told her I had been thinking about her often and that I was glad to learn that her surgery had gone well. Then I asked her, as politely as I could, if the doctors considered the operation a success.

"It was a horrible experience, Leeza, but they said they removed the entire tumor. Of course, we know there is nothing they can do to prevent it from growing again, and there is no guarantee that it will not." Then she paused and said, "I myself just hope that I am well enough in the spring to go to my village," referring to her cottage in Navolok.

"I hope you are, too, Inna. Do you feel any pain now?"

"My neck area is very tender, and the muscles near where they operated are sore. But generally I feel fine."

Emilia came over to us and asked her Aunt Inna to go outside and play in the snow. As Inna was obviously unable to, I volunteered to join Emilia. Inna encouraged her to go with me, but Emilia paused, quietly checking me out with her big, chocolate-colored eyes for a few moments, and then said, "*Davay.*" Let's go.

As we built what Emilia referred to as a "snow woman," Ilusha was busy trying to sabotage our efforts with snowballs. Fortunately I was able to ward off most of his attacks and make some defensive strikes of my own. At one point, I noticed Inna watching us through the kitchen window, smiling with delight.

When we came inside, there was a small *samovar*, "self-boiler," on the table; this is a traditional urn-like copper container Russians use for boiling water for tea.

As we gathered around the table, Olga filled bowls with a ladle of cabbage soup from a kettle and handed them to Shura, who cut a loaf of dark Russian bread. Inna's friend helped her walk over to a chair near me, and when she got close enough, I extended my arm so she could grab on to it while she sat down. It was then that I saw the wide bandage covering the back of her neck, concave in the middle where the tumor had been, and soiled on the edges with dried blood.

"Is it difficult to hold your head up?" I asked her.

"Not for short periods of time. My muscles are getting stronger each day."

"Have you ever thought about wearing a brace to support your neck?" I asked her.

"You know, Leez, an American friend already gave me one. But I decided it is better for me to hold my head up on my own for as long as I can. I am worried that if I start to rely on a brace, I will get used to it and then not be strong enough to hold my head up by myself."

Before I left that afternoon, Inna told me that she would be returning to Moscow at the end of that week and that we could begin our lessons a week from Monday.

I arrived for the lesson as planned, and it felt good to be back in Inna's apartment, sitting with her at the table. The energy in her voice was back and she looked much healthier than she had at Razdory. The bandage on her neck was smaller and not soiled. She said she was still getting her strength back, especially in her neck, but overall was feeling well. I had started to get the homework that she had assigned in December out of my backpack when she said she was sorry we didn't talk about my trip when I was at Razdory. She suggested we begin the lesson with my telling her about it in

Russian, which I did. Then she asked what else I had been doing since she last saw me.

I detailed an interesting but strange night I'd recently had with an American nanny, Suzy Crow, whom I was getting to know, and two Russians, Boris and Alosha. A professor of Suzy's had met them when in Moscow and had given her their names and telephone numbers.

"Alosha said that when he told his mom he was going to meet Americans, she told him to be careful because we were 'probably spies,'" I told Inna. "He is anti-Reagan and believes that the United States wants to blow up the Soviet Union. I tried to convince him that Americans want peace, but he would not hear of it. He said the Soviet Union would defeat us and proudly pointed out the Soviets' great victory in World War II. I responded that the victory might have been great, but that over twenty million Soviets died during the war, both soldiers and civilians. Alosha became angry and talked about how great a leader Joseph Stalin was during the war. I tried to tell him that it was Stalin who crippled the Soviet Union going into the war because of the thousands of high-ranking members of the Communist Party and military who he had killed during the purges of the 1930s. Alosha got very defensive and said Stalin had to kill his enemies because 'too many people wanted to live under a czarist regime again and they needed to be eliminated or Communism would not have succeeded.' Boris added that Stalin had had been 'like a father to us, a second Lenin.' How could he possibly think that, Inna?"

"The better question, Leeza, is how he could possibly not? He has not been taught anything to the contrary." Inna stopped, got up, unplugged the phone—to disconnect a possible listening device that was in it—and turned on the radio. She paused for a moment, looking as if she were deciding what to say, and then continued. "Boris and Alosha are products of the pro-Stalin indoctrination they have received their entire lives. It is as simple as that. I was also brought up with the same indoctrination and certainly not knowing the truth about Stalin. Even my parents, who knew some things, did not know the entire truth. They were afraid to." Then Inna got into a groove, like a jukebox after having been filled with enough coins to play its entire selection five times over. There was no stopping her.

"We are a society of people who have remained paralyzed from Stalin's years of terror. Not many here regard him, as I do, as a murderer in numbers that were far greater than the numbers attributed to Hitler for the simple reason that not many here have learned the truth as I have. How can they? The only truthful accounting we have had of the deaths in the Gulags during Stalin's time was by Solzhenitsyn.[1] Of course, both he and his book, *Gulag Archipelago*, have been banned from this country. He estimated over sixty million died in the Gulag.[2]

"A person can be arrested here for anti-Soviet agitation just for having a copy of his book. So it is not easy to learn the truth here, even for people who, like me, decide they must know it. I was able to get a copy of this book through the underground and only had two days to read it and then had to pass it on."

I couldn't believe it took Inna only two days to read a three volume book that took over ten years to write and that is considered one of the greatest nonfiction works of the twentieth century. This book was unlike anything that had ever been published before because it exposed the vast, and theretofore secret, network of

---

[1] *Gulag* or *GULag*, an acronym for the Russian term *Glavnoye upravlyeniye ispravityel'no-trudovih lagyeryey i koloniy*, "Chief Administration of Corrective Labor Camps," an Orwellian term for the massive system of Soviet forced labor and concentration camps, that burgeoned during Stalin's era.

[2] Leading historians of the twentieth century vary their estimates from 9.5 million (Alec Nove, *Victims of Stalinism: How Many?*) to 50 million (William Cockerham, *Health and Social Change in Russia and Eastern Europe*). In his book, *Great Terror*, British historian Robert Conquest estimated at least 20 million died: 7 million from 1930–36, 3 million during 1937–38, and 10 million from 1939–1953. American journalist Anne Applebaum, author of *Gulag, A History*, arrived at a more conservative number of 33 million people confined in the camps and 3 million deaths. Her book, published in 2003, received the Pulitzer Prize for General Non-Fiction writing in 2004 and was based on information from archives and other sources about the Gulags that only became available after the collapse of the Soviet Union in 1989. Her conclusion that "no figures reflect the cumulative impact of Stalin's repressions on the life and health of whole families" was consistent with what Inna was trying to explain to me.

labor and concentration camps that began in the Soviet Union under Vladimir Lenin in 1918 and reached a peak during Stalin's reign. The book was smuggled out of the Soviet Union on microfilm in 1968 but not published until December 1973, in France. Solzhenitsyn was arrested in February 1974 for treason, and the next day he was stripped of his citizenship and expelled from the Soviet Union. Around that same time, samizdat copies of *Gulag Archipelago* began circulating in the Soviet Union, one of which, over time, made it into Inna's hands.

"You can't even imagine it, Leeza, those two days I read Solzhenitsyn's book," Inna continued, becoming very intense and emotional. "I had a life before I read it that was based on a lie and then I had a life after I read it that was based on the truth. It is as simple as that. Well, because of that and other things I was coming to know, I knew it would be impossible for me to live here anymore. So in 1979, my son, his wife, and I decided to apply to emigrate. We were refused permission and then that was it for me—I was forced to quit my job at the Institute where I had taught for twenty years. I heard that my dear friend Sonya, whom I had known since we were students at the Institute, was the one chosen to denounce me at the faculty meeting. If she had refused to do this, she would have most likely been fired from her job. This, of course, was a very difficult situation for Sonya," Inna said empathetically. "I heard later that this is what she said at the meeting: 'Inna has been with us since she was a young girl and is leaving us . . .' and then she began to cry and left the room. Apparently this was acceptable to the school administration. Even they knew that it was indecent to expect her to enthusiastically denounce me.

"I remember coming home the afternoon Stalin died," Inna continued. "I knew something was wrong because my father was home from work early. He looked deep in serious thought, sitting in a chair, smoking a cigarette, and gazing out the window. I asked him if he had heard that Stalin died, and he did not respond to me at all. Then I asked him again and he said, without looking at me, 'Yes, I know, the dirty dog is dead.' His voice was so bitter it frightened me.

"I could not believe he was referring to Stalin, whom I had only regarded my entire life as our beloved leader. Why did he call this great man a dirty dog? I did not ask him any questions then, but little by little my father began to tell me more about Stalin, things he had kept from me all my life to protect me and our family. You see, if my parents said things to us and we repeated them to the wrong people, they would have been hauled off to the Gulag." She looked at me very seriously and then said, as if I did not believe her, "Absolutely, Leeza!"

"During Stalin's time, families were forever destroyed because parents were arrested and never seen again for words repeated by their children, and children's lives were ruined with the guilt of betraying their parents. When I was a kid, I had no idea my parents lived in fear because they simply could not risk showing it to me; they could not risk having me ask, 'Why are you afraid?'

"But as I got older, I heard and saw things that made me question all that I had been taught about Stalin, like the way my father reacted when Stalin died. Another example of this happened about a year earlier in 1952 when I, along with several other university students, were invited to a ball at the Kremlin because we had received the top grades for the semester. One of the students found a phone in an office, and we each took a turn to call our parents. I listened so proudly to those who called home and said, 'Hi, Mama' or 'Hi, Papa, I am calling from the Kremlin.' I excitedly took my turn, and when my mom answered, I told her so self-importantly, 'Mama, this is your daughter Inna calling you from the Kremlin.'

"'Hang up, Inna,' my mother demanded. I was so surprised that she was so angry. 'I will talk to you when you get home,' she said and immediately hung up. I did not understand her reaction and was embarrassed in front of my friends that she had hung up on me so abruptly.

"Even though the fear of my parents' generation was not something that was openly discussed, it was passed to my generation, and then to Boris and Alosha's generation—the young men whom you recently met. Everyone here knows they must consider what they can do or say in public. Even my nephew, Ilusha, who is only eight, knows what he can and cannot say. Last winter one of my American students gave me a pair of ice skates from Helsinki that her son had outgrown. I gave them to Ilusha. All the boys became so distracted the first day he wore the skates to hockey practice that they were unable to concentrate. Finally the coach asked Ilusha where he got the skates. He answered that he did not know, afraid to say that they were from an American.

"He came home from practice very upset and asked his mother what he should have told his coach. 'You should have told him the truth, that they were a gift from your aunt,' she told him. Leeza," Inna explained, "next year he will know exactly what to say. When he is fourteen, he will be even wiser, when he is sixteen very wise, and when he is eighteen he will be the wisest man in the world because he will know all the answers. You see, the system is there before you; you must simply find out how to survive in it, and then operate accordingly."

As I rode home on the trolley after my lesson, I started writing down what Inna said about Stalin on a blank page in my Russian-language dictionary. Suddenly, a vivid memory of an October afternoon stroll around Patriarch's Pond in the center of Moscow popped into my head. Inna and I had been discussing Mikhail Bulgakov's book *Master and Margarita*, and she suggested I visit the pond after the lesson. I knew from a Russian literature course that Bulgakov's book is considered a masterpiece of twentieth-century literature. Before his death in 1940, Bulgakov asked his wife to publish the manuscript if it would ever become possible to do so.

She kept it hidden until a brief period of tolerance for expression during Nikita Khrushchev's reign (1953–64) resulted in its first publication in *Moskva* magazine in 1966, and then in book form in 1967.

The Smiths had a copy of the book, so I had started to read it. I told Inna that I was finding it very difficult to understand, even though I was reading an English translation. She had read it and agreed that it was a very complex story. She explained that Bulgakov was a master at using layers of symbolism and satire to write critically about Soviet society at a time when "the harsh censorship under Stalin absolutely smothered his freedom to do so." I was reading the first chapter ("Never Talk to Strangers") and trying to understand a conversation two characters were having while sitting by Patriarch's Pond. She told me that Woland, the foreigner who approaches them, later reveals himself as Satan. We talked a little bit more about it, and Inna said she would be happy to discuss the book during my lessons. Then she said, "You know, Leeza, it is such a nice day, you could stop by that pond on your way home. Take the bus by the trolley stop on Osepenska Street to Maya-kovsky Square. Then just walk a block west on Sadovaya Street, and you will see it."

The pond was easy to find, and I was glad to be there. It was an oasis of tranquility amid the bustle of the city. The late afternoon sun was shining through trees covered with brilliant yellow, orange, and red leaves. Some had already fallen to the ground, so the crunching sound of people walking on them filled the warm, sooth-ing air.

The park was bustling with the activity of many people, all appearing to be in the same carefree mood as I. A middle-aged cou-ple was sitting on a bench—the woman leaning into the man's chest. Two silver-haired men were sitting at a table, smoking cigarettes and playing dominoes. Mothers and grandmothers were pushing babies in strollers on the sidewalk, young children walking beside them. Just ahead of me, two women, who looked to be in their twenties, were walking and holding hands—a platonic, common custom of Russian women. Not far ahead of them, an older man was napping on a jacket crumpled under his head as if a pillow, and his shirt was untucked, allowing his stomach to flop freely over the top of his pants.

I came upon a bench and sat for about ten minutes, holding my face upward to soak in the sun and breathing in what I knew was the last bit of warm air before the cold chill of winter set in. I watched an older woman, whose head was bundled in a black scarf dominated by a pattern of bright red flowers, stretch a net out into the water to collect leaves from the pond. Not a job that necessarily needed to be done, but one example why the Soviets claimed there was no unemployment. I could see the sweat on her brow as I got up and strolled by her.

Walking away from the pond, back toward Sadovaya Street, I noticed a frail and slender old woman shuffling toward me, slowly lifting one orthopedic-looking black shoe in front of the other, as if she were pulling it out of mud. Her posture and demeanor gave me the impression that she was at the end of a long life, yet she was tall—a little less than my height of five feet, eight inches. She wore a light blue coat that was buttoned snugly at her neck and fell loosely off her shoulders, like a shirt too big for its hanger. The coat stopped at her knees, revealing only the bottom portion of her chicken-thin legs, which were opaque with dark nylon stockings. Her hair was tucked completely under a white scarf, like a nun's habit, exposing only her face. As I got closer, I could see that her skin was shriveled with as many lines as on a crowded street map and sagged from her cheekbones into her chin like jowls drooping off a dog. It was her vacant expression that almost made me cry.

When we were almost side by side, she mumbled something to me, which I did not hear.

I stopped and asked in Russian, "Excuse me, please. What did you say?"

She turned her head toward me and leaned in so close that our noses were almost touching. "*Dyevushka*—young lady—I have *nichevo*—nothing," she said, almost in a whisper. She paused to grasp her next words. "My husband disappeared years ago. I had three very beautiful children. They are gone, too. I have no one. *Nichevo*." She looked at me but appeared not to see through her trance of sorrow.

I stood with her, attentively, tears swelling in my eyes. I did not distance myself from her nose. She stared into my eyes a few more seconds—long enough that I started to feel uncomfortable. Then she snapped out of her trance, and in the moment after she saw me, kissed my cheek. Her lips were smooth and warm, and no more of an intrusion upon me than if a butterfly had landed on my skin, and no less beautiful.

"*Spasibo*—thank you," I said, startled by her gesture. I stayed connected with her eyes and did the only thing I could do—I leaned in and kissed her cheek. Even now I remember how soft it was, like a baby's skin, yet lifeless as a wisp of cotton candy.

She looked at me, still expressionless, as if unable to feel a thing, and then, slower than the tick of the second hand on a clock, she turned her face away from mine and looked forward. Then she continued on with nowhere to go—no place to be; no one to see; lifting one heavy foot in front of the other.

My flashback of her and that fall day was jarred for a moment by the sudden stop of the trolley. I stared out the window into the dark falling on the February day and then vividly saw the old woman's face again. I tried to comprehend her suffering—her loneliness. I tried to comprehend the Communist country I was living in—its short history bulging with millions who had died, millions who had been taken away and never returned home, millions who had suffered unimaginable suffering, and the millions more whom all those millions had left behind . . . *it's unfathomable*, I thought. Then I realized there were signs of those millions of losses all over Moscow—as often as a leaf falling from a tree, as common as an old woman walking alone in the park.

CHAPTER

10

The Feeling That You Cannot Breathe

> The reasoned, quiet pleas of the two
> dissenters are an eloquent echo of all
> those, from Socrates to Zola, who
> risked their own freedom in order to
> defend the right of men to speak freely.
> —*Time*, "Protest on Trial,"
> October 25, 1968

T he first time I met with Andrei, Volodya, Natasha, and Uvol
after Daphne left was on January 21 to celebrate my twenty-
third birthday. We had spent a few minutes reminiscing about
Daphne when Volodya interrupted and changed the subject,
explaining he missed her too much to talk about her. He was
disappointed that I had not received a letter yet from her and
besides, he said, he was very tired and hadn't had any sleep because
he worked the night before at his watchman job at a lumberyard
outside the city.

Not too long after we first met Volodya told me that the watchman job was the only one he could find after he had quit the Komsomol—the level of the Communist party for ages fourteen to
twenty-eight—and a necessary stepping-stone to becoming a full-
fledged member of the party as an adult. He had also been a member of the Young Pioneers, the Communist club "for beginners,"
ages ten through fourteen. He explained that his reason for quitting

the Komsomol was not based on a specific event but rather because he felt disillusioned by it. "If you hear too much of the same thing, over and over again, you start not to believe it," he explained. Within only a few days of quitting, he was expelled from the university and dismissed from his part-time job. At first he thought he was just having bad luck in finding another job. Then he noticed that even if a job interview went well, he was treated rudely or ignored every time he followed up on the position. Finally, he called one person with whom he had a good interview the day before and asked why a decision had been made not to hire him. The man replied that a KGB officer came in after the interview and ordered the boss not to hire Volodya because he had chosen to quit the Communist party. "So now my life here is very difficult because I chose not to be a Communist," Volodya told me.

Uvol arrived about thirty minutes late to the party and, in a jovial way, made a big deal about giving me a chocolate torte he bought especially for the occasion. According to him, he had to search all of Moscow to find it, which is the reason he gave for being late. Then he stepped out of the room for a minute and returned with a rolled-up piece of white paper in his hand that was a little smaller than poster board size. He handed it to me as if he were handing me a newspaper and said, "happy birthday," giving me a big smooch on my cheek.

I unrolled the paper, not knowing what to expect, and found one of the most beautiful, thoughtful gifts I have ever received. Uvol had drawn caricatures of each of us with black ink in such fine detail that it looked similar to a pointillism painting. The caricature of me was in the middle, and off to the side of my left shoulder was a saucer cup with two smiling children sitting in it, representing Kjirsten and Laura.

He had drawn a black outline an inch in from the border of the paper; the caricature of himself rested on his back on the top line, with one foot on the line and the other dangling comfortably below it. His right arm was raised over his head, as if waving, and his left reached out toward me with a chrysanthemum-like flower. Natasha's caricature stood against the left border; she held a paintbrush in her hand that was taller than she. Andrei's caricature stood near the right border, holding his daughter Anya's hand. Above my right shoulder was the piano in Andrei's apartment with flowers and vines weaving across the front and an ornate candleholder on the top of each side with a candle billowing smoke into the air.

Natasha admired the drawing with me, commenting that she had not seen it in its completed form until just now. "He only found out yesterday morning that the party tonight was for your birthday," she explained, her face beaming with a smile. "Once he knew, he immediately began drawing and continued nonstop through the day, night, and into this afternoon until he finished it."

"Yes, Leeza, I did not get any sleep all night because of you!" Uvol added, in an overly dramatic way that drew laughter from all of us.

The name of each person was artistically written on each caricature, except there was no name on Natasha's character. I asked her to sign her name below it. She asked Uvol if it would be okay if she wrote on it, and he nodded yes. Then she took a black pen and surprised me by writing *tseloo-yu*, the Russian verb "I kiss you" instead of her name.

Suddenly, the room became quiet as all of us simultaneously realized that there was no caricature of Volodya. Uvol apologized profusely, explaining that he did not have enough time to include Volodya and that he could easily add him to the drawing. Volodya acted severely wounded in a teasing way and pointed out that Uvol had had enough time to paint Andrei's piano but not him. We all enjoyed watching Uvol beg for forgiveness, which Volodya eventually gave him.

As it was my birthday, I was the recipient of all the toasts that night. I tried to explain that the attention made me feel uncomfortable because my birthday had never been my own. This comment caused great and immediate curiosity.

"What do you mean, Leeza? Do you have a twin?" Uvol asked me.

I got a bit jumbled in my attempt to explain in Russian because by then I was under the influence of multiple shots of vodka and also because, while they were trying to understand me, they kept interrupting me, laughing, and not letting me finish my sentence.

"I was born on the same day as my brother and sister . . ." and before I could finish my sentence Uvol interrupted me and declared, "So, you are a triplet! *Bozhe moi!*" My God! "I've never known a triplet!"

When I told him, "*Nyet*—no—I'm not a triplet," he became very confused and asked me how that could be.

Then I made the mistake of trying to say the year I was born in Russian. Even if I had been sober, saying "one thousand, nine hundred and sixty two" in Russian would have been a mouthful, so it turned into a big mess and then an even greater mess when they all tried to help me. Finally I got it out, and they all understood I was born in 1962. Then, instead of trying to say each number in the year Jerry and Julie were born, 1960, I took a shortcut and said, "And Jerry and Julie were born two years earlier, on the same day."

Uvol's eyes lit up as soon as he understood, and raised his glass and wished me, my brother, and my sister a happy birthday.

Before I left, Volodya pulled me aside to tell me his gift to me would be to introduce me to someone very interesting. I, having by then become quite accustomed to making plans with my Russian friends without asking for any details, told Volodya that I would be happy to meet her at a later date.

It was a month later that Volodya made the arrangements for me to meet the "mystery" person he hinted at on my birthday. We met at the Dobryninskaya metro station and then rode together on a train going south to the Leninski Prospekt stop. It was not until we surfaced from the metro and started walking on Leninski Prospekt that he told me more about whom we were going to meet. "Her name is Larisa Bogoraz. Her apartment is just few blocks away," he said.

I had never heard her name before, so I asked Volodya who she was.

"Just a few days after the Soviet Union invaded Czechoslovakia in 1968, she went into Red Square in the middle of the day along with six other people and held up signs protesting our government's action. Plainclothes militiamen ran up to them within minutes, grabbed their signs, and started beating them up. Then they were hauled away by the KGB and arrested. Such an open act against the government was criminal. She spent four years in internal exile in Siberia and then returned to Moscow in 1972 where she has lived ever since."

Volodya pointed at the structure just across the street from us and said it was Larisa's apartment building. Then he stopped talking and motioned for me to be quiet by putting his index finger over his mouth.

A teenage girl about seventeen opened the door to Larisa's apartment and let us into a hallway cluttered with books and papers stacked on the floor three to four feet high against the wall. The girl said something to Volodya that I didn't hear and then walked down the hallway away from us. He told me Larisa needed a few more minutes to finish with her students and explained that Larisa had been a linguist before her arrest in 1968 and had supported herself over the years by tutoring high school students. That evening she was reviewing writings by the Russian poet Alexander Pushkin with three students in preparation for their college exams.

Five minutes later, Larisa called Volodya to come into the kitchen. We walked in as the students were leaving. They made eye contact with me, but we did not greet each other.

It seemed the smaller the Russian kitchen, the more furniture, papers, and other items were put into it, and that proved to be the case with Larisa's kitchen. There was a square wooden table in the middle with three chairs around it, which were similar only in that each was wooden and dilapidated. A fourth chair was a green stuffed armchair in which Larisa was sitting. She was a petite and slender woman, and looked at ease on the tattered fabric, which was especially worn on the spot behind her head and on the armrests.

She gestured for Volodya to sit on the chair next to her and for me to sit on the chair across from her. Volodya bent down and greeted her with a kiss on the cheek, and then introduced me, telling her I spoke Russian.

"Nice to meet you," she said as I sat down. She took a long drag on her cigarette and coughed while exhaling into the already smoke-filled air.

"It's nice to meet you," I replied.

Had I not known a thing about her, I would have concluded just by her face that her life had not been an easy one. She looked as if she hadn't had a good night's sleep in her entire life. The skin around her eyes was puffy and dark like a raincloud about to burst. Her gray hair was shoulder-length, wavy, and clipped back on the side in schoolgirl fashion with a couple of bobby pins. She was dressed in a black crewneck sweater so worn that the elbows were almost transparent.

I gave her a box of tea from a *Beriozka* store, as it was my custom to bring a small gift when I went to a Russian apartment for the first time. She was pleased to receive it and stood up, clamping her cigarette between her lips as she did, then gathered an eclectic group of chipped cups from a cupboard and set them on the table. Then she grabbed a kettle from the stove and set it by Volodya, gesturing to him with one hand to pour water into her cup while taking a puff from her cigarette with the other. She scooped a spoonful of dark red jam from a saucer on the table, stirred it into her cup, and then exhaled smoke across the table while pushing the jam toward me, past a saucer full of her cigarette ashes.

Volodya asked her how she was doing. She said all was normal with her, but she had recently received troubling news about a friend, Viacheslav Bakhmin, who was in internal exile in Kalinin, just two hours north of Moscow by train. I later learned that, like Irina Grivnina, he had been a member of the Moscow Working Commission to Investigate the Use of Psychiatry for Political Purposes. He was arrested and imprisoned in Moscow for three years, sent to a labor camp for three years, and was subsequently forced to live in Kalinin, away from his family in Moscow. All of that punitive action against him was apparently not enough based on what Larisa said next: Viacheslav had an eight o'clock curfew every night and was extremely careful about not violating it. One night as he was on his way home, a man walking toward him fell and asked for help. He stopped and helped the man get up. To his surprise, the man started to fight him. Two militiamen appeared and hauled Viacheslav into the station because, they said, *he* initiated the fight with the man he tried to help. By then it was after his curfew, which they warned him not to violate again. Viacheslav found out that the man who stopped him that night was known to the militia as an aggressive man and street fighter and had been arrested earlier that day. The militiamen told him he could either go to jail for three years because of his destructive behavior or he could help them that evening and then go free. He chose to help them and was instructed to do so by initiating a fight with Larisa's friend.

Since Larisa spoke so softly and quietly, Volodya often looked at me to make sure I understood what she was saying. When I didn't understand, he either repeated what she said to me again in Russian or tried to tell me in his limited English.

"Another night shortly after that, a stranger stopped Viacheslav on the street and asked him for a cigarette," Larisa continued. "He replied that he did not have one. The stranger punched him, and again the militiamen suddenly appeared, and he was arrested for "aggressive behavior and street fighting."[1]

At that point, a very old man shuffled into the kitchen with his head down and his hand following along the wall to guide him. Volodya, who appeared to be in awe of him, whispered to me that the man was Larisa's father; he had been a Communist during the Russian Revolution and was arrested during Stalin's purges in the 1930s. He spent many years in a Siberian labor camp. Volodya also said he was eighty-nine years old and almost blind. He was broad-shouldered, about six feet tall, and looked every bit his age.

A smile covered Larisa's entire face when she saw him. She stood up, went over to him, and said, "Papa, I have visitors this evening." We exchanged greetings just as a young teenage boy walked into the kitchen. Volodya smiled and said hello to him and then told me he was Larisa's son, Pavel. Larisa said something to Pavel that caused him to smile. She tousled the hair on his head, then asked him to help his "d-ye-d"—short for grandfather—back to his room.

Volodya asked Larisa if she had heard anything from her husband, whose name Volodya told me was Anatoly Marchenko. She said she had not and that it had almost been a year since she had been allowed to see him. "My husband should be allowed to see me three times each year, but he is denied these visits as punishment," she said in a discouraged tone. "Our son Pavel is growing up without his father."

Volodya explained to me that Anatoly had been arrested in 1980 for "anti-Soviet agitation" because of a book he had written, and

---

[1] I later learned that Viacheslav was released while still in prison during the pre-trial investigation as the result of a personal appeal made directly to General Secretary Mikhail Gorbachev on his behalf.

other dissident activities in which he engaged, and had been sentenced to ten years in a labor camp to be followed by five years in exile. He had only been in Moscow for a few years at the time of his arrest, having spent 1975–78 in a prison camp because of another book he wrote, the name of which I later learned was *My Testimony*. It is a sequel of sorts to *Gulag Archipelago*; in it Marchenko recorded his first experience in a labor camp, which was from 1961 to 1966. In doing so, he described the experience of his generation in the camps—the generation after Solzhenitsyn—and revealed to the world that such camps continued to exist in the post-Stalin era.

Larisa talked about other friends who were in camps and her efforts to communicate with and support their family members in Moscow. She mentioned one friend in prison who was very active in fighting for human rights, especially in fighting against the Soviet government's oppression of Jews.

We were with Larisa at her table for about an hour. I wanted to ask her about her protest in Red Square but was afraid any question I asked would reveal how very little I knew about the protest, and I did not want to embarrass myself or offend her. Years later I read about her in the *Moscow Times*—the article quoted a note she had smuggled out of a prison while still in Moscow after her arrest. She explained in the note what had compelled her to participate in the protest. She wrote, "I simply cannot act in any other way. You know, the feeling when you cannot breathe. . . ."

When we left Larisa's on that cold winter night and were walking toward the metro, the usually soft-spoken Volodya said emphatically, "The world is an organ, and the Soviet Union is the cancer within that organ," and then said nothing more as we reached the metro, descended into it, and got on a train going north to the Oktyaborskaya station.

As the train slowed approaching the station, I wanted to tell Volodya the enormous impact meeting Larisa had on me, but I was not able to find the words to convey what I was feeling. So

I simply thanked him for taking me to meet her, and then said, "I'm not the same person I was when we met here a couple of hours ago." He looked back at me with his wide, brown eyes that looked as sad as they had on the night he said good-bye to Daphne. He kissed me on the cheek before I stepped out of the train car. Then I headed toward the escalator to catch a train going east toward the Dobryninskaya station.

―∽∾―

I began my stay in Moscow on the side of left-leaning peace activists in the United States, who supported a freeze in the nuclear arms race between the United States and the Soviet Union. I was optimistic and believed the simplistic notion that if the American and Russian people came to know and understand each other, we could peacefully coexist. But one experience after another during my second year in Moscow chipped away at that optimism. As I rode the final stretch of the metro home from Larisa's, I felt whatever optimism I had left drop to the pit of my stomach. Then a thought, so contrary to what I had previously believed, blew into my mind as fast as the train whizzed along the metro tracks: a nuclear freeze between the United States and the Soviet Union would be dangerous for the United States. My country needed to arm and defend itself to whatever lengths necessary to be sure the Soviet Union would never impose its inhumane, oppressive, and paranoid form of government upon us.

As I lay in bed an hour later trying to fall asleep, I experienced a feeling that I'd never had before—the complete lightness of being an American. Of course, I had always known—in fact, I had only ever been taught—that I had the freedom to think, write, be, go, and do whatever, wherever, and whenever I pleased. That night I experienced the transformation from knowing all of that on an intellectual level to actually feeling it in my bones. I couldn't help but think that the rest of my life would always be easy. What problem would ever come my way that I couldn't overcome?

I better understood the comment Inna had made about the lettuce dryer—that she wished she had my worries. At that point in my life, the worst thing that had ever happened to me occurred when I was a senior in high school. My dad, who had only ever made a modest income as a printer, lost even that when the print shop where he worked for fifteen years burned to the ground. He was fifty years old and knew no other trade, but he managed by getting unemployment, tending bar at night, and taking any paying job he could find along the way until he finally got a job as a custodian at a community college. All the while, my mom had her job as a teacher's aide, and they managed to keep up with the mortgage payments and maintain the fundamental quality of their life. I could hear my mom say what she often had said, "Lisa, as long as we have our health, we have our wealth," and I realized she was absolutely right.

I wondered what was going through Larisa's mind in the quiet of night before she fell asleep. She must have been constantly worrying about her husband. Had he suffered that day? Was he well? Was he warm? Was he hungry? When would she hear from him again? When would Pavel see his father? How many other prisoners of conscience did she worry about, who had likewise been exiled so far away from their loved ones and their life's work because they had acted on what the blood flowing through their veins, beating through their hearts, and resounding in their minds had told them with certainty to be true—because they had acted on their *conscience*?

One of my favorite quotes is from Robert Kennedy's historic trip to South Africa in June 1966 during the darkest years of apartheid. He said, "Each time a person stands up for an ideal, or acts to improve the lot of others . . . he sends forth a tiny ripple of hope, and crossing each other from a million different centers of energy and daring, those ripples build a current that can sweep down the mightiest walls of oppression and resistance." Could Larisa and her "comrades" have been at all familiar with the prophetic words Kennedy spoke two years before their heroic and unprecedented protest in Red Square, or were his words intuitive to them? Certainly they could not have expected that the collective ripple they would make would be any more than the tiny ripple left by a tiny pebble dropped into a vast ocean. The oppressive policies in place under Leonid Brezhnev, who was the leader of the Soviet Union when they leapt against the dictates of their government on that summer day in 1968, guaranteed their protest would be snuffed out so quickly and completely that it would be nearly impossible for those in the Soviet Union and, for that matter in the West, to read a single contemporaneous word about it. There is no photograph that captures their magnificently defiant moment in history like the photograph of the moment when a student protester stood in front of four tanks in Tiananmen Square in June 1989.[2]

A few years later, I was fascinated to read a *Time* article dated October 25, 1968, and titled "Protest on Trial." It was a report on a trial that had occurred in Moscow two weeks earlier in which five of those who had protested in Red Square were sentenced to exile or imprisonment. The source of information in the article was a document that was secretly provided to a Western correspondent in Moscow, thereby defeating the Soviet authorities' attempt to silence news reports on the trial. The article also noted that a *New York Times* Moscow correspondent had been expelled from the Soviet Union the prior week for having sent a letter to the *Times* from one of the participants in the Red Square demonstration. That

---

[2]Fortunately, however, all the Soviet government did to quash Larisa's act of heroism has not precluded history from taking note of it. When I typed "Larisa Bogoraz" as a search term on Google while writing this in March 2009, more than twenty-five citations to articles about her appeared. There is a page on Wikipedia about her, which includes her biography and a small photograph of the sign, "For Your Freedom and Ours"—the sign that briefly, but freely, blew in Red Square in 1968. There is also a page on Wikipedia titled, "Red Square Demonstration," where the facts of the protest and the name of each protestor are provided (Larisa Bogoraz, Konstantin Babtsky, Vadim Delaunay, Vladimir Dremluga, Pavel Litvinov, Natalya Gobranevskaya, Victor Fainberg, and Tatiana Baeva), as well as the punishment each protester received. There is even a list of the slogans on the banners they carried ("We are losing our best friends"; "Long live free and independent Czechoslovakia"; "Shame to the occupants"; "Hands off [Czechoslovakia]"; and "Freedom for Dubchek"—the leader of Czechoslovakia).

letter described how the protesters were "mercilessly manhandled" by the police during their arrest.

The document contained the closing remarks made by two of those on trial, Pavel Litvinov and Larisa. The article introduced their remarks as follows: "The reasoned, quiet pleas of the two dissenters are an eloquent echo of all those, from Socrates to Zola, who risked their own freedom in order to defend the right of men to speak freely." This "transcript" of the courtroom colloquy between Larisa and the judge followed:

LARISA: I do not think that a critical attitude toward any specific action of the government and the Communist Party should mean a slandering of the system.

JUDGE: Do not speak of your motives. That has nothing to do with the court.

LARISA: I have to speak of my motives, since this question was asked of me. I did not act on impulse. I thought about what I was doing, and fully knew what the consequences might be. I do not consider myself a public person, still less a political one.

I thought some public personages might speak out publicly, but they did not. I was faced with the choice of acting on my own or keeping silent. For me to have kept silent would have meant joining those who support the action with which I did not agree. That would have been like lying. If I had not done this, I would have had to consider myself responsible for the error of our government. Feeling as I do about those who kept silent in a former period [the Stalin era], I consider myself responsible.

PROSECUTOR: The defendant has no right to speak of things that have nothing to do with the accusation and no right to speak of the actions of the Soviet government and people. I demand that Defendant Bogoraz be denied the right to continue.

JUDGE (to Larisa): This is my third reprimand to you. You are trying to speak of your motives.

LARISA: So far, I have not touched on my motives in the Czecho-slovak question. I do not admit guilt, but do I have any regrets? To some extent, I do. I regret very deeply the fact that with me on this bench is a young man whose personality is still unformed. I am speaking of Vadim Delaunay [a twenty-one-year-old student and poet sentenced to thirty-four months at hard labor], whose character may be crippled by being sent to a prison camp. I regret, too, that the gifted, honest scholar Konstantin Babitsky [a thirty-two-year-old Moscow philologist, who was banished for three years] will be torn away from his work.

VOICE FROM COURTROOM: Speak about yourself.

LARISA (to the judge): The prosecutor ended his summation by suggesting that the verdict will be supported by public opinion. I, too, have something to say about public opinion. I do not doubt that public opinion will support this verdict as it would approve any other verdict. The defendants will be depicted as social parasites and outcasts and people of different ideologies.

Those who will not approve of the verdict, if they state their disapproval, will follow me here to this dock. I know the law, but I also know it in practice. And therefore today, in my final plea, I ask nothing of this court.

—◦◦—

Before I fell asleep the night I met Larisa, I tried to imagine what it was like for her to walk into Red Square at noon on that August day, knowing full well that only moments later her life as she knew it would come to an end. I was in awe of her courage and absolute sense of conviction to do what she believed was right.

Now I imagine her on a cliff, high above the water below, hav-ing arrived there with the certainty that she had reached her desti-nation—the only place where she knew she could breathe. And so when the time came for her to jump, she did not doubt that she should, she could, and she would soar, unafraid of where or how she would land. Because it was only in the act of jumping—only in the act of expressing her opinion—that she knew she would be free.

The Moscow Helsinki Watch Group

> Never doubt that a small group
> of thoughtful, committed people
> can change the world. Indeed it is
> the only thing that ever has.
> —Margaret Mead

"*On myortvyi chelovek,*" "He is a dead man," was all my taxi driver had to say when I asked him his opinion about the death of Konstantin Chernenko—the leader of the Soviet Union who died the day before, March 10, 1985, at the age of seventy-four. Chernenko had come to power only thirteen months earlier, when his predecessor, Yuri Andropov, passed away on February 9, 1984. Andropov, who was seventy years old when he died, had been in power for only fifteen months.

Chernenko's death gave way to Mikhail Gorbachev, who, at the age of fifty-four, at least had the potential for a term longer than his two predecessors. It seemed, from my observation, that the Soviets had slept through the transition of power from Andropov to Chernenko, but Gorbachev's liberal reforms and ambitious anti-alcohol campaign—which he launched soon after taking power—generated great interest among my Russian friends.

Already by the end of March, there was talk that Gorbachev was going to make drastic cutbacks on the production of vodka, implement harsh penalties for drinking in public, and even try to halt the thriving tradition of making homemade vodka. It did not take long for jokes about Gorbachev to spread. Andrei told me the following one day: "A man was waiting at the end of a line to buy vodka. He grew very impatient and angry and finally told the man ahead of him that he was going over to the Kremlin to shoot Gorbachev. But after only a few minutes he returned to the line. The man ahead of him asked if he had shot Gorbachev. He answered, 'No. The line over there is even longer.'" Uvol had this to say: "We used to be able to get to work at one in the afternoon and say we drank all night and everyone understood, even the boss. Now we have to get to work by noon!"

Inna told me this joke when I saw her a few days later: "Now, under Gorbachev, the first time you are caught at work drunk, you are fined 100 rubles and the second time, 200. The third time you are caught, the punishment is severe. They will take your internal passport and write on it that you are Jewish."

In fact, it was this joke that led into a broader discussion about Jews in the Soviet Union, because I asked Inna why "Jewish" would be written on an internal passport and how the notation could adversely affect someone. "When Stalin imposed internal passports in 1933, he required Jews to state their nationality as "Jewish" on the fifth point or spot on the passport. We must show our internal passports when applying for jobs or for the university and so our nationality is always taken into consideration by those in charge of making the decision. Jews are very aware of this, because all of us, either ourselves or our friends or a relative have not been allowed to advance, at one time or another, because of the fifth point on our passport," she explained.

"My friend told me a story about a Jewish girl who went to get her internal passport. When the official issued it, he did not notice her last name and in the spot for nationality wrote 'Russian' instead of 'Jewish.' When the girl arrived home she happily showed her parents that 'Russian' was stamped on her passport and exclaimed that this could create many opportunities for her. Her father became silent. Her mother took her passport, ripped it up, and flushed it down the toilet. Her parents then instructed her to return to the passport office and get a new passport. The poor girl went back and explained she lost her passport and this time was honest—she told them her nationality was Jewish."

—⁂—

When I met Gary in March, he was not at all in a joking mood. We had seen each other once in January and once in February, and each time he was worried about whether his plan to get admitted into a psychiatric hospital would succeed. Then the first week of March he called me at my apartment, something that he had never done before.

"Leeza, I go this week on my vacation."

"Your vacation?" I asked, not yet understanding what he was really trying to tell me.

"Yes, my vacation I told you about," he said, then paused to give me a moment.

"Oh, yes, *that* vacation," I said, my tone of voice conveying I understood he was referring to the hospital.

"Can we meet tomorrow night?"

"I'll have to juggle some things. What time?"

"Seven o'clock at our same place."

"I need more time. How about eight?"

"Okay, see you at eight."

We met at the Kievskaya station and then rode together to the Arbatskaya station. As we were riding the escalator up out of the metro, Gary reached into his jacket, pulled out a cigarette, put it in his mouth, and lit it.

"I have never seen anyone smoke in the metro," I observed.

"Because if they catch you, you have to pay five rubles," he explained.

"But I really don't think I have ever seen anyone smoke," I persisted.

"Because no one can afford five rubles."

—◦◦—

Once we got outside and started walking north to Bolshaya Nikitskaya Street, Gary told me he wanted to show me one of his favorite places in Moscow. We had walked only a few blocks more when he said, "There it is," pointing to a large church across the street and telling me it was the Church of the Great Ascension. Gary walked over to a bench directly across the street from the front of the church and invited me to join him. The main building of the church was painted yellow, and it had four white pillars at the entrance. Its dome was wide and round and more typical of one that would sit atop a government building than the classic onion-domed tops of Russian Orthodox churches. A white bell tower stood separately to the north of the church.

Gary told me the Russian poet Alexander Pushkin was married there in the early 1830s, in a ceremony that was marked by three bad omens. First, a major force of wind blew out the traditional groom's candle Pushkin was holding. Then Pushkin dropped a cross from the pulpit. The last ominous sign was when one member of the wedding party dropped to the floor during the exchange of rings between the bride and the groom.

"And did the omens prove true?" I asked.

"Of course. Pushkin was killed just few years later fighting in a duel."

"So why are you telling me these things tonight of all nights? Have you come here looking for a bad omen?"

"No. I like the place because on the outside you can't know people are not allowed inside," he replied.

"It is not a church where people can actually worship?"

"No, of course not. This church died long time ago under Stalin."

I was not surprised. One of the first things I learned about Soviet ideology was that it was based on atheism and aggressively antireligious. As soon as the communists overthrew the Russian monarchy and came to power in 1917, they did everything they could to destroy Russian Orthodox Christianity, which had been Russia's official religion since 988. Monasteries were shut down, churches were closed, and religious leaders were killed or sent to labor camps. Those who insisted on still trying to practice their Christian faith were often branded as mentally ill and sent to psychiatric hospitals.

"Are you nervous about going into the hospital?" I asked him.

"No," he replied. "Why should I be? One month with crazies will be better than two years in Afghanistan. I will survive the hospital. I am lucky man because my mom gets me into hospital."

"Do you know how long you will be there?"

"I cannot know, but I hope before summer begins. When I get back we go on picnic to Arkhangelskoye. Have you heard of this place? Just twenty kilometers from Moscow. It was built in the late 1700s and is fantastic. We call it the Russian Versailles. You will see how the rich Russians lived under the czar—fountains, flowers, and sculptures."

"It sounds great. I'll remember that and hold you to it."

We sat and talked for another fifteen minutes and then agreed to call it a night. Gary suggested it would be a more direct route for me to take a bus to the Octyaborskaya metro station and offered to ride with me. Our good-bye on the bus, surrounded by strangers, was awkward. Even if the words had come to me, I could not have spoken them to him out of concern that those around us would hear what I was saying. So I gave him a kiss on the cheek and told him I would be thinking about him often. In the moment our eyes connected before I turned to step out of the bus, I saw his familiar twinkle as he smiled at me and I smiled back.

Only a week later I received a call at my apartment from Gary's mother. When she introduced herself at the beginning of the conversation, I immediately thought something bad had happened. However, she explained that she had just visited Gary and told me not to worry, he was doing fine. She was calling because he wanted me to come with her the next time she visited him. She suggested we meet at a certain metro station and travel together to the hospital, which was located on the outskirts of Moscow. Without giving it any thought, I agreed to go with her, and we made plans to meet the following Tuesday afternoon at three o'clock.

As soon as I hung up the phone, I had second thoughts. One should never be spontaneous in the Soviet Union. Psychiatric hospitals were off limits to foreigners. I remembered Irina Grivnina and her work to expose the forced incarceration of Soviets who criticized their government, and I knew I would not be welcome there for that reason alone. If I did go, I would have to dress like a Russian from head to toe in order to go in unnoticed. Would I have to register my name? Would I have to answer questions? Would my Russian sound authentic enough, or would my accent reveal I was an American? What if I got caught? Would I get kicked out of the country? How much trouble would it cause the Smiths? As upsetting to me as these questions was how awful it would be to see Gary there. The thought of it all spooked me.

But how could I *not* go? He was my friend and had asked me to visit him.

Fortunately, I had a lesson scheduled with Inna the day before I was supposed to meet Gary's mom and decided to talk to her about it. I told her all my reasons for not going to see him and she agreed that, as an American, I would be forbidden to enter a psychiatric hospital. We talked about what could happen if the Soviet authorities stopped me from entering and about my concern that it would cause trouble for the Smiths. But I explained that, nonetheless, I felt obligated to visit him because he had asked me to. Inna responded empathetically. "You see, Leeza, now you understand. It is never as simple here as doing what you believe in your heart you should do. You must always consider the consequences of your actions."

I knew she was right, and I knew I couldn't go.

"Are you ready to begin?" Inna said. When I replied that I was, she asked me to hand her a book near me so she could find the page in it for me to read. I picked up the book and under it was an autographed photograph of U.S. Senator Gary Hart.

"Leeza, I had an important visitor yesterday, Senator Gary Hart," she told me in a matter-of-fact way before I had a chance to ask her about the photograph. She explained that Naum's only child from his first marriage, Olga, had been allowed to emigrate with her husband from the Soviet Union in 1976. Naum had applied with them but was denied a visa. He insisted they leave without him. Olga settled in Boulder, Colorado, and once there, succeeded in getting her senator, Gary Hart, involved in pressuring the Soviet government to allow Naum and Inna to emigrate. "He was here to visit Naum and me yesterday," she said, smiling. "He seemed to know a lot about our situation and told us he would keep fighting for our visas."

As Inna began telling me about Naum, I realized we had spent very little time talking about him. I knew they had only been married for a couple of years but did not know how they had met. I thought it was an opportune time to ask—and she gladly began to recall their courtship: "I first met Naum in 1981 to discuss how I should appeal the government's refusal of my visa application. He was recommended to me as someone who would know how best for me to proceed. We met at an American journalist's apartment, Annie Garrels. She was a correspondent here for ABC News and was one of my students. Do you know her, Leeza?" She paused for a moment and I nodded, confirming I knew to whom she was referring. "Naum immediately impressed me as a very intelligent and kind man. And although he is twenty years older than I am, I found myself quite attracted to him. Things moved fast between us, and I moved into his apartment after only a couple of months. Soon after that we were married," she smiled, and the look in her eye showed how smitten she was with him.

"He had been a very successful mathematician before he applied to emigrate to Israel in 1975," she continued. "He was refused permission, because the government claimed he knew 'state secrets' based on calculations he had done in the development of the Soviet atomic bomb over twenty-five years earlier. This reason is often used by our government to deny visas to scientists and mathematicians—that they have classified information. But the truth is any classified information Naum once had is now outdated and obsolete. Since at least 1955, his findings have been openly published in scientific journals here. Sakharov wrote a letter to the Federation of American Scientists in 1977 on his behalf, stating without a doubt that any information Naum had access to in the 1950s was no longer classified."

"Naum worked on the atomic bomb?" I asked.

"Yes. After the war, he worked in a mathematical section of the Institute for Problems in Chemistry of the Academy of Sciences with a very accomplished physicist, Lev Landau. They worked together on calculations regarding the formation of the Soviet atomic bomb. He and his colleagues received the State Stalin Prize in 1952 for this work." She explained it was the highest honor awarded each year by the government for achievements in several areas, including math and science. "Naum continued his work for over twenty more years, mainly at the Academy of Sciences, but was expelled from the Academy when he applied for a visa in 1975.

"That is when he became involved in the Helsinki Watch Group. Have you heard about this group, Leeza?"

I had not quite lifted my jaw off the table at learning of Naum's work in the development of the Soviet atomic bomb. Although I was embarrassed that I had not heard of the group before, I swallowed my pride and asked her to tell me more.

"Our leaders signed an international agreement in Helsinki in 1975, which is known as the 'Helsinki Accords.' The Soviets persuaded the West to recognize borders the Soviet Union had claimed in the Baltic States and in Poland after World War II. In exchange, the Soviets agreed, along with all nations that signed the agreement, to afford its citizens basic human rights and freedoms.

"For a few individuals here, who had been fighting our government for human rights, this agreement became a manifesto. In 1976, they formed a group in Moscow to monitor our government's compliance with the promises it made in the agreement. The original group had twelve members, and it became known as the 'Moscow Helsinki Watch Group.' Naum joined a year later with a few others.[1]

"Even though it had the right to exist by the very terms of the agreement, from the moment it was formed in 1976, the Soviet authorities would not tolerate this group. Some members were arrested for such things as treason, spying, and anti-Soviet agitation. Some were sent to psychiatric hospitals. A few others were stripped of their Soviet citizenship and forced to leave the country. It was only a matter of time before it was crushed completely," Inna continued. "Absolutely, Leez. By the time I married Naum in 1981, almost all of the members of the Helsinki Group— eighteen people—were in prison or had been forced to leave the country. By 1982, Naum and only two other members had become so harassed by authorities that they had no choice but forced to dissolve the group.

[1]The Helsinki Watch Group was founded by Yuri Orlov, and originally consisted of eleven others: Lyudimila Alexeyeva, Mikhail Bernshtam, Elena Bonner, Alexander Ginzbury, Pyotr Grigorenko, Alexander Korchak, Malva Landa, Anatoly Marchenko, Gregory Rosenstein, Vitaly Rubin, and Anatoly Sharansky. Additional members were: Sofia Kalistratov, Yuri Mniukh, Victor Nekipelov, Tatiana Osipova, Felix Serebrov, Vladimir Slepak, Leonard Ternovsky, Yuri Yarym-Agaev, Viaschelv Bachmin, and Alexander Podribinek.

"By Naum's count, during the time the Helsinki Group was active, it issued almost two hundred statements on such concerns as emigration, the rights of Crimean Tatars and other minority groups, and the forced incarceration of dissidents in psychiatric hospitals."

She told me in detail about one statement the Group issued regarding the results of a study of Jewish high school graduates who applied for admission to the prestigious mathematics department of Moscow University. The study, done in the late 1970s, was conducted by two math teachers, Valery Senderov and Boris Kanevsky, who suspected Jewish applicants were being denied admission since so few Jewish students were in the program. Fifty out of one hundred applicants in one year were Jewish, yet only five or six of them were accepted to the university. "You would have expected the Jewish applicants to do well on the exam because they had all excelled in advanced physics and mathematics high schools and many won national competitions," Inna explained.

"Naum told me that one student, who the university officials believed was Jewish, received poor grades. When his mother provided documents to the university that proved her son was not Jewish, his grades were changed, and he was admitted to the university. Of course, the university admitted to none of this."

"How did the university officials know whether or not an applicant was Jewish?" I asked.

"Students had to present their internal passports during the application process," Inna replied. "The Helsinki Group was concerned about this case not only because it proved that Jews were being intentionally excluded from receiving an advanced education, which they were qualified to receive, but also because the two authors of the study were arrested and sentenced to jail and exile for anti-Soviet agitation.

"You know, Leeza, Naum is well known in the West, in part, because of his work with the Helsinki Group, and so we have received invitations from many countries for me to come for medical treatment—Sweden, France, Israel, and the United States. Every time I apply for a visa to travel for such treatment, I am denied. We believe, in Naum's case, the government does not need to resort to arresting him and sending him to Siberia to punish him for fighting for human rights. Instead, it denies me, his wife, a visa to travel to the West to receive medical treatment. That in itself is brutal punishment.

"Naum would like to believe the sacrifices the members of the Helsinki Group made and the suffering those members endured for fighting for human rights had some effect, not only on the leaders of this country, but on our fellow citizens, but we have no way of knowing."

To say that I left Inna's apartment that afternoon in awe is an understatement. I couldn't believe the wispy-haired, scattered-looking man who had greeted me at the door over the last few months was one of the leaders in the fight for human rights in the Soviet Union. And while there was absolutely no sign at that time that the Soviet government would ease suppression of those advancing the fight for human rights, an article published by the National Security Archives at George Washington University on May 12, 2006, to mark the thirtieth anniversary of the formation of the Moscow Helsinki Watch Group noted:

> Although the early 1980s became the worst years for the Soviet human rights movement, we know that the ground prepared by the Helsinki groups became the fertile soil for Gorbachev's perestroika after 1985. Thus the story of the signing of the Helsinki Final Act and the founding of the Moscow Helsinki Group becomes a story of unintended consequences for the Soviet regime, which links the events of the mid-1970s with the end of the Cold War and the collapse of Communism in Eastern Europe and the Soviet Union.

An Average American

May the road rise up to meet you.
May the wind always be at your back.
May the sun shine warm upon your face,
and the rains fall soft upon your fields.
And until we meet again,
may God hold you in the hallow of His hand.
—Irish Blessing

As March came to end, I was busy making plans for my mom's visit to Moscow. She was scheduled to arrive on April 4, and I was so excited that the day, which had seemed to be so far away, was now just around the corner. The girls were also very excited about having my mom visit, as it was rare for them to have a guest from the States.

My mom was going to be in Moscow for ten days, and I had arranged an activity for almost every one of them. I planned on taking her to a performance at the Bolshoi Ballet and on a day trip to two of Russia's oldest cities, Vladimir and Suzdal. They had been the center of Russia from the eleventh through the thirteenth centuries and were very important in the development of Russian language and nationality. I thought my mom would also enjoy getting out of Moscow and traveling by train through the Russian countryside.

Of course, I also wanted her to meet my Russian friends and had made arrangements for us to spend time with each of them. Galya and her mother could not wait to meet her and thank her in person for sending the Orwell book. I arranged to see them Friday night. Natasha also offered to host a gathering on Saturday night. Finally, I made plans to take my mom to meet Inna at my regular lesson time on Monday.

On Thursday morning, Joan drove me to the airport; we arrived about twenty minutes before my mom's flight landed. I was beside myself with excitement as I waited by a wire fence in the main hall that separated those arriving from those waiting to greet them.

At first I didn't recognize her because she was not dressed in her usual casual attire. Instead of jeans, sweater, and comfortable shoes, a purple wool cape covered my mom's shoulders and dropped over her waist where it blended into the lighter shade of her purple velour pants. Dark lenses from her sunglasses covered her eyes. Somehow she managed to walk swiftly, in spite of black leather boots with spike heels, the likes of which I had never seen her wear before. Loose brown curls, accented with modest highlights, bounced naturally around her face. She looked very much the part of a seasoned international traveler, rather than someone who, just the day before, had been in the heart of middle-class, Midwest America.

The sight of seeing my mom entering my life in Moscow overwhelmed me. Her movements to the passport and visa inspection area, where she replaced her dark sunglasses for her regular wire-rimmed frames, seemed to play out in slow motion. She passed through the checkpoint and started walking in my direction—and only then did she see me. I ran to her, and we hugged. When we broke our embrace, I stepped back and looked at her, then touched her face to make sure she was really standing there in front of me.

Then I experienced the pleasure of introducing her to Joan, and they warmly and affectionately greeted each other. I did not have any plans for that first day, as I suspected my mom would be tired from her trip, and she was. She enjoyed meeting the girls and had brought them each a Cabbage Patch doll, which was all the rage in the States at that time. I also asked her to bring them some candy, and they were thrilled when she gave them grape-flavored Bubble Yum and long sheets of paper with colored candy dots on them.

The next night with Galya, Victoria, and Vera turned out to be one of my most memorable experiences in the Soviet Union. I decided to take a taxi in order to spare my mom the hour-long trip by public transportation. On the way, I told her how grateful Galya and Victoria were to her for sending the book about Orwell and that they considered her their hero. "But all I did was mail you a book," my mom responded, not grasping how such an ordinary act on her part could produce such an extraordinary result on the other side of the world. As we walked down the pavement to Galya's apartment, I noticed my mom had stopped a few paces behind me. So I backtracked toward her and asked her what was wrong.

"Just give me a minute, Lisa. I'm a little nervous," she whispered. She reached for my hand and held it tight, and I realized what had become routine for me was anything but that for her. It was the moment of a lifetime. "I remember when I was a kid," she continued, "we did duck-and-cover drills in grade school. Unlike a steady ring for a fire drill, when the alarm blasted on and off, we knew it was the signal that we were about to be bombed by the Soviet Union. So the teacher helped us all scurry under our desks and duck for cover. Now here I am, in Moscow. I can't quite believe it."

"I can't either, Mom, but I am so happy you are." We stood together a few seconds more, and then I put my arm around her and said, "Now let's go and meet my friends. You will love them, Mom. I promise, you will."

What I had tried to verbally explain to my mom was conveyed without words the moment Galya and Victoria greeted us at the door. Galya hugged my mom as if she were a long-lost friend and then stepped aside and let her mother do the same. Victoria held my mom a little longer and a little tighter than Galya had, and then pulled back away to kiss her on the cheek. She looked into my mom's eyes and said, "Thank you, Helen, from my heart" in English, as if she had rehearsed it over and over again just to get it right, and she had. Both women smiled as brightly and warmly as the midday sun. Victoria took my mom's hand and said, "Please come, we have been waiting for you." The two did not leave each other's side for the two hours that followed.

Once in the apartment, we walked down the hallway past Galya's room to Victoria's room at the end of the hall. Vera was standing near the door to greet and escort us to our chairs. She, in her typical fashion, was shy but very sweet, and was as pleased as Galya and Victoria had been to meet my mom. Victoria introduced us to a man she said was her good friend, Leonid, whom I had never met before. He appeared to be in his early- to mid-fifties. As I watched the two of them interact in a tender and familiar manner, I suspected their relationship was an intimate one.

A long table was set up in the room, and I was sure it fit only because they had cleared out some furniture. It was covered with an incredible feast of traditional Russian and Georgian food. Victoria's mother gave a description of the dishes on the table to my mom—with me jumping in to translate as best I could when necessary—as we all breathed in the smell of garlic, dill, raw onion, and kolbasa.

"This is called *khinkali* and is a dumpling filled with meat. I learned to make them when I was a child in Tbilisi, Georgia." While Victoria briefly explained to my mom where that was, I was a bit captivated by the *khinkali*, which I had never seen before. It was in the shape of an oversized Hershey's Kiss and just as I was wondering how you would go about eating it, Victoria said, "Pick it up with your hand and eat around the top first." She pointed to one other Georgian item on the table, a large piece of rounded bread that she called *khachapuri*. She explained it was typical for Georgians to eat this cheese-filled bread with every meal. The main dish was a beef shish kebab. There was an assortment of vegetable dishes: eggplant, beets with dill sprinkled on them, and *stolichny* salad—the dish that no Russian table ever went without.

Victoria offered the first toast of the evening, which was to my mom. She switched from Russian to English as her voice became full of emotion. "Your act of kindness, Helen, saved me. Thank you." Many other toasts followed—to friendship, the future, and world peace. Galya gave my mom a wooden egg about the size of an adult fist with a religious scene that she had painted herself. My mom was in awe of the gift, and she exclaimed it was "absolutely beautiful." Then she hugged Galya, telling her she had never seen anything like it.

As the night progressed my mom was growing visibly tired. I asked her if she wanted to go, and she said, "No, but it is getting late, so we'd better." As I announced that it was time for us to leave, my mom surprised me by saying it was her turn to give a toast. She explained that her ancestors on both her mom's and her dad's side were from Ireland. "I can't remember the words exactly, but there is an Irish blessing that goes something like this: 'May the road rise up to meet you, the sun shine warm on your face, and the wind be at your back, and, until we meet again, may God hold you in the palm of His hand." Her words were heartfelt, clear, and she moved her eyes around the table so she could connect with each person as she spoke. She absolutely amazed me. It was one of those moments meant to be lived through and written on your soul.

Saturday night we went to Natasha and Uvol's. Everyone was so friendly and jovial, causing my mom to feel immediately at ease. I tried to keep up with translating, but hand gestures and facial expressions seemed to carry the night. We had a blast.

On Monday afternoon, I eagerly brought my mom to meet Inna. Inna smiled graciously as she opened the door, but waited to greet us until we were in the apartment. I made the introductions as I took my mom's coat, and then Inna invited her to come into the study.

"Helen, it is such a pleasure to meet you. Leeza has told me so much about you. Please sit down," she said as she pointed to a chair at the table. "Leeza, there is a torte in the kitchen. Can you bring that in with the kettle from the stove and the jar of Nescafé? Or do you prefer tea?" she asked my mom.

"Coffee is fine, thank you."

"I am so impressed you traveled all this way to see your daughter," I heard Inna say as I walked out of the room.

I was in the kitchen for only a few minutes, but when I was walking back into the study, the wonderful sight of the two of them together, engaged in lively conversation, stopped me in my tracks. They seemed so familiar and comfortable with each other—as if they had been meeting on Monday afternoons to chitchat for years. I hesitated in interrupting them. After a minute or so more, Inna noticed me in the doorway and motioned me to come in.

"Please set the torte and coffee down on the table," she told me. Once I had done that she asked me to get something for her that she had put behind the door to the study. I had no experience with Inna giving me orders, but she did it in a way that reflected how comfortable she was with me, and I felt as comfortable with her. It was if she and I were the hosts, and my mom was our guest.

I looked behind the door and found a *matryoshka* doll about a foot tall. I carried it over to Inna, and she took it from me, only to immediately hand it to my mom.

"Helen, this is for you. It is an example of traditional Russian folk art," Inna explained. "There are many smaller dolls nested into the larger dolls. See," she said, twisting the waist of the doll and taking out a slightly smaller second doll and continuing until five dolls later she pulled out a tiny doll, half the size of my pinkie finger. Inna explained she had bought it at a market and that it was hand-painted by a Russian peasant woman.

"It is beautiful! Thank you so much, Inna. And I have a gift for you, too," my mom replied as she reached into her purse and retrieved a book of poems by Emily Dickinson, which I recommended she bring for Inna.

"Oh, thank you, Helen," Inna said, truly delighted with the gift. "Leeza must have told you Emily Dickinson is one of my favorite authors." Inna looked at me and smiled. I poured the water into the cups, and they each scooped and then stirred in a couple spoonfuls of Nescafé. Inna asked me to cut the torte, and I served them each a piece.

Then they started up their conversation again, seemingly oblivious to my presence. I simply enjoyed listening to them chat—they seemed perfectly at ease with one another. After we finished our torte, I cleared the plates, took them into the kitchen, washed them, and tried to stay out of their way.

When I returned to the room, Inna asked me to sit down and join them. Then she said, "Helen, I have enjoyed getting to know your daughter. She has such a busy life here and so many friends, and she is a good student."

Toward the end of our visit, Inna remarked that she and Naum get many visitors from the West. "Because of my situation and all those who are trying to help us, we are fortunate to have many guests," she explained. "But you, Helen, are the first average American I've ever met." Her remark caused me to laugh first and then immediately feel concerned that my mom might have felt slighted by being called average. Inna, noticing my reaction, quickly explained her comment, "I mean average in the sense that people who visit Naum and me usually have a purpose for seeing us. They are good reasons, but nonetheless, some other motive than just being with us. They are diplomats, journalists, visiting politicians, or students like you, Leeza. But Helen, you have come to me straight from the Midwest of America, and I have learned so much from you."

Then she became very serious and said, "Spending this time with you, Helen, has made me understand that the tragedy if I die here would be that average Americans like you would never know my story. Other Americans like you should know the reality of my struggle, of our struggle here."

Inna's comment about my mom was the turning point in my friendship with her because it made me start thinking about what I could do to help her tell her story to all Americans. Although I had come to really care about Inna, I had not ever before thought about personally getting involved in helping her. In part, this was because I never thought there was anything I could do to help her get a visa. The idea of telling her story to Americans, however, was something I could do. I just had to think of a *way* I could do it.

That night I had an idea and wondered whether I should discuss it with my mom or whether it would only worry her after she returned home. In the end, I could not resist. So often in Moscow I wished I had my mom there to talk to, and now there she was, right in my bedroom. I sat on the floor next to the bed and started to whisper to her what I was thinking. At first she looked at me strangely. "Why are you whispering?"

I knelt up close by her and, continuing in a whisper, said, "I need to be quiet because we just assume there are listening devices in the apartment."

She looked at me in disbelief, but I whispered again, "I'm serious, Mom."

Her eyes widened a bit as if she understood, and then she asked, her voice lowered to a whisper, "What are you thinking about doing?"

"Remember what Inna said today, about what a tragedy it would be if she died here without average Americans knowing her story? I want to help her tell her story. Maybe I could interview her with Paul's video equipment and then I could try to publicize her plight with the tape of the interview when I return to the States."

"Where would you interview her?"

"I'm not sure, Mom. We will all be leaving for the States in a few months, so maybe whatever I plan, I would arrange to do it my last week here."

Swimming in the Daylight

> I learned that courage was not the
> absence of fear, but the triumph
> over it. The brave man is not he
> who does not feel afraid,
> but he who conquers that fear.
> —Nelson Mandela

In mid-April, a day or two after my mom left, I received a call from Gary. He had just returned to Moscow from the hospital and wanted to see me. We arranged to meet the following night. At first, I almost didn't recognize him. He had a small frame to begin with, so his weight loss was remarkably noticeable. A scruffy beard covered his face, making him look older than he was. But it was his eyes that startled me. They had lost their sparkle and looked weary and defeated.

The first question he asked me was why I had not come to visit him. I tried to explain the reason, which had seemed so valid a month earlier, but in front of him, my logic crumbled.

"I'm very sorry, Gary. It just was not possible for me to visit you there. It is not a place where Americans are allowed. Was it awful?" I asked, trying to move the conversation away from me.

"Oh, no, it was like cruise on Volga River," he replied. At least he had not lost his sarcasm.

"Tell me about it," I insisted.

"I had to come up with an act so doctors believe I was crazy, so the first few days I was very quiet and watched the guys around me. They keep to themselves. One guy made loud noises. I decide to copy him. I got from being to myself, very quiet, then weird laugh, very loud. The worst part was injections, two a day for two weeks."

As Gary spoke, I remembered what Irina Grivnina had told me: "Without the injections, it is possible to keep your mind." I wondered if draft evaders received a different type of injection than dissidents. I wondered if Gary had kept his mind intact.

"Did the injections hurt or make you feel strange?"

"I have a black-and-blue ass from injections. You like to see?" he offered jokingly. "They made me tired, help me sleep all day."

"Now what?"

"No Afghanistan."

⸺◦◦⸺

The next time I saw Inna, she spoke with delight about my mom and what a warm and genuine woman she was. I told Inna my mom felt the same way about her. Their meeting strengthened the bond Inna and I had already formed.

"I must tell you about a short story I read on the train to my village about a fish that was perhaps too wise," Inna said to me as we sat in the study. "The story is by a well-known nineteenth-century Russian satirical writer Saltykov-Schedrin and is about a small fish that spends all of his life afraid of the big fish. The little fish did not want to swim during the day for fear of openly exposing himself to the larger fish, which he feared would eat him. So the fish safely lived his life burrowing under a rock during the day and coming out only in the dark of night to search for food. As he grew older, he began to imagine more and more what it would be like to swim in the daylight, free of the fear that he would be eaten by the larger fish. He became very preoccupied with this thought and tried to muster the courage to swim during the day. Then one day, while sleeping under a rock, he dreamt that he was swimming, freely and without fear, in the daylight. The feeling was so real, so extraordinary. But at the peak of this feeling, the fish died."

Inna's eyes were full of tears as she finished the story. I was holding back my own.

"You know, Leeza, I realized that the story is about me. I am like that fish."

"I know, Inna."

"Only for me it is not too late. I myself became brave later in my life, but it made me extremely happy. I am not afraid of anything."

"Inna, you are swimming in the daylight."

There was silence. Perhaps Inna, like I, was thinking about the one thing incomplete about her dream was that she was still in a stream in the Soviet Union.

"I have something important to tell you, Inna. I have been thinking a lot about what you said when my mom was here, that it would be a tragedy if you died in the Soviet Union without average Americans, like my mom, knowing your story. Remember?"

"Yes, I remember," Inna answered, showing great interest in what I was saying.

"Well, I want to give you a chance to tell your story." I explained my idea in a very quiet voice. "I want to interview you with the Smiths' video camera. I can send the tape to Appleton through a friend of mine who is an American diplomat, so the tape won't be intercepted by the Soviet authorities. Then, when I get back to the States, I'll try to try to get it on the news and show it to as many people as possible."

I waited anxiously for her reaction—both to my idea and to my desire to try to help her.

She reached across the table, turned the radio on, and became very serious—almost stern—in her reply: "This could be very dangerous for you to do, and you must be sure about it. Of course, if it was done right and if I said the right things, it might help us. But I will have to think about it and talk to Naum."

_⚬·⚬_

The next week, when I arrived for my lesson and sat down at the table next to Inna, she picked up an envelope next to her and pulled out two airline tickets from the Swedish airline S.A.S.

"Inna, are you leaving Moscow?" I asked excitedly.

"No. Naum and I just received these tickets to Stockholm from a Swedish diplomat. We have everything we need to go: the tickets, an invitation from the Swedish Minister of Health guaranteeing all of our expenses, and a hospital willing to admit me for treatment. So, we have everything except a visa from my government allowing me to go.

"Leeza, I am sorry to sound so desperate, but I am ready to carry a sign into Red Square demanding our release. My son is so upset. He wanted to go on a hunger strike for me, as a way to fight for my leaving here, but I told him not to do it. He cannot jeopardize his job, which is hard work and requires all of his strength. And he cannot afford any trouble now. His wife is expecting their third child. I told him that I myself would do a hunger strike. But he would not have that. So, we called a truce.

"Maybe I won't use these tickets now, but someday, Leez, I will leave here. I only hope that when I do, I will not have to be carried out on a stretcher. I want to walk by myself onto the plane."

"You will get to leave here, Inna. And when you do, I'll be there when you land."

"I hope so, Leeza. Let's go for a walk," she said. She was quiet until we had walked about a block away from her apartment building.

"I talked to Naum about your idea to interview me and he and I are in agreement. At this point, we are willing to try anything to get my visa so that I can leave for medical treatment. I also talked to some of my friends who are American journalists, and they agree an interview is a good idea. But they suggested that if I am really serious about telling my story, I should do an interview with an American correspondent, that is, it should be done professionally. They said if it were done on a home video camera by an amateur, the quality might not be good enough for the networks in the States to use it. But, this is your idea, so I want to know what you think."

I thought for a moment and then answered enthusiastically, "The most important thing is that you get the chance to tell your story, and the chances of that would be greater if a reporter did the interview. I think it would be great! A major network might only air a few minutes of it on the evening news, but it would still be worth it. Maybe I could get a copy of the tape and try to do something with it when I get home."

"How many people would see it if it were on the evening news?" Inna asked, thinking over the idea.

"I'm not sure. The correspondent would know better, but I'm sure the number's in the millions."

"Really, Leez? I have thought about it. Naum and I are so frustrated. But each day we wake up with the hope that with treatment in the West, I can survive. It is still not too late for me. And if the interview is a success—if it is shown on your national television—not only will average Americans hear about my story, but we are sure our officials will see it, too. But I am not afraid of that. I want them to see it. And if they get angry and want to punish me, what could they do to me that is worse than ignoring our plea for visas and denying me medical treatment that could save my life?"

I walked Inna back to her apartment and then continued on, but not in the direction of the tram stop, because I was too upset to go home. I walked a few blocks north and came to the base of the Moskvoretsky Bridge and started walking over it toward Red Square, pausing about halfway to take in the view of the Kremlin. The epicenter of the Soviet government and communist rule, the Kremlin had been the czar's Moscow residence before the Revolution. The grand Kremlin Palace, the building in which the governing body of the USSR met, was ironically surrounded by churches built in the 1400s, including Assumption Cathedral, which was the mother of all of Russian churches.

As I stood there, staring at the sun's reflection off the churches' golden onion domes onto the river below, I felt so sad and hopeless about Inna's situation.

"Why, God, do you allow such evil to exist? Why is Inna just dying here?" I asked out loud.

I stood there for a few moments, immobilized by emotion. Finally I started walking again and made my way past St. Basil's Cathedral and into Red Square. A huge red banner of Vladimir Lenin was hanging on the façade of one of the buildings on the Square. The sight of it felt suffocating to me. All I could think about was Inna sitting at her table with airline tickets to Sweden without any chance of using them. A group of young Soviet soldiers were marching in formation toward me as I walked by the State History Museum, on the east side of the square. The very sight of them turned my stomach, and I could feel the blood rush to my face as they marched closer. When they were about ten feet in front of me, I imagined them being shot down by a machine gun firing behind me. Within moments they walked by, leaving me feeling completely astonished and frightened by my imaginary reaction to them.

I decided to take the metro home and got on at a station on the north side of the Square. It was about four o'clock in the afternoon, and the crowds were beginning to get heavy. I managed to find a seat near a window and retreated into my thoughts as the train descended into the dark tunnel. The Smiths were starting to talk about when they were going to pack up and leave Moscow. Joan was intending to leave as soon as the girls got out of school, at the end of June. I had thought that would be my plan, too, but based on the visceral reaction I had just experienced, and how intense living in

Moscow was feeling to me, the end of June seemed too far away. My tank, which had been full of adventure and energy when I arrived in Moscow in October 1983, felt almost empty. I wanted to go home.

I talked to Joan that night about leaving Moscow by the end of May. I explained I was feeling burned out. She was very understanding and said they would be fine without me those last few weeks.

Around that same time, I had lunch in the snack bar at the American Embassy with a group of women I knew from my job in the Consulate. Karen Glass, the wife of an American diplomat, started talking about an American family that had taken a cruise from Odessa across the Black Sea. She said she was thinking about taking a similar trip, and even had an Intourist brochure. One thing led to another, and before I knew it, I was making plans to leave the Soviet Union by ship from Odessa to Athens, Greece. From there, Karen would fly to Germany for the summer, and I would fly to Amsterdam to see Daphne for a few days before continuing on to the States.

I saw Inna the next week. We sat in her kitchen, and Inna made tea. She cut a few slices from a dark loaf of bread and offered me fresh jam for both the tea and the bread. "The jam was made by a woman in my village, Leez," she said proudly.

"Inna, I have something to tell you. I am going to be leaving Moscow at the end of May."

"You will be returning to the States for good?" My news took Inna by surprise.

"Yes, I will. The Smiths are leaving a couple of weeks later. I am running low on energy, and I think I've had enough." I told her about my travel plans.

"Excellent! You will have to send me a letter and tell me about it," Inna responded enthusiastically.

"I just hope that your interview will be arranged before I leave."

Inna got up and took something off a shelf and returned to the table with it. It was a magic slate pad. In a quiet voice she asked, "Do you know what this is?"

"Of course, I drew on those when I was a kid."

"We call it a Jewish notebook here," she laughed and explained, "We can immediately peel back the cover and erase what we write. It is very useful and efficient." Then she wrote on the pad: "May 29. Mark Phillips—CBS news—here—May 29."

"That's fantastic!" I whispered.

"It's a nice day. Let's go out for a walk." As soon as we walked across the street from her apartment building, Inna began talking about the interview.

"What do you think Americans would be most interested in hearing about? I want to keep it simple, yet talk about the whole issue of refuseniks and Jewish emigration, not just about myself. You will have to help me prepare," she sounded uncharacteristically worried and anxious, and I understood why. This was her chance, perhaps her one and only, to tell the world about her fight for medical treatment. It was an opportunity for her to fight for her life.

While it felt strange for me to be giving Inna advice, I tried to tell her something that would lessen the pressure she was obviously feeling. "Inna, you're so kind and honest. Just be yourself. Talk as if my mom is across the table from you, and you are telling her about your life here and about your friends. As my dad would say, you just have to get up to bat and take a swing."

"Ah, yes, you are referring to your American sport, baseball," Inna said.

"Yes, Inna, but more than that, my dad was referring to life presenting an opportunity, and just giving that opportunity your best shot."

We saw each other a few weeks later, which turned out to be my last scheduled lesson with her. She gave me some of her worksheets and a book of short stories in Russian that she suggested I read over the summer. Then she presented me with a book called *The Itinerants*, which contained a collection of paintings by Russian Realist artists from the second half of the nineteenth and early twentieth centuries. Inna knew I loved that era of Russian painters. She inscribed it as follows: "Dear Leeza, Keep us in your mind and in your heart. Love, Inna. P.S. By 'us' I mean all of us."

We then talked about my plans for the summer. I explained I would live in Appleton with my parents for three months, and then return to my senior year at the University of Minnesota in September. "I hope to find a job and earn some money for school while I am in Appleton. I also have to find a place to live in Minneapolis, so I'll be busy."

I asked if everything was still on schedule for her interview, and she nodded her head yes, indicating that it was. Then she offered to walk me outside. It felt so good to just be walking with her on that warm, sunny day. Neither of us spoke for a while, both of us enjoying the comfort we felt just walking together without talking.

She paused on the small bridge near the tram stop, by the place where we first met.

"I have decided to get my hair done the morning of the interview, and I will wear the sweater I am wearing now because it covers my neck," Inna said. "And I think I will have just a swig of vodka before the interview begins to calm my nerves."

I smiled and told her she would be great. "Inna, I'm just so glad that you're doing the interview. You know I'll help in any way I can, but it seems to me that everything is arranged. What I am trying to say is I don't need to be there, if I am going to be in the way."

"You know, many people from abroad visit Naum and me, and we are very lucky because most offer to help us. But of all those people who come and go, there are only few who we can really depend on. For example, we have a friend who is a doctor in France, and we rely on him for medicine. He sends it to us regularly through a French diplomat.

"Leeza, *dorogaya*," she smiled, referring to me affectionately as "dear" in Russian, "Naum and I discussed the tape, and we agreed we want you to be responsible for it. We want you to have a copy of it so you can do what you are able to do."

I had tears in my eyes and felt the true weight of what she was telling me, which felt not like a burden, but rather like an exceptional honor.

"Inna, that's the most important compliment I have ever been given," I replied. "I'll never forget it, and I won't let you down."

CHAPTER

The Interview

> In keeping silent about
> evil it gets buried so deep that it will only rise
> up a thousand-fold in the future.
> —Alexander Solzhenitsyn

On my last Monday in Moscow I got up early to say good-bye to Smiths, who were going to Helsinki for the week. Getting the girls out of bed and helping with their breakfast had always felt like a pleasant routine rather than a job, and there was nothing any different about that morning except suitcases were by the door instead of the girls' school backpacks. We deflected saying good-bye by talking about getting together over the summer. They would be in Minneapolis with Joan's mom before relocating to Geneva, Switzerland. Kjirsten, who was such a tenderhearted child, became very sad when Paul finally took charge and declared it was time for them to go. I gave her a hug and held her tight, telling her I would miss her very much, but that I would see her during the summer. I had been managing to hold back the tears, but when Laura ran into my arms, and I had to go through it again, I lost it. I had to pause and compose myself before I could say how much I would miss her. Joan and Paul had always made me feel like a member of their family, and I felt that more strongly than I had ever before when I said good-bye to them. As I watched the four of them walk down the hallway toward the elevator without me, a sharp pain overcame me, knowing that I would no longer be a part of their everyday life.

On Monday afternoon I met Natasha, Uvol, Andrei, and Volodya, even though we had plans to be together Wednesday night for my going-away party. Natasha said she had a gift for me and did not want to wait to give it to me. I suggested we meet at Gorky Park, because it was a pleasant spot along the banks of the Moscow River and a convenient place to get to from my apartment. I had enjoyed taking Laura and Kjirsten to the amusement park there, and we even went in the winter to skate on the walkways, which had been purposefully flooded and frozen with ice.

As soon as we walked through the arched entrance to the park, Natasha handed me a large object, about fourteen inches wide by twenty inches high, loosely covered by a plastic bag. I lifted up the plastic bag and discovered a painting from her apartment. It was of a clown sitting on a chair in an empty room. Behind the clown, a curtain flowed from the breeze coming through an open window. The clown's head flopped back, and he looked deflated. I had admired the painting since the first time I had seen it that night at Natasha's apartment, after the babushka had died. I felt such a strong connection to the subject of the painting because it depicted how I often felt during my second year in Moscow, finally getting home after a long day with a chance to be by myself and think about all the things— many seemingly incomprehensible—I was experiencing.

I had taken a photograph of the painting a few months earlier and mailed the film to the United States to be developed, intending to make an enlargement from the negative when I got home. When I received the photographs back in the mail, I brought them to show Natasha. We both agreed that none of the photographs was a good duplicate of the painting, but that was the end of our discussion about it.

"Oh my gosh, Natasha, is this your painting?" I asked, overwhelmed.

"No, this is your painting. I painted a copy of it just for you. Now you will have one on your wall in your apartment, and I will have one on mine."

"Thank you. I can't believe you did this for me."

We walked leisurely through the park, as if time were on our side, and talked about my plans for the summer and when I would possibly return to Moscow. I had no idea when that would be, but told them someday I would be back. Volodya was very happy I was going to see Daphne so soon after seeing him, because he believed I would be able to transport his energy to her. He had written a letter to her that I promised to hand deliver.

Monday night I went to Galya's. She and Vera had prepared some food and offered vodka and champagne as we chatted about my plans and when I might return to Moscow. When the inevitable moment came for me to leave, I hugged each of them— Victoria, Vera, and Galya—and then I hugged each of them again. Outside, I bent over, put my hands on my knees, bowed my head, and cried. I had never before experienced saying good-bye to a friend without knowing when and if we would meet again. I considered running back to see them once more but knew it would only be worse to have to say good-bye a second time, so I made myself put one foot in front of the other and walk away.

Tuesday night I met Gary at Smolenskaya Square at the west end of Arbat Street. We walked east to a café with outdoor seating and each had a dish of ice cream. Our friendship had been strained since his return from the hospital. He had become introverted, no longer exuding the charisma that had made it so easy to be with him, and I sensed his disappointment in my not visiting him while he was away.

He insincerely asked about my travel plans, so I only told him the basic itinerary. I wanted to tell him I would come back in a year or so after I graduated from college and try to bring him to the

United States. But I couldn't bring myself to make a promise I wasn't sure I could keep.

Our good-bye was unemotional and matter-of-fact. He told me to come back soon. I responded that I would try.

"You must write me about your trip," he said with a pleasant smile on his face. Then, without saying another word, he turned around and walked away from me. I took a few steps in the other direction, to take a bus home, and then turned to see him one last time. But he had already disappeared in the crowd.

Wednesday, my last full day in Moscow, was the day of Inna's interview. About mid-morning, I went to the American Embassy to say good-bye to some friends and have lunch with my coworker Sandy. As she talked about her own plans to leave Moscow at the end of June, I became preoccupied with thinking about Inna and her interview. I suddenly worried about what would happen if the KGB stormed in during the interview and hauled us all away. I had not told any American about it and wondered what I would do or who I would call if I found myself in jail. So I decided to tell Sandy about the interview and asked if I could call her if any trouble arose. She agreed without hesitation and then jokingly added, "If you're allowed to make a call."

I took a taxi to Inna's apartment. I had the driver stop a couple of blocks away from the apartment so I could walk the rest of the way. This was my lame attempt at ditching any KGB agent who might have been following me—as if a KGB agent who had been following me would not know exactly where I was going and why.

When I got to Inna's apartment, Nancy Traver, an American correspondent for *Time*, met me at the door and let me in, putting her finger over her mouth indicating I should be quiet. Her husband, Andy Rosenthal, the Moscow correspondent for the Associated Press, was also there. I knew they were both good friends of Inna and Naum's but had never met them before.

I walked a few feet into the hallway and peeked through the doorway into the study. Inna was sitting at her table, facing the hallway, and the CBS reporter, Mark Phillips, was seated in front of her, with his back to us. The room had been transformed into a television studio. Two bright lights shone on Inna, and there was a large microphone in front of her on a stand. The cameraman stood just behind Mark's left shoulder, and his camera was rolling.

The sight of it gave me goose bumps. She noticed me and smiled. I reached my hand out and cheered her on with a thumbs-up. Her face was a bit flushed and she sounded nervous when she talked, but soon she relaxed and settled into her natural cadence. I listened with great attention to every word she spoke.

"This is an interview with Inna Kitrosskaya Meiman," Mark began. "Inna, you have prepared a statement to make, but let me just ask you, what is it that put you in this situation that you're in now, and what it is you're trying to do?"

"Oh, I wonder if I can read my statement first," Inna asked nervously, not ready to answer questions.

"You can begin with whatever you like," Mark encouraged her.

Inna cleared her throat and began: "Before me is an American magazine, *Newsweek.* 'Living with Cancer' is an article that attracted my attention. It is about a courageous American woman, Helen Barlet, and her fight against cancer, which is supported by her family, friends, and an army of medical workers, as well as American society. Being a cancer victim myself, my feelings were in turmoil as I read the article. But I am not going to compare my case to hers, because they are completely different.

"What I am going to talk about is that cancer is something that the patient has to fight in order to survive, and I want to talk about how I am trying to fight my cancer. Before I go into that, I want to introduce myself and tell you who I am.

"My name is Inna Kitrosskaya Meiman. I am fifty-two years old and Jewish. I was born in Moscow, and I've lived here all my life.

I have never left the Soviet Union, because I have never been allowed to. I went through college in Moscow, majored in English. I was a teacher of English for almost thirty years. I must say that I had a pretty good job by our standards. I earned a master of science and have written college textbooks for English. I have translated a few books on art from Russian into English. I was very successful in my professional career.

"Then, in 1979, I decided to immigrate with my son and his wife to Israel. In our country, the desire to emigrate is considered an unforgivable treachery. If a person has applied to emigrate, the government considers him unworthy of any decent job, not to mention teaching jobs. So, under pressure, I quit my job, and my son and I started waiting for our visas. Two years passed before we were summoned to the Moscow visa office. An official told me very pompously and importantly that we had been denied permission to emigrate. I asked why and was told, 'Your relatives in Israel are not close enough for you to go and join them.' That was that.

"We became refuseniks and joined a very large group of people in Moscow and elsewhere in this country whose lives are very harsh and miserable. By the way, we are nonexistent, because when our government officials are asked about refuseniks they always respond that we do not exist.

"In 1981, I married Naum Meiman, a professor of mathematics, a doctor of science, and himself a refusenik since 1975. He is seventy-four years old. He is an active fighter for Jewish emigration and also a fighter for civil rights. He is a member of the Moscow Helsinki Watch Group.

"In 1983, I fell ill with cancer. People know now so much about cancer. They also know that diagnosis is always more or less unexpected. I put my hand on the back of my neck one day and discovered a lump. I have a very big cavity there now, so it is hard for me to hold my head up for a long time. I had an operation to remove the tumor, which was a horrible experience under local anesthetics.

"In May 1984, I had another tumor in the same place. This time, I went to the All Union Cancer Center for an operation. I had another tumor in November 1984, followed by a third operation in January 1985.

"Now to the point of my story. My diagnosis is sarcoma of the soft tissue at the back of my neck. The site is not typical, and it is dangerously close to my brain and to the spine. The doctors here, who are willing to operate on me again when necessary, cannot offer me any other treatment except surgical.

"We know by now that operation is the most important, essential part of treatment, but we also know that there is other treatment in the West, such as cautious radiation or some sort of isotopic treatment. This we learned from our friends who live in the West and from my husband's daughter, Olga Plam, who lives in Boulder, Colorado. She, by the way, has not seen her father for ten years.

"We were sent invitations from many friends to come for treatment. For example, here are invitations from Sweden, Israel, France, and the United States. I would like to read just one. 'You are cordially invited to Sweden in order to undergo medical examination. I guarantee all expenses here in Sweden. Welcome and warmest greetings.' Signed, Karleen Arland, Member of Parliament, Former Minister of Health.

"We were very hopeful when we received this invitation. My husband went to the visa department and left an application for permission for his wife to travel to the West for medical treatment along with the invitation. A few weeks later, a visa official summoned him and told Naum that they cannot even consider the application because travel abroad for medical treatment requires a letter from the Soviet Ministry of Health, testifying the treatment is necessary.

"Of course, my husband rushed to the Ministry of Health. He was received there by the Head of the Foreign Relations Department, Doctor Shubov, who told him, even with some sympathy, that they are strictly forbidden to give any letters of this sort.

"So, my husband went back to the visa department and demanded an appointment. Another two weeks passed before he was actually seen by the head of the visa department, Colonel Kuznetzov. The colonel was very angry with Naum. He said he would never consider his application because treatment needs a letter from the Ministry of Health. When Naum explained to him that he had been to the Ministry of Health and that he was told they were forbidden to give such a letter, he got even angrier. Then my husband told him, 'All right. It is a vicious circle, but we must find a way out. Allow my wife to go on a guest visa and she will get the treatment she needs. You allow Soviet people guest visas, don't you?'

"'Of course we do,' the colonel said, 'but now that I'm informed your wife wants to go for treatment, I would not allow it.'"

"I find it difficult to comment on. It is a brutal answer. Who would be able to understand such logic? I hope that the American people do not believe that our medical system is up-to-date on the latest achievements and advances of the American medical system. It is not. Our government officials, themselves, go for treatment in the West; they invite doctors here and are treated with special medical departments full of Western equipment and medication. They can do it because they are high-ranking officials. But this is not available to average Soviet citizens and certainly is not available to me at all.

"I want to make two points very clear. Point number one: the doctors here have done their best to help me, and I am grateful to them. Point number two: the treatment in the West might not prove effective at all. We are well aware of this. What I am fighting for and what I am really desperate about is my right to use my chance to survive. I am also fighting for a wider issue of human dignity, and though I have been talking about myself, I would gladly and happily talk about many other people."

"Let me ask you one question," Mark Phillips broke in. "Why are you trying to broadcast your fight now? Do you think it will help?"

"First, I think there might be a chance that if American people hear a story about a person from Moscow and her plight, that might make some high-ranking government officials here very ashamed of themselves because, at the moment, it is not a matter of politics, it is a simple matter of health. It is a matter of visa for treatment," Inna answered."

"Yes, but people say that this is very much a matter of politics, that people like yourself, in the refusenik community, are hostages to the current political standoff between the United States and Soviet Union and that's why they are still here."

"Of course," Inna responded. "You know how refuseniks are being treated here. We do not have any right for anything. I don't know how to explain it. But that doesn't make it sound any easier or better or make them sound more human, does it?"

"You were saying earlier that it is also a sign of increasing desperation on your part," Mark said, getting her back on track.

"Surely. What else can I do? There were so many invitations from the West. There were so many people talking to our authorities about my case. There has been international publicity. I heard that Simone Veil, the French Minister of Health, spoke about me in a meeting last week in Paris. We were featured on a French television station last year. The day before the story was to air, the station received a letter from the Soviet ambassador in Paris. He asked them not to show it because, he claimed, it was all untrue. He said the people who it is about are criminals. This letter was read before they showed the film.

"What can I say? We are criminals because we are fighting for civil rights, or for the right to survive or for the right to live? Is that criminal in any way? I have no more words," Inna said, visibly upset.

"Then we will stop here," Mark replied.

"Do you think I missed anything?" Inna asked.

"No. I'd just like to keep it to what we have talked about—your particular situation, the way you relate to the general refusenik situation and to the broader political problems, as well as your current sense of desperation. You and your husband have run up against a stone wall from the authorities for years, yet you still have a comfortable life by Moscow standards. Are you not afraid that this kind of publicity now could jeopardize what you have?"

"We might jeopardize what we have now. But we don't care. We have so little time. My health is so poor that it doesn't matter really. We've come to the limit when we feel that it doesn't matter whether we have our apartment and our life here in Moscow or not. Being in and out of the hospital over half of the year is too much of an experience to care about personal comforts and convenience. The only thing we care about is to try to survive."

"Your case is an extreme example of a situation many people find themselves in here, not just refuseniks, but people in the Helsinki Watch. We are approaching the ten-year anniversary of the signing of the Helsinki Accords. The Soviet authorities maintain that they are, in fact, complying with the Accords, while the Accords are not being enforced the way they ought to be. Do you have any response to that?" Mark asked.

"I don't even know how to respond. We hear it on the Voice of America very often that when our authorities are asked about human rights, they say they have no comment. Or, if they do comment, their answer is always the same. For instance, in response to questions about Jewish emigration, they say, 'We have no problem with Jewish emigration. We have no refuseniks. All those who want to leave have left.' What can you say to that when you yourself and all of your friends here are dreaming about leaving every day? And it is not ten people, or a hundred people, it is thousands of people. The number is really great. Could you tell a very high-ranking official, look here, you are lying? He knows very well that he is lying, because they are dealing with us inside this country very harshly.

"For example, if a Jewish person comes and asks for work, and they see a gap in his working career, they immediately ask, 'Did you apply to emigrate?' Most of them, not even high-ranking officials, are aware of the refusenik group. But to the West, they pretend that we do not exist.

"I might as well say it, I thought maybe it would not be the right thing, but I have read that cancer can be caused, in part, by pressure and stress. Although I was already a refusenik and under pressure when I married Naum, when I came to live with him I met many wonderful people who I would not have otherwise known. By then, most of the members of the Helsinki Watch Group were in prison, but I came to know their wives and children. And I came to live a new life. Though I knew a lot about how we live here and our system, at first, it was so unbearable to me to see all this suffering, unnecessary suffering, and unnecessary cruelty. You ought to be very tough and very strong to see it, to hear it and to try to understand it. I think, it might not be fair to say, I don't know, but my impression is that this was too much for me, that, as a result, I developed my illness." With this Inna concluded the interview.

The cameraman shot stills of Inna's bookshelf and the textbook she wrote on the English language. Then she took the book from the shelf and paged through it in a scholarly fashion. The camera pointed to the other side of the room and focused on a picture of Naum's daughter Olga and her son—the grandson Naum had never met.

As the cameraman began to pack up the equipment, we all discussed the logistics of getting the tape out of the country.

"My friend has offered to mail it to the States through the diplomatic pouch," I offered.

"Thank you, but we have a person who will carry it out by hand this week," Mark responded.

"Mark, will you please arrange for a copy to be sent to Leeza and to Naum's daughter in Colorado?" Inna asked. Mark agreed, and I gave him my parents' address in Appleton. A few minutes later, Naum walked the CBS crew, Nancy, and Andy to the door, and they left.

"What did you think, Leez?" Inna asked me as we sat together in the study. She looked relieved that it was over.

"You did a great job. You told your story, and you talked about the plight of other refuseniks. You said it all."

Naum returned to the room with a bottle of wine.

"We have a bottle of Israeli port wine that we have been saving for a special occasion, and this is certainly it," Inna said. Naum opened the bottle and poured three small juice glasses full, and then we each took a glass.

"First, we must offer a toast to you," Inna replied "because this interview was your idea—you wanted to help me tell my story." The sparkle in her eyes was as bright as the sun shining off the glass as she lifted it and proclaimed, "Naum and I wish you success and happiness."

We raised our glasses and then I tapped mine with Naum's and then Inna's. The port was heavy and sweet, and a rush of warmth flowed up into my face after I had a couple of sips. Then we raised our glasses again, congratulating Inna on the interview. Naum told Inna he was very pleased and thought it went very well.

I had been so focused on the interview that the thought of saying good-bye to Inna didn't occur to me until the moment I had to do so. All the time I had spent with Inna was now coming to a grinding hault, and there was nothing I could do to slow down time. *Would a day ever bring me back to her apartment?* I wondered. If so, would she be on the other side of the door, so happy to see me? Would Naum shuffle by the doorway, interrupting us only to speak to me briefly in English before going about his own business?

Inna reached on the chair next to her and handed me a gift that was wrapped in brown paper.

"Go ahead and open it," she said excitedly.

It was a book titled *Medieval Bestiary*. As I looked at it curiously, she explained that she had been hired by the publisher to translate it from Russian into English. "It was a great challenge to translate such language. I was very proud when it was published last year. So was Naum. He went out and found several copies to buy. We want you to have one."

I paged through the book and read the inscription: "Be happy and content and full of the joy of life. Love, Inna."

"Thank you, Inna. I have something for you too," I said. I walked out into the hallway and grabbed a bag I had brought with me. "Here," I said, as walked back into the room and pulled out my winter coat. Inna had always admired it because it was so thick with down feathers and was reversible, khaki on one side and maroon on the other.

She was reluctant to accept it, "Really, you want me to have this beautiful coat?"

"Yes, I really do. If it doesn't fit you, you can give it to your sister."

"Very well, thank you, Leeza," she said and then changed the subject. "We thought it would be helpful for you to have a list of names and addresses of our friends in the West who we know will be interested in the tape," Inna said. She held a small black address book in her hand and started paging through it, pausing when she found a name she wanted to give me and then read it to me. By the time she got done, my list included U.S. Senators Richard Lugar, Paul Simon, Patrick Moyniham, Ted Kennedy; Representatives Timothy Wirth, Norman Lent, and Tom Lantos; Robert Bernstein of the Helsinki Watch office in New York; and friends from Moscow who had emigrated to the United States, Lyudmila Alexeyeva and Pavel Litvinov.

"Let them all know when you have the tape, and maybe they will be able to help you," Inna suggested. "Now, Leeza, let's talk about you. When are you leaving tomorrow?"

"My flight from Moscow leaves at seven o'clock in the morning, and the ship from Odessa leaves at four o'clock in the afternoon. I am going to a friend's for a party tonight, so I don't think I'll get too much sleep."

"You'd better go," Inna declared, reluctantly.

As she spoke those words, I instantly froze in my chair. Taking a deep breath, I tried to summon the strength to move through the last moment I would be with Inna, possibly forever.

The sound of children's voices playing in the courtyard blew through the window with a breeze. I looked at my watch. It was already 4:30 PM, and I still needed to return to my apartment before going to Natasha and Uvol's that evening.

"Yes, I'd better go," I said. I stood up and started walking toward the hallway. Inna and Naum followed behind me.

As I turned to face them, my stomach tightened as if bracing for a knockout punch. The sunlight stretched into the hallway and brightened their shadows. Inna saw I was fighting back tears and said, "Leeza, please don't get me started or I will never stop."

I hugged Naum and then Inna, carefully resting my hand near her neck. Then I kissed her cheek and pulled myself away from her embrace.

I did not say good-bye. Instead, I said a single Russian word, *uvidimsya*, which means, "We will see each other again."

"Yes, Leeza, *uvidimsya*," Inna replied, tears flooding her eyes.

PART II

MINNEAPOLIS

CHAPTER

The CBS *Evening News*

> George Schultz devoted most of his
> speech to the allegations of Soviet rights abuses,
> "the most important promises of a
> decade ago have not been kept."
> —*The New York Times*,
> July 2, 1985

The night before my departure, I did not return to my apartment until close to eleven o'clock, exhausted from the emotions of having to say good-bye and a little tipsy from several farewell toasts of vodka and champagne at Uvol and Natasha's party. All I wanted to do was brush my teeth, wash my face, and collapse into bed. But my closet and dresser were still full of clothes that needed to be packed, and so I began at a slow and deliberate pace, trying not to feel too overwhelmed by the task at hand. When dawn started to creep in through the window, I felt besieged by a nauseous chill brought on by exhaustion and a hangover that was well under way. I drank some water, kept working, and managed to finish in time to lie down for an hour before dragging myself and my luggage downstairs to wait for my cab.

All went smoothly with our departure from Moscow, and Karen and I arrived in Odessa on schedule. We took a cab to the port from which our ship would sail. As we got our bags out of the cab, I had the good sense to give Karen the journals I kept while in Moscow. Her diplomatic status immunized her and her bags from inspection by the Soviet customs officials—my nanny status afforded me no such protection.

My bags were subjected to a thorough search, which immediately yielded letters Gary gave me to mail once I was out of the Soviet Union. They were at the bottom of my shoulder bag under a vinyl-covered cardboard flap. After a customs official discovered them, he pointed to a mailbox across the room, assuring me that the Soviet postal system was very efficient. I felt sick to my stomach as I dropped the letters into the box, knowing that the Soviet authorities would retrieve them and trace them back to Gary.

The discovery of the letters intensified the search through my bags. One official actually looked between the photographs in my wallet and even peeled apart two small paper hearts glued together, which had been a present from my five-year-old niece for Valentine's Day. Fortunately, I had tucked Volodya's letter to Daphne in the journals I gave to Karen. The fact that I had nothing in my suitcases or on my person that I should not have had did not prevent a slow and intense burn from rising up the back of my neck; I realized the only thing remaining for them to search was my body. I tried to look calm as the thought of that terrified me: I leaned against a counter, my chin resting in my hand, trying with all my might to seem indifferent and as if I had all the time in the world. I was very relieved when, about five minutes later, the customs officials finally concluded their search and let me through.

That feeling lasted for only a moment, however, because the first thing I saw as I passed through the door outside to the dock was an enormous red Soviet flag flapping in the wind. In other words, I hadn't just cleared customs and boarded a plane bound for the West—for the next three days I would be on a Soviet ship and, technically, still on Soviet territory.

Each day of my trip brought me closer to home—from Odessa across the Black Sea with port stops in Sofia and Istanbul, then to Athens, where Karen and I took a ship to the island of Crete and stayed in a hotel for the night. We returned to Athens for a night, and then I continued westward to Holland, where I spent a few days with Daphne. As nice as it was to see her, visit the town where she went to college, and spend an afternoon at her family's cottage in the countryside, I was preoccupied by the feeling of wanting to be home with my own family. I was so excited the night before my flight home that I could barely fall asleep.

My excitement only increased every hour the next day as I got closer to Appleton. When the connecting flight from Chicago O'Hare pulled into the gate in Appleton, I jumped out of my seat before the seatbelt light was turned off, just so I could be the first one off the plane. As soon as I got into the airport, I saw my parents, who were standing in front of a group of about twenty people. I rushed into their embrace and cried tears of joy. I was finally home!

In the days that followed, I found it difficult to acclimate to my life in America. The United States was in a recession, and there was talk among my family and friends about how financially tight and difficult life had become. Yet I marveled at the ease of my friends' and family's lives—the comfort and privacy of their own homes, the convenience of one car and often two in their driveways, and their spacious backyards with lush green grass, flowers, and bushes.

Within the second week at home, I got a part-time job as a cashier at a Kwik-Trip gas station close to my parents' house. While my desire was very strong to do something for Inna and Naum, I knew any action I took on their behalf would be based on Inna's interview tape. It would be my vehicle—my tool—to publicize their plight, so I put my efforts on hold until I received it.

I had not yet heard from Mark Phillips. Although he told Inna he would send me a copy of the tape, I assumed he had forgotten about me. My calls to the CBS office in New York to determine if they had the tape were frustrating, because not a single person I contacted there had a clue about it.

In early August I received a letter from Nancy Traver. She had offered for me and Inna to send our letters to each other through her. I opened the letter and read with much anticipation:

Dear Lisa:

There is news about Inna. She is at her dacha now, but I spoke with Naum last night. Inna had a fourth operation on July 26. It was apparently successful by Soviet standards. There was no incidence of infection. Of course, the operation did nothing to solve her problem completely. She still requires treatment in the West. Naum said that this operation has left her unable to care for herself. They again removed a portion of her neck muscle and now the weight of her head is a burden for the neck to support. However, she is by no means incapacitated. But, because of Inna's inability to care for herself, Naum feels it is necessary to obtain an exit visa for himself as well as Inna, in the event she receives permission to seek treatment in the West. Both want to immigrate to Israel now!

Regarding the videotape, it was confiscated. A second copy was sent out. Nothing unpleasant because of the interview has happened to Inna or is expected to. After the first filming by CBS, NBC requested and received an interview from Inna. ABC received an interview from Naum alone. All copies of those interviews are now in the States.

Inna and Naum recently sent a letter to Gorbachev. Naum, alone, sent a letter to the Soviet Foreign Minister, Andrei Gromyko. Naum now thinks it best to publicize their case BY EVERY MEANS POSSIBLE. He now calls for the widest publicity possible.

Naum suggested that you write to Sen. Lugar, who is head of the Foreign Relations Committee, Sen. Paul Simon and Sen. Mathias. He especially spoke of Gary Hart and thinks Hart should try to talk to Gromyko and then publicize that effort.

Lisa, I am sure you know most of the above, but Naum was most insistent that I take notes and send everything to you. He spoke very highly of you and is hopeful that you will be instrumental in bringing this to justice.

I hope you are enjoying life in the USA.

Nancy

This information about the tape's confiscation triggered my memory about how meticulously my bags had been searched when I was in Odessa and I wondered if the tape was what the customs officials were trying to find as they rummaged through my personal belongings. Regardless, the letter jolted me from the transition I was making back into my life in the States as if there were neither the distance of time nor miles between me and Inna. I reread the sentence quoting Naum several times, "He spoke very highly of you and is hopeful you will be instrumental in bringing this to justice." I tried to be hopeful, too, but for the first time began to worry about what I could possibly do to help them, with or without the tape.

Nancy's letter gave me an idea—if the videotape was in the States, maybe the local CBS affiliate in Green Bay could help me track it down. I immediately called the station and explained my desire to locate the tape. The receptionist transferred me to a reporter. The reporter said he could not help me locate the tape, but he would like to interview me about Inna that afternoon and get the story on the news that evening. We agreed the focus of the story would be on a local woman's return from two years in Moscow, her friendship with Inna Meiman, and Inna's fight for a visa to leave the Soviet Union for medical treatment. He said there was a chance the CBS national office would see the story and be interested in doing more with it.

An hour later the television crew was at my house, and in what felt like an out-of-body experience, I gave my first TV interview. As promised, the interview was on the news that very night and watching my first public attempt at telling Inna's story was exhilarating. But that feeling diminished over the next few days when I heard nothing from the CBS office in New York and was no further ahead in determining the whereabouts of Inna's tape. I reread Nancy's letter, and the urgent tone prompted me to write to the people on the list of names Inna and Naum gave me, to which I added my own Wisconsin representatives at the same time.

I made twenty copies of a photograph my mom took of Inna and me the day she was at Inna's apartment. I cut myself out of the photo, leaving a nice passport-size photograph of Inna, which I glued to the upper left-hand corner of a legal-size yellow paper. Next to the photo, in black marker, I wrote: "It is not a matter of politics; it is a matter of Inna's life or death." Then I wrote the same letter, by hand, twenty times because I thought a handwritten letter would personalize my plea:

> I last saw Inna Meiman on May 29, 1985. I worked in Moscow for two years as a nanny for an American family. I was fortunate to get to know Inna and her husband, Naum, during my second year there. Many of you to whom I am writing have met Inna. My prayer is that those of you who have not will someday have the chance.
>
> Inna underwent her fourth operation on July 26 to remove a tumor from the back of her neck. It is a type of cancer Western medicine could treat and potentially cure. The Soviet government has refused Inna and Naum an exit visa each time they have applied to emigrate. The Soviet government has refused Inna the right to fight for her own life. As Naum reminded me in a recent letter, "Inna has received invitations from Switzerland, France, Sweden, Israel and the United States for medical consultation and treatment. In a couple of cases, travel expenses would be assumed by the inviting country."

I feel very strongly that the "real" cancer Inna is fighting is the Soviet government. What is the cure for a government that does not value the life of one of its citizens? That is what I am asking you. You have the means and influence to bring this issue, this case, to the attention of the Soviet government.

You are part of a democratic institution that I have learned to appreciate and very much believe in after living in the Soviet Union. I refuse to accept that my government is powerless in this matter. I urge you to contact your colleagues who are aware of this case and inform those who are not and, together, call for immediate action from the Soviet government. As Naum told me to tell his friends in the U.S.,

"It is very simple; we are running out of time."

I am eager to answer any questions you may have and to discuss the Meimans with you.

Sincerely yours,

Lisa C. Paul

I also wrote to Nancy and asked her to contact Mark Phillips about the status of the tape and included a letter for her to deliver to Inna. Then I tried to settle into the rest of my summer in Appleton, spending time with family and friends.

I was cooking dinner with my mom a few days later when she asked me to turn the television on in the living room so she could listen to the evening news. The channel just happened to be on CBS, and Dan Rather just happened to be introducing a segment:

Ten years ago this month an international human rights agreement known as the Helsinki Act was signed by thirty-five nations, including the Soviet Union. On the anniversary of this important agreement, our Moscow correspondent, Mark Phillips, examines how the Soviet government has complied with the agreement and whether or not the quality of human rights has improved for the Soviet people during the past decade. From our Moscow bureau, here is Mark Phillips.

Mark began by profiling a Russian Orthodox priest. Then he said:

> In addition to those still being persecuted for their religious beliefs, there are many Soviets who are denied permission to leave the country, even to undergo lifesaving medical treatment in the West, such as Inna Meiman. She has been repeatedly denied a visa since 1979 and, now, four operations later, her plea to leave is a desperate one.

Then Inna's face appeared on the screen . . . on my television . . . in my living room . . . in Appleton, and she said: "The treatment in the West might not prove effective at all and we are well aware of that . . ."

"Mom! Mom!" I yelled. "Oh my God, come in here. It's Inna! She's on the news!"

My mom rushed in and stood by me, and we both watched the rest of the segment, mouths agape and not able to believe what we were seeing. Just as I had remembered, Inna stated, "What I am fighting for and what I am really desperate about is my right to use my chance to survive. I am also fighting for a wider issue, for human dignity. And although I am talking about myself, I could have gladly and happily spoken about many other people. This fight for my own right is actually part of a wider fight for human dignity."

After the segment concluded, I spoke to my mom with a new sense of determination: "I can't believe it. Mom, Inna's story made it on national television here, all because of you and your visit. And after all these weeks of trying to locate the tape, now I know CBS has it. I can call there tomorrow and ask them to send me a copy, and when I get it, I'll be able to do something to really help Inna!"

CHAPTER

"Please God, Let Me Help Her"

Each one prays to God according to his own light.
—Mohandas Ghandi

Imade no progress in locating the tape the next day or for the rest of the summer. I moved to Minneapolis the second week in September to start my final year of college. Launching my effort to help Inna remained at the top of my list of things to do, and I began to think I would have to come up with a plan even if I did not have a copy of the tape.

At the end of September, my parents forwarded me a letter from Inna, dated September 5, that was sent to their address via Nancy. Inna was responding to a letter I had written to her in August:

Dear Leeza:

I have received your first letter and I know that there is another one, but Nancy and Andy have just come back from Europe so I'll get it later today. Since they are coming, I am writing to you so that I can give my letter to them to take this afternoon.

Leeza, I am very glad you are returning to your studies—I think it's a break from your "Russian period" and it will do you good. You are intelligent and purposeful and I'm sure you'll be a credit to your country (not to mention your parents and relatives, and friends, me amongst them!). I am also very well aware of the fact that due to your life in Russia you do have an appreciation of how lucky you are to be American, no matter what our press says about your "poor" country. You know me well enough to realize that I am not being mealy-mouthed about America and spiteful or bitter about my own country. But to be frank, I wish my son were American, or Israelite, anyone but a Soviet (he wouldn't like me to call him Soviet, though).

Back to our Soviet reality. Yesterday on television they showed a very unusual thing. They stopped people on the street and asked for their opinions on what to expect of the Geneva Summit. Only one very pretty girl was cautious and volunteered nothing beyond, "Of course, we want peace," the rest were very big-mouthed saying things, rather than repeating what they hear on TV or in newspapers in a very knowledgeable way, that is, they didn't seem to think even for a second that what they are being fed is not authentic, to put it mildly (or to avoid what they call, "slanderous insinuations"). Whether one should blame them or not for their militant blindness and bluntness is a moot question to me. That I have reached a different stage in life does not in itself make it possible for me to judge other people (and they make up by far the biggest part of population, clearly the overwhelming majority). But I am certainly sorry for them, and that's it!

My situation is rather a tough one. The July operation made me much worse off. Besides there is a new tumor, which they refuse to operate on now. They offer me chemotherapy (they had told me two years ago that it is useless in my case) and I don't want to go for it. I have been eating nothing, but drinking carrot juice for thirty-one days. I am eating a little again now, in case I do go for chemotherapy. But one thing is very important for you to know—I am very optimistic and hopeful and as long as I can preserve my optimism, I am safe. What I mean is, I will survive as long as I keep my spirits up. So, Leeza, don't be upset, just keep hoping like I do, will you?

I don't want to go in for expression of thanks for politeness sake. We both know how things are. Please keep well and happy. Write soon.

All my love,

Inna

A new tumor that was inoperable? The news was bleak, and I felt so desperate to help her. Then I remembered Mark's promise to mail a copy of the tape to Naum's daughter, Olga, who lived in Boulder, Colorado, and I decided to give her a call.

When I called and introduced myself, Olga said her father had spoken to her about me and was glad I had called. Best of all, she told me that she had just received a copy of the tape. She promised to make a copy and send it to me as soon as possible.

Each day, my anticipation in finding the tape in my mailbox grew. In the meantime, however, I received a letter from my friend, Teresa. I had sent her some letters to deliver to Gary, and she had met with him a few times before she returned back home in August. The news she reported to me was very upsetting:

> I met with Gary at a metro stop near the center of the city and we walked for a quite a bit. It was a beautiful summer night. Gary was thin. When we reached a fairly deserted park area, he began to tell me a tale that made my stomach so nervous, I thought I'd be sick. Apparently, a "friend" had turned him into the KGB, saying Gary was not only a black marketer, *but* also an American sympathizer. He explained it

like this: On a sunny Saturday afternoon two weeks before, he was lying on his bed recovering from a party, when the phone rang. It was the water delivery man calling to ask if he could deliver the family mineral water supply in fifteen minutes. Gary told him he could and then returned to his room and fell asleep. Suddenly, he heard a bang on the door. "Water delivery," rang from a man's voice. In a half-asleep manner and without hesitation, he began to open the door. In an instant, the door was flung open and he was thrown against the wall. "Well, well . . . Igor . . . our American sympathizer, you capitalist pig." Six men came in and began ransacking his apartment. They identified themselves as KGB and, while ripping the American flag off his wall, they accused him of everything from black marketeering to attempting to marry an American girl. They said that they knew of his American girlfriends. As you can imagine, he denied everything.

The head of the gang said, "My, my. . . . look at this war museum" and quickly began taking Gary's treasures from the shelves on his wall. They drilled him about the "We must have change" writing on his wall. He told them it meant nothing. They knew better and beat him around, all the while cursing him out and telling him, "You will never leave the USSR!" They told him he would be under close guard from that day forward. At that point in the story he started to cry and there wasn't anything to be said.

On such a gorgeous summer night, sitting in a small park amidst old women gossiping and children playing near the bench we sat on, it was difficult for me to believe his words, but his face told me all he said was the truth. I couldn't even cry, I was silent. We both just sat in a daze until the rustling of the branches behind us gave away the presence of an unwanted, theretofore unseen young man. We quickly walked out of the park and I said that it was time to go home. He walked me back to the metro and we said good-bye.

I didn't tell anyone about this incident but it's been heavy on my mind as you can imagine. We had arranged to meet again in a week. I was supposed to phone him and speak in Russian. . . . Emotionally, between saying good-bye to my Russian friends, and his news, I wasn't sure I could handle another meeting with him. But, I finally decided and called at the time agreed upon, but there was no answer. He never came in contact with me again. That night he told his story is, of course, one of my worst memories of Moscow. I just thought you should know about it because you were much better friends with him. He spoke of how much he missed you.

Sadness, regret, and horror raged through me as I read the letter. I remembered being forced by the Soviet militiaman to mail Gary's letters at customs in Odessa. What had I done? What could I do now? With Teresa no longer in Moscow, I had absolutely no way of privately contacting Gary. Calling him from America was not an option because the last thing an accused "American sympathizer" needed was a telephone call from America. Of course, I relived those days in Moscow when I had thought about marrying him—how complicated it all seemed there, how the choice was not mine to make at that time. My heart was heavier than it had ever been before. There was nothing I could do for Gary other than get on a plane to Moscow and find him, and that was impossible.

Yet I could do something to help Inna, and fortunately the tool that would aid me in doing so arrived in the mail a few days later—the tape of Inna's interview. As I was rushing off to my part-time job

Inna, 1955.

Inna and Lev, 1959.

Inna at "her village," Navolok, early 1980s.

Members of the Moscow Helsinki Watch Group, 1976 or 1977. Back row, left to right: Naum Meiman, Sofia Kallistratova, Petro and Zinaida Gringorenko, Natalia Velikanova, Father Sergei Zeludkov, and Andrei Sakharov. Front row, left to right: Henry Altunyan and Aleksandr Podrabinek.

Inna and Naum, 1981 or 1982.

Inna and Naum with fellow refusenik and human rights
activist Ida Nudel. Date unknown.

January 21, 1964: my second birthday and my sister,
Julie's, and brother, Jerry's, fourth birthdays. My
oldest sister, Therese, back right.

Laura, me, and Kjirsten, January 1984.

- Studying Russian on the hillside
in Tbilisi -

- To Inna -
I wish you had _my_ worries!
Love y.sa

Me on a trip to Tiblisi, Georgian Republic, November 1984.

Me in front of Lenin's Tomb, December 1984.

Uvol's drawing, January 1985.

Inna's niece, Emilia Kister, in Razdory, February 1985.

My mom and Galya's mom, Victoria Chalikova, April 1985.

Natasha, Andrei, my mom, Volodya, me, and
Uvol, April 1985.

Inna and me at the table in her study, April 1985 (photograph taken by my mother).

My mom and Inna, April 1985.

Flora Litvinov's painting of Anuta's hut, a gift from Inna to me in September 1985.

Postcard to me from Inna, September 1985.

10.

— Ага! Вот через эту трубу я и проберусь
в дом! — обрадовался волк.
Он осторожно влез на крышу и прислушался.
В доме было тихо. «Я все-таки закушу сегодня
свежей поросятинкой»,—подумал волк и, облиз-
нувшись, полез в трубу.

С. Михалков

Художник К. П. Ротов.
Иллюстрация к сказке «Три поросенка».

А 02458. 11.II-64 г. З. 1016. Т. 400 т.
Типография № 5 Главполиграфпрома
Госкомитета Совета Министров СССР
по печати. Москва, М.-Московская, 21.
Цена 2 коп.

Liza!
Nothing special is meant by
this card, just to refresh
your Russian.
Inna

Inna and Naum in their Moscow apartment, October 1986.

Me at my press conference, ending my hunger strike, U.S. Capitol, January 7, 1986.

Opinion

Lisa Paul's commitment

It is good that Lisa Paul is not holding her breath as well as fasting in her effort to convince the Soviet Union to allow a Soviet woman to travel to the United States for cancer treatment. The Soviet record of responding to such voices in the wilderness is so poor as to be no response at all.

Paul, however, is hoping that the U.S. media can turn her lone voice into a crescendo, that Soviet officials will hear it and allow Inna Meiman to receive the travel visa which she needs to save her life.

If the Appleton native's hunger strike somehow, miraculously succeeds in getting medical treatment for Meiman, it will be an accomplishment of major proportions given the Soviets' recent history of releasing citizens whom they want to stay home for any variety of reasons.

For a dozen years Meiman has vainly tried to secure her visa. U.S. senators have prodded Soviet officials without success. Complicating Meiman's case is the fact that her husband dealt with secret mathematical calculations 30 years ago and there is a possibility that Meiman herself might know some of those "secrets." Because Meiman is a Jew and the Soviets have a terrible record of allowing Jews to emigrate, her obstacles to travel are magnified many times.

But while Paul expects to end her fast this week after a 25-day diet of fruit juice and vitamins, she still has high hopes that Soviet officials will respond with a visa for Meiman.

What is there about Americans that allows them to have such high hopes for success in the face of such likely adversity?

In Paul's case, there appears to be an enduring faith in the media's ability to force a bureaucracy to make the only sensible decision. The fact that the Soviets haven't listened to such media pleas before might augur poorly for Paul's chance this time.

Then again, if more Lisa Pauls would take the time and trouble to get involved in such fashion — even in some manner of less pain and commitment — who can say what might be accomplished?

An example of my hometown support: editorial,
Appleton *Post Crescent*, January 1986.

Me greeting Inna at Dulles Airport, January 19, 1987. Photo from the Associated Press.

Lisa Paul helps her friend Inna Meiman from a wheelchair after Paul's successful fight to bring the ailing Soviet woman to the United States for cancer treatment.

Associated Press

Inna at Dulles Airport, January 19, 1987. Photo from the Associated Press.

A poster of Naum at Dulles Airport, January 19, 1987.

The Georgetown Retirement Residence.

Inna in her Georgetown apartment,
February 7 or 8, 1987.

Lev Kitrossky (right) arriving
at Ben Gurion Airport in Israel,
May 6, 1987.

Misha Plam, Olga Plam, and Naum Meiman in Boulder, Colorado, April 16, 1989.

Me, Olga Fookson (Inna's sister), and my husband, Ross Puppe, in Milwaukee, Wisconsin, January 2002.

Olga Plam (middle); her son, Yegor (left); her daughter-in-law, Annie (right); and her grandsons, Aaron and David; Bolder, Colorado;
October 1, 2010.

Levi Kistrossky and family, Israel 2007. First row: Mariam, Inna-Shifra, Dina-Hasya,
Nechemia, Gedalia, Leah, and Elisheva. Back row: Levi and Yosif.

in a dorm cafeteria, I put it in my backpack, planning to watch it at the library after my shift.

When work finally ended, I held on to the tape like I was carrying the Olympic torch on its final mile as I biked on my five-speed yellow Schwinn—which I had owned since seventh grade—across campus to the Walter Library.

The audiovisual room was filled with garbled voices of students reciting their foreign language lessons aloud. I spotted an available VCR in a carrel at the end of the aisle with an empty seat next to it. *Perfect*, I thought, *I'll have some privacy.*

I placed my backpack on the chair next to mine, took off my shoes, put headphones on, settled into my chair, put the cassette in, pressed play, and waited. Within a few seconds I heard Mark Phillips's voice and then Inna came on the screen. For the next twenty-five minutes, I was so glued to the screen that if a fire alarm blasted and the library evacuated, I would not have moved. At times I reacted as if I was hearing her story for the first time; at others, I joined in and finished the sentence with her ". . . but what I am really fighting for is human dignity."

While the interview played, it felt like I was back in Inna's apartment, sitting right next to her. But when the tape ended, my heart sank with the reality that she was still so far away and that her situation had not changed at all for the better since I last saw her. My desire to help her was stirring like a volcanic force within me, and I knew I needed to get outside to let it erupt.

I walked out of the library, onto the campus mall, and toward Northrop Auditorium, which was just ahead of me at the center of the north end of the mall. I walked up a few steps and then stood between two of the ten majestic white pillars at the base of the auditorium, which were lit as bright as day. I knew now was the time for me to take action. I finally had the tape, so there was no more reason to delay. I took it out of my backpack and as I held it,

I was overcome with a feeling of absolute powerlessness. A voice cried out from the pit of my stomach, "What on earth can you possibly do with this?" I slid my back down along a pillar to a seated position and was brutally honest with myself—I couldn't do a damn thing with it; I had no money, no connections, and truly no time to accomplish what I had been thinking I would do with it for months. That realization scared me to death and I started to cry.

Tears streaming down my face, I had a flashback to the time when I stood with Inna on the small bridge by her apartment discussing the final arrangements of her interview; I had promised her I would not let her down. I also remembered Irina Grivnina and Larisa Bogoraz and all they had sacrificed to fight for what they believed was right. How would it be possible for me to look into their eyes and explain to them my reasons for failing Inna? In that moment, in the middle of campus, I realized my conclusion that I was incapable of doing anything to help Inna was ridiculous. I was young and free and an American. I had absolutely nothing to lose. I would not, for example, get expelled from the university, sent to exile in some remote part of the United States, or incarcerated in a psychiatric hospital for taking some sort of action for Inna's freedom.

Suddenly a surge of energy flowed through me as I realized whatever action I took could not be defined or limited by the lack of my external resources—it would have to come from my internal resources. So, what *were* my inner resources? First, there was the love of my family, who I knew would support me. Second was my brand-new realization that to do something and fail was better than doing nothing at all. And third, and perhaps most important, was my faith. All that I had been taught through years of Catholic upbringing—including Catholic grade school—started flowing through my mind: "Seek and you shall find," "Ask and you shall receive," "Knock and the door shall be opened." Then I remembered a verse from a song,

"All that I have and all that I offer comes from a heart both frightened and free. Take what I bring now and give what I need, all done in your name."

Could it be as easy as that, I wondered, *to just rely on my faith and trust that it would lead me exactly in the right direction?* Calm came over me as I discovered the answer to what I would do for Inna would have to come from prayer, and I started to do just that: "Please God, let me help her. I'm right here, willing to do whatever I possibly can . . . please, let me help her."

I walked down the stairs of Northrop and back to the library, and unlocked my bike from a rack. I pedaled south along the mall, over a pedestrian bridge across Washington Avenue, and then east for a mile or so toward my apartment. As the cool autumn wind brushed against my face while I pedaled, I started praying some more: "Please God, let me help her, let me help her, let me help her," I said, over and over again, tears flowing down my cheeks until I got home. It was about 9:00 PM, and I went right up to my room. I tried to do some homework, but all the thoughts in my mind were swirling around what I could do for Inna. Maybe I could plan a protest march for Inna from the campus to the State Capitol building in St. Paul. . . . No, the Minnesota state government was not the target of my protest. Maybe I could try to have an "Inna Meiman Day" on campus, on which I would show her interview and ask students to write letters to Gorbachev urging her release. . . . No, not dramatic enough. Dramatic . . . that is what I needed to do, something dramatic enough to call immediate attention to me so that I, in turn, could publicize Inna's situation.

Then an idea darted through my mind that surprised me and gave me pause. What about a hunger strike? I could do it during my winter break. But what did I even know about hunger strikes? I knew that Soviet refuseniks and prisoners of conscience, such as Sakharov in Gorky, put their lives at stake when they resorted to such action. I also knew that there was no way Inna would ever approve of my risking my well-being for her, and neither would my parents. Perhaps a hunger strike without the extreme goal of starving myself until the Soviets permitted Inna to leave Russia, might be plausible. I could use the hunger strike as a vehicle to call attention to the Soviets' refusal to issue Inna a visa for medical treatment. The more I thought about it, the less crazy it seemed.

I decided it was best to sleep on it and see what the morning would bring.

Faith, Hope, and Love

> Man must evolve for all human
> conflict a method which rejects revenge,
> aggression and retaliation. The foundation
> of such a method is love.
> —Dr. Martin Luther King, Jr.

I woke up in the morning and before even getting out of bed, I realized I had to turn my idea of going on a hunger strike over in a spiritual sense because it was so much bigger than myself. So I set out on a spiritual journey that began with going to mass on Sunday morning to the Newman Center—a Catholic student organization on college campuses throughout the United States.

The sermon that day seemed to be tailor-made for me. The message was that our personal resources, whatever they may be, are always enough when God calls us to serve—that what we have to offer is always sufficient to do God's work.

Over the next few weeks, the Newman Center became the place I went to collect my thoughts and pray. My favorite spot was the balcony of the church, where I sat a few feet away from the base of a large and beautiful stained-glass image of Jesus. I stopped by often after class, usually for ten or fifteen minutes, sometimes to just think, other times to pray. Within two weeks or so of the hunger strike idea, I asked God for a sign to let me know if I could really go through with it. The sign came to me as soon as I walked down the stairs from the church balcony into the lobby and saw a poster on a bulletin board with these words on it: "The purpose for which you are brought together is to live in harmony, hold all that you have in common. You are not without blame if by your silence you permit a brother to be lost. —The Rule of St. Augustine."

I had also got into the habit of randomly paging through a small New Testament Bible, which I kept on the nightstand next to my bed. Somehow, I consistently opened it to I Corinthians: "There remain then, faith, hope, love, these three, but the greatest of these is love." It made perfect sense to me that these principles would have to be the foundation for any action I took for Inna, so I committed myself to striving for each one of them.

In the third week of reflecting on the hunger strike, I decided to talk to Professor Adel Donchenko about showing the tape of Inna's interview on campus. She had been my Russian language professor the year before I went to Moscow, and it was she who made the announcement about the nanny job. She suggested I call Steve Feinstein, a professor of Russian history at the University of Wisconsin–River Falls and who was also involved with a group in Minneapolis active for Soviet Jews. She thought he would be interested in Inna's interview and might have ideas about how I could publicize it.

I called Steve that same day, briefly telling him about Inna and how I had met her while living in Moscow. He was interested in the fact that I had just lived in Moscow and invited me to show the tape at the next meeting of the Minnesota-Dakotas Action Committee for Soviet Jewry, of which he was the director.

"What does the committee do?" I asked.

"We are working to get every Jew who wants to leave the Soviet Union *out* of the Soviet Union," he replied emphatically. He explained the committee was part of a nationwide organization that engaged in many activities to support and bring attention to the plight of Soviet Jews, such as rallies or marches. The committee also organized letter-writing campaigns to U.S. elected officials to pressure the Soviet government to release a specific Soviet Jew.

I went to a meeting the following week. And even though most of the people sitting in the room had heard about the plight of Soviet Jews before, they watched Inna's interview with great interest and asked me many questions. At the end of the evening, Steve invited me to talk about Inna's case at synagogues throughout the Twin Cities, and I readily agreed to do so.

I left the meeting with a strong sense of support and understanding about my desire to help Inna.

By the first week of November, I felt sure enough about going on a hunger strike that I started to tell some of my closest friends about it. Mary Jo Zapp, who was from Appleton and graduated a year ahead of me in high school; Julie Boulay, also from Appleton; Dotti Piotrowski, who had been my roommate the year before I lived in Moscow; and Dotti's high school friend, Amy Doyle all met at Julie's apartment. The first thing I did was show them the videotape. Then I revealed my plan to go on a hunger strike. They were, needless to say, surprised by it, and skeptical, but they assured me that they would support me 100 percent.

Another friend, Jenny Micke, was in medical school at the University of Minnesota. I thought she could be a good resource on what it would be like physically to not eat for an extended period of time. As we were talking, she remembered a friend of hers who had gone on a fast and who was also a doctor.

I spoke to the doctor on the telephone for an hour. She explained that her fast had been a spiritual journey for personal atonement. When I told her my purpose for not eating, she encouraged me to take fruit juice and vitamins, as she had done, because the toll on my body would not be as great as it would be on just water.

She also told me the best way to prepare for not eating would be to begin eliminating specific items from my diet three weeks before the day I planned to go on the strike. She explained that by slowly eliminating the intake of products that produce toxins the body is able to purge the toxins in advance of the actual fast and minimizes headaches and other adverse symptoms that come with a sudden stop in eating. Beginning the third week out, I was to eliminate junk food, caffeinated beverages, alcohol, and sweets from my diet. The second week I was to stop eating meat and dairy products. The final week, I was to eat only fruit, bread, and soup broth, and to drink lots of water.

I went to the meeting of the Minnesota-Dakotas Action Committee the first week of November and, as I was leaving, decided to tell Steve Feinstein about my hunger strike. He asked me several questions about it and seemed impressed that I had thought it all through quite thoroughly. He said he and the committee would, of course, support me. He also suggested I call Lori Fink, a reporter from the *Minnesota Daily*, the University of Minnesota's campus newspaper. When I called her, I told Lori that I had recently returned from spending two years in the Soviet Union. She was immediately interested to learn more about my experiences in Moscow, and we agreed to meet the next week. I decided to wait until then to tell her about the hunger strike.

By November 8, the hunger strike idea had evolved enough that I wrote Inna a letter about my plans. I decided that I would begin my hunger strike on December 14, the first day of my winter break. I wanted to allow at least a month for us both to correspond about it:

November 8, 1985
Dear Inna,
I finally received a copy of the interview you did with CBS.
It was good to "see" you again. Watching it, I realized that

my commitment to you and need to do something about that is greater than ever.

I have given much thought to what I am about to say to you. I have talked to several people about this, but most of all, I am growing stronger in both my mind and heart to do this. It seems that the politicians here are only able to do so much for you. I keep asking myself, "What can I do?" My answer is no more than what people in Washington are already doing for you. The alternative then is what I can do to try to tell your story to as many people as possible—some kind of protest I could make to draw attention to me so I in turn can give the attention to you.

And so, after five months of being home and thinking about that question, I feel that I have finally found a solution. Let me also say, that I, personally, will not rest, will not be content enough to get on with my life and discover my future ambitions here until I try to do something for you.

With all seriousness, more than I have ever felt about anything, I am considering going on a hunger strike on December 14 on your behalf. It is during my Christmas holiday, after my first semester exams, so I would not be jeopardizing my studies. The timing is good because it will be after the Geneva Summit (the media may be more receptive to this type of story) and during the holiday season, also a good time for such a human interest story.

Although a month is not that far away, I do have time to get prepared and organized, and to get other people involved. Steve Feinstein, who is the chairman of the Minnesota Action Committee for Soviet Jews, has already offered me his support and said that he will help me in any way that he can.

I will be in Minneapolis because this is a large metropolitan area and I am confident I can get publicity here. If or when a TV station wants to interview me, I will tell them that is great, but it is not my story, it's Inna's and ask them to play at least a minute of your tape on their newscast. As public interest picks up, I would also make known ways for people to write to you and to the Ministry of Health. I also thought of telling them how to call you personally. Do you think that is a good idea?

I am realistic in that my goal behind this is not so much your exit visa but more on a basic level, on what I can accomplish, to get publicity, to protest against the Soviet government.

Another thing to my advantage is that this would be a little unique—not the hunger strike, those have been done before—but my connection to you. I am not a relative and I am not Jewish and that could result in greater interest in why I would do such a thing.

As far as how this will affect me personally, I am young and have the rest of my life to do and learn and be whatever I want to. The rest of my life can't make sense if I don't stand up and fight for you now. I have never been one to live by what the future may hold. I live in the present and you are very much a part of that.

As far as how long I will actually be on the hunger strike, that I can't really know at this time—as long as it takes for me to make my point. On the other hand, if I find that on the sixth day I physically can't do it, I'll stop. I am not worried about that BECAUSE THE POWER that is leading me to do this will also get me through it.

Maybe you could get in touch with your Western correspondent friends and tell them about this. Maybe they would be interested enough to get involved, to contact their offices here to send a reporter my way. I also want you to know that my mom and dad will support this, whatever I feel I have to do, they will understand. My entire family will be behind me, my friends already are. So, that is what I am working toward. I'm being very reflective, prayerful, and serious in doing so. Very simply put, you are special people, friends of mine. Inna, you must have the right to fight for your life. As you said in the tape, it is a matter of human dignity.

I'd appreciate any suggestions you have.

I'll end with a quote by Helen Keller, "Keep your face to the sunshine and you will not see the shadow."

I hug and kiss you,

Leeza

I continued on my spiritual journey as the primary way to prepare for the hunger strike. The weekend before Thanksgiving I went on a retreat sponsored by the Newman Center, where I had two significant experiences.

The first was a friendship I made with a woman whose room was next to mine. She had a son my age and was a free-spirited artist who believed the mind and body to be one. She invited me to her room on Friday night, and we chatted as we each had a glass of wine. I soon felt comfortable enough to tell her about the strike. To my surprise, she was against the idea, mainly because she saw it as a punitive act against my own body. She did not believe that any cause could justify depriving the body of so many nutrients for such an extended period of time. The more I tried to convince her of all my reasons for wanting to go on the hunger strike, the more I freed myself from any doubt that it was the right thing for me to do.

The second experience occurred after a Sunday morning session. We were given time alone to present our prayers to God. I chose to sit in a room with a large bay window, where I looked out at the snow-covered lake still hazy from the morning fog. A plain wooden cross, about eight feet tall, stood just at the edge about thirty yards from where I was sitting.

I prayed as earnestly as I could for God to give me the strength and courage I would need to sustain the strike. I knew my actions would have to reflect Inna's positive and hopeful spirit . . . only I didn't feel so positive or hopeful. Mostly painful memories of Moscow swirled my mind: not visiting Gary in the psychiatric hospital, the night Daphne left, meeting Irina Grivnina and Larisa Bogoraz. But most of all, I remembered the hate that consumed me as I walked by the soldiers in Red Square that spring afternoon after I left Inna's. I shut my eyes for a few seconds, and when I opened them, I saw an image of Christ on the cross—the image of what had always been taught to me as the greatest love possible. In that moment, I realized that was the place within me from which my hunger strike had to come—love, not hate. As I watched the fog rising off the lake, my own pain lifted with it. My entire body felt like I had become submerged in a warm, soothing bath as feelings of faith, hope, and love flooded over me—the feelings that would sustain me in the days and weeks to come.

Ripple of Hope

> You are not without blame
> if by your silence you permit a
> brother to be lost.
> —The Rule of St. Augustine

Itold my parents about my hunger strike when I was home for Thanksgiving weekend. I did so on that Saturday afternoon, which was like any other Saturday afternoon at my parents' house— my mom was getting ready to go to four o'clock mass and my dad was in the kitchen cooking dinner. We were not a family of serious sit-down discussions, so requesting one with my parents got their immediate attention.

"It's about Inna and Naum. After I received the tape of the interview Inna did with CBS, I knew I had to do something dramatic to draw attention to me so I could draw attention to her." I paused, took a breath, and continued, "I decided I am not going to eat," padding it first, then paused again. "Actually, I am going to go on a hunger strike over my Christmas break."

"What?" My mom asked, completely stunned.

"A hunger strike. It will be an act of protest against the Soviet government. Mom, you know I have been trying to think of something to do for Inna since I got back from Moscow. I think a hunger strike would get media attention. I spoke with a doctor who said that the body can survive on fruit juice and vitamins for over thirty days without any complications, so I will do that and not just drink only water."

"Oh, Lisa," my mom said, very concerned. "What if you get sick or too tired? What about your own health?"

"Then I'll stop. My plan is to start on December 14, the first day of my Christmas break and take it one day at a time. I hope that I'll be able to do it for the three weeks of the break, but if I feel I can't continue, even after two or three days, I'll stop. I am not going to put my own health at risk, so you don't have to worry about that. But I need to try to do something now, something that might give Inna hope."

"And if you're successful and attract attention, how do you think that will affect your career?" my dad asked. "Do you think you could ever go back to Moscow to work or study?"

"I don't know how it might affect my career. If I didn't get a job for that reason it probably wouldn't be the right job for me anyway. I know my future is important, Dad, but it is like I wrote to Inna—the rest of my life will not make sense unless I do something for her now."

By the end of our conversation, it was clear that they both understood I had thought everything through carefully and that it was something I was prepared to do. They offered me their full support and made me promise to stop as soon as I felt physically uncomfortable or unable to continue, which, of course, I agreed to do.

I called Inna the next week to make sure she had received my letter about the hunger strike. I was meeting with the reporter from the *Minnesota Daily* the next day and wanted Inna's approval of my plans before I made any public announcement. I was relieved my call got through and happy to hear Naum's voice on the other end of the line. We exchanged greetings and then he said he would help Inna, who was in bed, to the phone.

A few minutes later, Inna greeted me and asked me about my exams.

"I take them next week, so I am studying."

"I am glad that you cannot see me now," Inna said, her voice sounding weak and tired. "I am fighting, though, and I will continue to fight."

"Did you get my letter?"

"Yes, I am so touched by your thoughts and what you are doing. I have sent you a letter explaining all my feelings. You should receive it soon. In the meantime, take care of yourself and be careful. I need you to be healthy and with me. Maybe it would be best if you limited it to no more than ten days," she suggested.

"I will be careful, Inna, and I promise you I will stop as soon as I don't feel well."

"I'll try to call you on the fourteenth, but they may try to block the call."

Within a week later, I received a letter from Nancy:

Dear Lisa,

Inna asked me to send just a short note to you regarding a few things she forgot to tell you when the two of you talked by phone. She asked that during your hunger strike, people should not phone her. She is afraid that if a lot of people start phoning her, her phone will be disconnected. If people want to write a letter, they should send it to Mikhail Gorbachev.

She said you plan to go on the hunger strike beginning December 14. She wonders if it might be better to go on strike on behalf of all people suffering human rights abuses in the Soviet Union, rather than just on her behalf. She asks that you think about this suggestion.

Best regards,
Nancy

Around that same time, Jill Goldenberg called and introduced herself as an aide to U.S. Senator Paul Simon, a Democrat from Illinois. Her mother, she explained, lived in Minneapolis and received a letter from the Minnesota Action Committee about me and the CBS interview. Jill told me Senator Simon had met the Meimans while in Moscow, was active on their behalf, and was interested in their case. He wanted to know if I had received any recent news from them. I told her that Inna was continuing to fight her illness and that the Soviet government was still denying her a visa to travel to the West for treatment.

"I do have some news about me, though," I said, deciding to take advantage of the opportunity to get word about my hunger strike to a member of the U.S. Senate. I informed her of my plan to go on a hunger strike and its purpose to call attention to Inna's plight. She told me she was sure Senator Simon would be willing to help in any way he could.

⁓

I set out two goals for my hunger strike. First, I wanted to attract significant local publicity in Minneapolis and Appleton, which I was believed was within my reach. The second goal depended on the first, but was less tangible. I wanted to achieve one form of national media coverage because national attention would be most likely to draw the Soviet government's attention to me and, thus, to Inna.

I met with the reporter from the *Minnesota Daily* and took the first exciting step toward launching publicity about my strike. When I told her about my plan, she immediately offered to make that the focus of her story. She said it would run on December 7, the Friday before finals week, and the last day the paper was published before winter break.

I was both nervous and excited when I set out on campus the morning of December 7 to pick up the *Daily*. When I did, I was thrilled to see a photograph of me holding a photograph of Inna on the top half of the front page and a few columns about my hunger strike below it.

That article prompted a reporter from the Minneapolis *Star Tribune* to give me a call. He had read the article and wanted to do a story about my hunger strike. He interviewed me on the telephone and arranged a time for a photographer to come to my apartment to take my photograph for the story the next day. I asked him if the story would be able to run on December 14, the first day of my strike, and he said that he would try to make that happen.

And so a "ripple effect" began—a phenomenon that was to last throughout my hunger strike.

⁓

The week before my hunger strike was simultaneously the most stressful and exciting week of my college career. It was almost impossible for me to study for my final exams as there was so much to do for my hunger strike. I was also preparing physically, as the doctor had advised, and was down to eating only fruits, bread, and soup broth.

By Tuesday afternoon, it was obvious to me that I was not ready to take my two remaining exams. I spoke to one of my professors and was relieved to learn I could take an incomplete in a course with no adverse ramifications if I completed the course within a year. So I took two incompletes and focused all of my extra attention on launching my hunger strike.

The eve of my fast, Friday, December 13, I went shopping with my roommate to stock up on a supply of fruit juices. There was a nice selection of natural fruit juices and I bought a dozen quart bottles, thinking that amount would easily get me through the first week. I also stocked up on vitamins—a one-a-day multivitamin, calcium, and vitamin E.

I had butterflies in my stomach as I tried to fall asleep—as incredible as it seemed, I couldn't wait to stop eating the next day. I reached for the New Testament on my nightstand and searched for one final piece of spiritual guidance before I went to sleep, and I found it. It was the story of Lazarus. Martha and Mary had sent a message to Jesus to come to Bethany right away when their brother, Lazarus, became ill. But Jesus did not get there until a few days later, after Lazarus had died. Martha, overwhelmed with grief, greeted Jesus as he was entering the city. She told him, "I know if you would have been here, my brother would not have died." As Jesus arrived at Martha's house, her sister, Mary, expressed the same faith. He was so deeply moved by this belief in him that he asked to be taken to where Lazarus was buried. Once there, he ordered the stone be removed from the entrance of the tomb and Lazarus to rise from the dead. Lazarus did rise, which demonstrated the power of faith and love.

After reading the story I knew I had to have a similar faith in conducting my hunger strike. I wanted to believe that, if God was with Inna, she would not have to die in Moscow. So I decided the spiritual goal of my hunger strike would be to move "the stone" blocking Inna's exit from the Soviet Union one inch each day with my love and faith. I hoped that by the end of my fast I could say, "Look, God, here is what I was able to do with all my love and faith, and I believe you can move it the rest of the way and let her go free."

Fruit Juice and Vitamins

People say, "What good can one person do?
What is the sense of our small effort?"
They cannot see that we must lay one brick at a time,
take one step at a time; we can be responsible
only for the one action of the present moment.
—Dorothy Day

The sound of the newspaper hitting my apartment door woke me up at seven o'clock on Saturday morning—Day 1. I ran downstairs, got the paper, and went back up to my room, where I sat on my bed and eagerly searched through the paper.

"U Student Starts Hunger Strike for a Sick Soviet Friend" was the headline on the second page of the second section of the paper and, in the middle, a photograph of me next to a samovar and holding a photograph of Inna. The article ran the width of the page and went a third of the way down. The first sentence read: "Inna Meiman of Moscow is dying of cancer, unable to get treatment in the West, and Lisa Paul of Minneapolis is starting a hunger strike today in protest."

After I read the article, I went down into the kitchen and unceremoniously poured my first class of juice. I also drank a glass of water, knowing I should drink as much water as possible each day. Then I called my mom and announced that I had officially began my hunger strike, and excitedly told her about the article in the paper.

While she admitted she was worried about me and wanted me to be careful, she was swept up by my enthusiasm and congratulated me on getting started. She told me to call her each day to report how I was feeling and any progress I was making in getting media attention.

The doctor I previously spoke to suggested I walk at least a mile every day to help release toxins that my digestive system would no longer be doing because it would not be digesting any food. She also advised me to dress warmly because the lack of calories burning through my system would reduce my ability to stay warm.

So I decided to walk that afternoon to a Kinko's and made copies of the *Star Tribune* article and of Inna's address to distribute after each mass at the Newman Center, the first being at four o'clock that afternoon. I was nervous but prepared and ready to finally start telling people Inna's story. I was scheduled to talk after communion. This was my debut at public speaking, and I was full of nerves as the priest introduced me; I felt all eyes upon me as I walked to the podium. I put my paper down, adjusted the microphone, and began, attempting to make frequent eye contact with the audience as I read my speech:

Hi. My name is Lisa Paul. I am a senior at the University majoring in Russian Area Studies. The past two years I lived in Moscow where I worked as a nanny for an American family. The memory I have of that experience is fortunately filled with the many Russian people I met during my stay, especially those who came to be my close friends.

It is a privilege to tell you a little more about one of those friends, Inna Meiman. Inna is fifty-three years old and is very ill with cancer. Since she became ill in 1983, she has had four operations to remove a tumor located on the back of her neck. Soviet medicine no longer offers Inna a means to treat her illness. In the meantime, she has been invited by several countries, including Israel, Sweden, France, and the United

States, to come for medical treatment. Because medical technology is more advanced in the West, there is the possibility that such treatment could help Inna. But the Soviet government has repeatedly refused Inna and her husband, Naum, an exit visa—denying Inna the right to fight for her own life—as Inna has said her right for human dignity.

Today I began a three-week hunger strike to protest what the Soviet government is doing and to let it be known to others. I am not doing this thinking that it will result in her visa. I am doing this for Inna and Naum, to let them know how much I care about them and their struggle. I am doing this for me, because of my values, my commitments, and because of my faith. And, I am doing this for you—so that any attention I receive as a result of my protest will enable me to tell you and other Americans Inna's story.

My hope is that you would be willing to write Inna a short note of support, encouragement, or even a New Year's greeting. You can tell her that you are a friend of mine. How great it would be for Inna at this very critical and desperate time to know that other Americans care. How nice it would be for the Soviet authorities, as they censor her mail, to know of that concern, too. I will be in the lounge after mass and am eager to give each of you Inna's address. There was also a very informative article about me in today's *Star Tribune*. I will have copies available if any of you would like to know more about my cause.

Heat radiated off my face as I walked down from the altar and out the side door into the lounge. I listened as the congregation sang *all three verses* of the last song. I displayed Inna's address and copies of the newspaper article on a table in front of me and then waited, wondering if anyone would take an interest.

Soon, the singing voices were replaced with the sounds of people chatting after the mass ended. A few people came into the lounge and then more through the side door. Eventually the room was full of people. Several people shook my hand and wished me luck, some stopped to chat, others just took the information and left. One woman said she had two children and would ask each of them to write to Inna. I spoke at both masses on Sunday, and was likewise greeted with a favorable response.

I had been told that the first two days of the fast would be the most difficult, but the speeches at the Newman Center energized me and distracted me from thinking about how I was physically feeling. It was Monday before I knew it, and I had made it through the first forty-eight hours without any major hunger pains.

On Monday—Day 3—I wrote a letter to send along with a copy of the *Star Tribune* article to several national magazines and television stations. On Tuesday—Day 4—I called the local *USA Today* office in St. Paul. I briefly explained who I was, what I was doing and why. I mentioned the story in the *Star Tribune*. The first woman I spoke to transferred me to an editor, and I repeated my pitch. She was interested and gave me the name and number of an editor in the national office in Virginia. I immediately called that office, and that editor was also interested in my story. She said she would have a reporter from the St. Paul office call me the next day to schedule an interview. The reporter followed through the next morning and came to my apartment, along with a photographer, early that afternoon. He said he would send in the story by the end of the day, but could not tell me when it would run.

On Thursday morning, I was invited to do a live telephone interview with a popular local radio station, WCCO, and called in at 7:15. I had also called the local television stations in Minneapolis early in the first week. Those calls resulted in two stations sending their reporters to my apartment to interview me on camera, and the

LISA C. PAUL 171

story ran on two of the local networks on Thursday night. Each showed a clip of Inna's interview.

I started settling into a routine—each day was filled with at least one activity to keep the ball moving forward, whether it was writing a letter, photocopying information, or conducting an interview. Each day's accomplishment was my "daily bread" and kept me going.

I communicated often with Senator Simon's aide, Jill Goldenberg. She told me that Senator Simon was going to make note of my hunger strike and include the entire *Star Tribune* article in the Congressional Record.

On Sunday, December 22—Day 9—I rode home with a friend to Appleton. For the first time since my fast began, I was forced to sit still and do nothing for the five and a half hours it took to drive across the middle of Wisconsin. I felt invigorated by how well things had been going and relieved by how normal I felt. At the same time, I was ready to be home with my family; I couldn't wait to see my parents again.

When we finally drove up my parents' driveway, I rushed out of the car and into the house, greeting them as enthusiastically as I had when I returned from Moscow. As my mom held me in her embrace my knees went weak, like I had just run a big race. My brother, Tom, looked astonished when he saw me. He said he was expecting that I might look weary and thin after not having had any food for nine days, so he couldn't believe I looked and acted completely normal. I took out a small container filled with vitamins and joked, "Here's my dinner, what are you guys having?"

My mom handed me what I considered an early Christmas present—a letter from Inna. She said it had arrived the day before. It was Inna's response to my letter in which I informed her of my plans to go on a hunger strike, and I was grateful to receive it:

December 4, 1985
My Dear Leeza!

I have sat down to write you and answer with a worried mind and an uneasy heart. This state of mind and soul (so uncharacteristic of me, unfortunately) is due to my absolute inability to react to your news and your decision in any clear and determined way. My first impulse was to try and stop you! But after I have read your letter ten times, I realized you are not asking me for approval or permission, you are trying to do more than anyone has ever done or wanted to do, you are trying to help me by making a sacrifice. Going on a hunger strike, no matter how short or long, is a very hard and difficult thing to do physically, not to mention the moral strain of all of it! And this makes me very worried! Please, Leeza, let's be honest with each other and merciful. I ask you to be merciful to me and to stop doing it *as soon as* you feel any discomfort. And will you?

I want to tell you (but only you) that my state of health is poor. I've been on carrot juice for thirty-one days, lost a lot of weight (nothing to regret, as you understand), and in mid-October felt much better than now. Then the pain returned. Now two beautiful people, a husband and wife (homeopaths and herb healers), are trying very courageously and devotedly to help me. All day I apply compresses to my poor neck, drink all sorts of herb drinks and try very hard to be cheerful and brave!! But actually, I am in bed most of the day. Naum is trying to be helpful and so on. All this *does not* mean that my condition is very critical, it is critical because of the pain, but if I understand correctly, there is no real danger at the moment, and if the growth is arrested then there is time for curing me.

Leeza, I tried to be very frank with you as to the gravity of my situation. I also want to tell you that I am sure I'll survive, that this isn't the end yet. So, maybe, you'll change your decision and do the hunger strike when things are really bad. Please, think about that, too.

Now, if you are determined to go on with it, then, please, do be careful of how you go about it! From my experience, I know that the most painful thing is to stop eating and you *must be* extremely careful. You must start with a little home-made juice, then a little porridge, and no animal food at all during the period which is equal to the period of hunger. Please, for my sake, do it all attentively and seriously!

Of course, Naum and I are going to help you in any way we can. I have already written to my friends in America. But our mutual friends here tell me for the hunger strike to be effective it ought to be made in Washington. Leeza, I don't understand such things, so decide for yourself. The main, key thing is that for Americans my case ought to show how inhuman and paranoid our government is. I don't want you to starve *just* for me. I want you to do it for a *cause*, for all those trampled down most cruelly and heartlessly, whose names are not known and whose lives are ruined!! After all, my case is not that tragic, I have never been to prison, and except for some pressure I haven't been actually persecuted.

Leeza, in mid-October Teeny Zimmerman and Marjorie Kampleman (you know that their husbands are diplomats at the American Embassy) came to visit me. We had a nice party and I told them the short story about the fish. I am sure you remember this story, which is quite applicable to me. After I told the story, I offered a toast, first to those who were born brave, then to those who became brave, and finally to those who become brave before dying. But most of all, my heart went to the people who, like the fish, died without being brave at all.

I myself became brave late in my life, but this made me extremely happy and unafraid of death, this is God's truth. Unfortunately, I fell ill and haven't done half of what I meant to but I am sure there is time yet. Leeza, please, do not consider that the situation is a tragedy; difficult, yes, but it is still not a tragedy. I am very lucky I have such good friends, like you and your family and wish you great success in what you have planned. I would still like to emphasize again, that your fight for me should be for all those deprived of civil rights and for all those who are repressed. Leeza, I also decided to organize a small demonstration, but not now, in January, after you finish your fast. I ask you to be sensible and to proceed carefully.

I am with you every minute of your experience. Naum gives you heartfelt greetings. I strongly hug and kiss you,

Your Inna

Monday, December 23, was my first full day in Appleton, and it was fantastic. I had contacted Ellen Kort, a friend of my mom's with media contacts, a week before and asked her to send out press releases for me. Her work proved to be effective. By nine o'clock on Monday morning, I had scheduled interviews with each of the three local television network affiliates and a reporter from each was at my house at 9:30, 10:30, and 11:30. Then I called in and did a live radio interview with a local station over the lunch hour, and in the afternoon I spoke with a reporter from the *Post Crescent*, the Appleton newspaper.

At one point, during all the commotion of that day, I received a phone call from New York from a friend of the Meimans who was a Moscow bureau correspondent for *Newsweek*. She explained she was in New York for the holidays and that Inna asked her to call me. "She and Naum send their love. They told me to tell you that they are thinking of you every day and to be sure to take care of yourself."

On December 24, the article about me appeared in *USA Today* on the second page of the paper, with a nice photograph of me holding a snapshot of Inna. So, eleven days into my fast, I reached my goal of receiving national media coverage. I was thrilled!

The emotional high I had been on since arriving in Appleton ended on Christmas Eve. I went to mass with my parents and my brother Tom. Then we went home where the three of them ate dinner and, afterward, we exchanged a few presents. From there we went to a party at a neighbors' home, where I found it difficult to be around the spread of holiday foods—not so much because of physical temptation, but because of mental frustration and social isolation that comes with not eating.

About thirty minutes later, my older brother, Jerry, came over to say good-bye to me because he was going to his girlfriend's house. It was only ten o'clock, but I felt fatigued, as if dawn was approaching. My parents were having a good time, and I knew they would easily be there until midnight. So I asked Jerry to take me home and he said he'd be happy to.

We were quiet during the ten-minute drive across town. For the first time since I started my hunger strike I was worried that I had gotten in way over my head.

As Jerry walked me to the back door, I looked at him and started to cry. "Jerry, I can't believe what I am doing."

"Lisa, we can't either. What you're doing is so great. We are all so proud of you." He put his arms around me and gave me a hug. Then he offered to come in and talk for a while, but I just wanted to go to bed, so he said good night to me and hugged me one more time.

My presence in the house did little to disturb its stillness. I walked through the dark rooms and up the stairs to my bedroom. The wind rattled the windows as I got in bed and curled up under several blankets. The back of my neck burned. Then, for the first time since the night I watched the tape of Inna's CBS interview at the library on campus, I cried for Inna and her desperate situation, and then for me because I questioned if I had started something I didn't know if I could finish. I prayed for faith—faith to believe what I was doing would make a difference. I prayed for a sign to know I should and could keep going. Eventually, I dozed off.

My mom woke me up at about four o'clock that morning. "Lisa, there is a man on the phone calling from Norway. He said he just saw Inna in Moscow this morning."

I picked up the receiver. "Hello, Lisa," a male voice said and introduced himself to me. The overseas connection was good. "I was just in Moscow this morning at the Meimans' apartment," he explained. "All Inna spoke about during my visit was you. She asked me to call and relay her greetings to you as soon as I got home. She is worried about you and told me to tell you to stop your hunger strike if you feel weak or ill. How are you feeling?"

"I feel great. It's so nice of you to call me."

We talked for just a few minutes and then said good-bye. I hung up the phone, and my mom came and sat next to me on the bed. "Is everything okay?"

"Yes. He was actually with Inna in Moscow today. She asked him to call me when he got back to Norway and he did, right away. Inna is doing everything she can to communicate with me, Mom, and let me know how much she is thinking about me. I feel so close to her," I said and started to cry.

"Oh, Lisa, honey. You must be so tired. Are you sure you can keep doing this?" my mom asked.

"Yeah, I am now, Mom. I worried about it all night and wondered if I could really keep this up. Now I know I can. Just getting that call, tonight, when I needed it most, meant so much to me, because I feel that Inna is right here with me, right here giving me her strength."

20

Capitol Hill

Each time a person stands up
for an ideal, or acts to improve the lot of others . . .
he sends forth a tiny ripple of hope.
—Robert F. Kennedy

I slept in late on Christmas morning. As I lay in bed I realized my angst the night before was the result of pushing myself beyond what it could handle without a daily supply of food. I needed to respect my limitations.

I relaxed and enjoyed my parents' company until my brothers and sisters arrived in the afternoon. I kept up with the activities but decided to avoid feeling left out during dinner by taking a nap. As my family members enjoyed their meal, I dozed off, imagining I was mixing my mom's baked peaches in a blender in order to qualify them for my juice diet.

My aunt Margaret called the next morning to tell me there was a short article about me in the *Milwaukee Sentinel* by the Associated Press. The headline was: "State Woman's Hunger Strike Praised" and the article stated: "A Soviet woman, struggling to win an exit visa from Soviet authorities, said she is 'touched and overwhelmed' by a young Wisconsin woman's hunger strike on her behalf."

"Isn't that nice they interviewed Inna in Moscow?" my aunt asked.

"Yes, it was nice," I replied, gratified as the ripples of publicity I was attracting grew bigger and bigger.

In contrast to my busy schedule the day before Christmas, my only plan the day after was to see the movie *Out of Africa* with a high school friend. Just before noon, I received a call from Bill Taylor, another person who had just visited Inna and Naum. He told me he was the director of the Center for National Policy Review at Catholic University Law School in Washington. He had read the article about me in *USA Today* while transferring through the airport in Montreal, Canada.

"Lisa, not only are you doing a great thing for Inna personally, but you're making an important public statement on behalf of all Soviet Jews, and I congratulate you. Is there anything that I can do to help you?"

"Well, I'm trying to get all the publicity I can and have been pretty successful so far, but I have not had any coverage out East. Do you have any contacts there who would be interested in doing a story about me?"

Bill told me he was involved with the Union of Councils on Soviet Jews, a U.S. organization that was dedicated to the freedom of Soviet Jews: "Let me call my friend there, Mark Epstein, who is the director. I am sure he would be interested in doing something, perhaps a press conference here."

"I've been working with Senator Simon's office and know he would be interested if a press conference could be arranged," I suggested. "My contact there is Jill Goldenberg."

"Very good. I will talk with Mark, and we will call Jill. I'll try to get back to you later this afternoon."

As promised, Bill called back a few hours later, just before I was to leave for the movie. He said Mark was very interested in arranging a press conference in D.C.

"Wow, that's great," I said, amazed it was falling together so quickly.

"We both talked to Jill, and it does not seem possible to have it before January 4, the day you are planning to end your fast. We would like to schedule it for January seventh."

It was immediately obvious to me that a press conference would be more compelling if I was still on the hunger strike, so I pointed that out to Bill.

"Lisa, we are certainly not asking that of you."

I was still used to the idea of fasting, so I was confident that I could prepare myself to go a few more days beyond the original end date of January 4. Besides, my approach had been to take it one day at a time, which was proving to be effective. I had not experienced any adverse physical symptoms and felt strong.

"Bill, if the press conference is scheduled for the seventh, I'll extend my fast until then."

"Are you sure you feel well enough?"

"Yes, I feel fine, and ending my hunger strike with a press conference in Washington would be worth not eating for a few more days." I considered extending it even further, but I knew Inna would not have approved if I did.

The day ended on another high note. When I returned from the movie my mom excitedly exclaimed that there was an article in the *Post Crescent* about my strike. The article was titled "Appreciation—Lisa Paul's Hunger Strike Moving to Inna Meiman's Stepdaughter," and the byline was the Associated Press. It began: "From a north Boulder condo to an Appleton duplex to a Moscow apartment—that's where the hearts of Olga and Misha Plam are reaching this holiday season." Olga was quoted stating that many people were trying to help Inna and Naum, but that nothing was working. "Both their names are on every possible list. Whenever a U.S. official goes to the Soviet Union for a high-level meeting, their names are mentioned." In response to the question of whether my hunger strike gave her hope, she said, "It does. But I'm afraid to say so because I'm afraid to put too much burden on Lisa. She is doing a wonderful thing."

That evening I insisted on cooking a chicken stir-fry dinner for my parents. They were uncomfortable with the idea until they saw me enjoying the process of washing, cutting, touching, and smelling the food. Once the meal was ready, I went upstairs and packed while they ate.

My ride back to Minneapolis left at nine o'clock the next morning. I was sad to leave my parents, but we were all excited about the press conference in D.C., which created a lot of positive energy when we said good-bye. My mom told me to take care and not push myself too hard and then started to cry when she tried to tell me how proud she and my dad were of me. My dad carried my suitcase to the car and embraced me firmly before I got in.

"It's like your mom said, we are very proud of you. You know we will be right there with you wherever you go," he said, patting his right hand over his heart.

"I know, Dad. I love you so much," I said as I hugged him. I got in the car and as we backed out of the driveway, he stood on the sidewalk in an unlaced pair of wool-lined snow boots and an unzipped navy blue down winter jacket. Black hair snuck out just below his gray Russian fur hat, a gift from me the year before, and wisped over the top of his ears. I waved to him and he waved back, smiling and giving me two thumbs-up.

The week of December 30, I was busy working with Jill Goldenberg and the Union of Councils to arrange the logistics of the press conference. The Union of Councils offered to pay for my flight and booked the reservation for me. I was scheduled to leave Minneapolis on Sunday, January 5, and return on Tuesday night, January 7. Winter quarter classes began on Monday the 6th, so I would miss only two days of school. The Union also offered to pay for a hotel room, but I opted to arrange to stay with my friend Teresa—the same Teresa whom I knew in Moscow—

who was living in D.C. and going to school at George Washington University.

In addition to planning the trip to D.C., there was plenty to keep me busy in Minneapolis. I did another interview with the reporter from the *Minnesota Daily*, which was scheduled to run on the first day of winter quarter classes. I also continued to market my story to other possible media outlets.

On Friday, January 3, I was a guest on *Almanac*, a weekly public television talk show in the Twin Cities. I had sent the producer a copy of Inna's tape in advance of the show, and they aired a clip of it during my interview, which was a success overall.

On Saturday, my friend Julie helped me put together an outfit for my press conference, which consisted of her navy blue skirt, light blue blazer, and white blouse. I finished the outfit off with a pair of navy blue dress shoes. Julie and our friend Amy took me to the airport on Sunday and were set to pick me up when I returned on Tuesday night.

When I arrived in D.C., I took a cab from National Airport to Teresa's apartment in Georgetown. It was great to see her again, and she was surprised to see how strong and energetic I was.

On Monday morning I met with Bill Taylor and Mark Epstein at the Union of Councils' office. Like Teresa, they were amazed that I did not appear weak or weary from my fast. On Monday night, I went to see my friends, Greg and Kathie Guroff, who I knew in Moscow and had traveled with to Austria in 1984. They lived in Chevy Chase, Maryland, just north of D.C.

I called Kathie from Appleton after the press conference was arranged and told her about my hunger strike. I wondered how she and Greg would react to my news, as this revealed a side of me that was different than the nanny they knew in Moscow. Greg, who was then working as Deputy Director of the President's Initiative on U.S.–Soviet Exchanges at the United States Information Agency in D.C., was an expert on the Soviet

Union. He received his PhD in Russian Economic History from Princeton and had taught Russian Studies at Grinnell College before working in Moscow. I highly respected both his and Kathie's opinion.

When I called, I briefly told them about my friendship with Inna and the goal of my fast to call attention to her plight. They were both very supportive and insisted we get together during my short trip to D.C. We agreed to meet at their house the evening of January 6.

I arrived that evening at 6:30, as we had planned, and intended to spend an hour or so with them and leave before dinner. The evening was relaxing and enjoyable. I told them more about Inna, and about Naum's involvement in the Helsinki Watch Group. They were familiar with the Meimans and well-informed about the Soviet dissident movement. Greg told me that while he wasn't sure if my fast would get Inna out of the country, he admired what I was doing, an encouragement that meant a lot to me. I invited them both to attend the press conference; Kathie said she'd be sure to attend, but Greg told me that meetings in the morning would prevent him from being there.

When I got back to Teresa's, I started writing my speech for the press conference. I had tried to work on it in Minneapolis and on the plane, expecting it would flow as easily as had everything I had said, written, and done for the past twenty-four days. But I couldn't write a thing. The reality that I was going to be delivering a speech at a press conference in the U.S. Capitol the next day caused all my circuits to jam. I persisted, however, and finally pounded out a first draft. Then Teresa helped me work through a second draft.

Finally, at midnight, we turned out the lights and I tried to sleep, but I was wide awake. I ran through a checklist in my head of the next morning's schedule: leave Teresa's at 9:30, Union of Councils at 10:00, Capitol Hill at 10:15, press conference at 10:30. Then suddenly the words for my speech came to me. Not wanting to disturb

Teresa, I went into the bathroom to write. I worked through another draft and quit at about 1:30 AM. I was nervous about staying up so late and expending energy that I didn't really have to burn—so I set the alarm clock for 8:30 instead of 7:30. I ended up dozing off thirty minutes after the alarm went off, and Teresa didn't even stir. We didn't get up until almost 9:00 AM. That proved to be a mistake. Unlike the control with which I greeted each day of my hunger strike, I woke up on Day 25 feeling rushed and disorganized. I had intended to practice my speech in front of Teresa before leaving, but we ran out of time.

I was, in fact, almost late for my own press conference. I called Mark Epstein just before Teresa and I left her apartment at about 9:45 and suggested we meet at the Capitol, but he insisted we meet at his office. So we dashed outside and fortunately got a cab right away. I fine-tuned my speech in the cab, revising some parts after reading them out loud to Teresa.

We stopped briefly at the Union of Councils office and then the four of us took a cab to Capitol Hill, arriving almost on schedule.

All the last-minute panic I had been feeling came to a halt as I walked into the Capitol rotunda and fully grasped what I was about to do. I paused, looking up at the mural in the dome's center just as I had when I visited D.C. as a young girl, and at that moment a wave of awe and humility washed over me as I thought about all I had accomplished with my hunger strike. Then I bowed my head and silently thanked God that my hunger strike had brought me to this place.

I was still not completely confident about my speech, so I asked Teresa to read it one last time when I saw her in the conference room. As she read, I glanced at the two dozen or so people in the room. I recognized only a handful—Teresa, Bill Taylor, and Mark Epstein. There were also aides for Senators Hart, Durenberger, and Congressman Sikorski present. Senator Durenberger's aide invited me to meet with the senator that afternoon and I was happy to accept.

Jill Goldenberg introduced herself to me, expressing her pleasure in finally meeting me in person, and congratulated me in what I had accomplished with my hunger strike. She also told me that there were approximately ten reporters present—including those from the Associated Press, National Public Radio, and the *Wall Street Journal.*

Then Bill Taylor came over and showed me my seat at the front table. There was a television to the side of the table, with a VCR because I had asked to play a clip of Inna's interview during the press conference. Mark Epstein walked up to the podium, which held eight microphones, and announced we were going to start in a minute or two.

I started feeling nervous as I sat there waiting and just as I was thinking how nice it would be for my parents to be there, I felt a tap on my shoulder. I turned and standing there were Greg and Kathie. They each gave me a hug and wished me luck, which was exactly what I had needed to calm down.

The press conference began. Mark Epstein read a statement from Senator Simon and another from Senator Hart. Then, in what was one of the proudest moments of my life, Mark showed a clip of Inna's interview. As I heard her voice say words that had become so familiar to me, I drifted off, remembering what had become a defining moment for me—the afternoon Inna told me she wanted me to be responsible for the tape and I told her I would not let her down. I almost started to cry, but I knew my speech was next on the program, so I stayed relatively composed.

The tape played for about five minutes and then Mark introduced me. I was calm, almost stoically so, as I stepped up to the podium, knowing this was my moment—my time at bat, as my dad would say, and I was ready to hit a home run:

The memory I have of my stay in the Soviet Union is fortunately filled with the many Russian people I met, especially those who became my close friends. Not all of my friends were of refusenik status. In fact, I did not go to Moscow seeking these people out. I became friends with a young man who at the time was having difficulty finding a job because he quit the Young Communist League. Through an American friend, I got to know two women my age. We usually saw each other once a week. I knew a "black marketer" who was eighteen years old. Our relationship was based on friendship, not business. Through an American professor, I became friends with three Russians, Natasha, Andrei, and Uvol. The time I spent with them was often spent around a kitchen table with food, drink, and laughter.

Then, in August of my second year, I met Inna Meiman. I was only familiar with Inna's name as a possible Russian tutor. Our weekly lessons began very seriously; we would chat a bit in English after each lesson. I began to realize that the conjugation of a Russian verb was not as important as what we discussed in English. We began to spend more of our time talking with each other, about each other. As I found out more of Inna's story, I was awakened to the plight of many refuseniks. I met some of Inna's friends . . .

A rush of emotion overwhelmed me as I remembered the night I met Irina. I paused for what seemed to me like minutes, trying to control the tears that were about to burst out of me. I took a couple of breaths, told myself to keep reading, and, in a matter of a few seconds, gained my composure to continue:

I met some of Inna's friends, each one with their own story to tell, each one surviving with hope despite their personal struggle for justice. I felt the strong consequences of repression through these people. Their strength and spirit amid their struggle was inspiring to me then, and is a part of me today.

I appreciate that people here have told me that they admire my courage. Yet, in comparison, my decision was relatively an easy one to make. I met a woman who spent years in prison and exile because she protested the 1968 Soviet invasion of Czechoslovakia. She stood up with everything to lose, and she did. This, of course, continues to be the result for any Soviet citizen who dares to stand up for their beliefs or for their rights.

Inna Meiman's current situation is desperate. After four operations since 1983, new signs of a cancerous growth have appeared. Inna has thanked her Soviet doctors and said they have done all they can for her. Medical technology in the West offers advanced treatment and hope for a cure. She has received invitations from the West for treatment, including France, Israel, Sweden, and the United States. The Soviet authorities, by repeatedly denying Inna an exit visa, refuse Inna the right to fight for her own life; as she has said, her right for human dignity.

Since my return to the U.S. this past summer, I have been very preoccupied with Inna's plight. Though I felt frustrated, as an American citizen I realized that I have the right to speak out against this injustice. To remain silent was intolerable to me. Today I am ending a twenty-five-day hunger strike that has been an attempt to focus attention, not only on the Meimans' struggle, but to the issue that they represent.

In a letter from her on December 20, Inna wrote: "For Americans my case ought to show how inhuman and paranoid our government is. Do not starve yourself for just me, starve for a cause. For all those here who are trampled on and treated so cruelly, whose names are not known and whose lives are ruined. Though my case is critical, I have never been to prison or persecuted."

In closing, I would like to thank Steve Feinstein and the Minnesota-Dakotas Action Committee for Soviet Jewry for their support and Senator Paul Simon and his office for their assistance. I am grateful to Mark Epstein and the Union of Councils for Soviet Jews for organizing this today on my behalf. The understanding of my friends and family has been very important to me; my parents' support throughout all of this has been incredible.

If by my hunger strike Americans have become more aware of Inna's plight, and if by my action I have been able to give voice to the many people in the Soviet Union whose voices are silenced, then it has been my privilege to accomplish that.

I sat down, letting out a deep sigh. Then the questions began, and there were many. How much weight had I lost? "About eighteen pounds." What did Inna think of my hunger strike? "She is worried about my health but very supportive." If Mikhail Gorbachev was here what would I say to him? "Can I swear? Seriously, please let her go today!"

The conference ended about 11:15 AM. Several people congratulated me and wished me luck. After the crowd dispersed, Jill gave Teresa and me a private tour of the Capitol, which included bringing us out on the Senate floor. After the tour, Teresa and I walked out of the Capitol into the bright January sun.

It was time for me to end my hunger strike. Teresa suggested Au Pied de Cochon in Georgetown, a French restaurant where a Soviet spy had recently ditched CIA agents and gone back to the Soviet side. We took a cab and arrived there shortly before noon.

Before I could stop her, Teresa told the bartender I was breaking a twenty-five-day hunger strike. He was hesitant to believe us, but Teresa convinced him. He handed me a beer and eagerly presented me with a basket of French bread. Then both he and Teresa waited to see my reaction. They did not have to wait long. While I had been advised to gradually reintroduce food into my system so as not to get sick, all the discipline I had exerted over the last three weeks had been exhausted. I watched powerlessly as my hand reached for the bread and brought it to my mouth so I could take a bite. Then Teresa raised her glass, toasted my success, and then we both took a sip of beer.

I took a spoonful of creamy potato soup and, at that moment, I experienced the euphoria of eating again. I had another sip of beer and finished the cup of soup and could have easily enjoyed consuming more but knew I needed to ease back into eating again. Plus I had several appointments to keep that afternoon, so we decided to go back to Teresa's apartment, where I relaxed for a few hours.

I returned to the Capitol building at 4:30 that afternoon to meet with Senator Durenburger. He wanted to learn more about Inna's case and what he could do in the Senate to help her. I explained that it was important to keep pressure on the Soviet authorities and suggested he join Senators Simon and Hart in their continuing efforts. Our meeting, unfortunately, was cut short as I needed to be at a TV studio at 5:15 to prepare for a live hook-up with a Milwaukee evening news program and then my flight was scheduled to leave at 6:45. It was a mad dash from the studio to the airport, but I made it just in time for my flight to Chicago, where I transferred to a plane headed to Minneapolis. It wasn't until after 11:00 PM that I arrived home.

A small group of friends gathered at my apartment—Julie, Amy, Mary Jo, and Dotti. They insisted I open the bottle of champagne they had bought, an offer I couldn't refuse. I was exhausted but still on an emotional high and so happy they had all made the effort to celebrate the end of my hunger strike with me. Physically, I felt fine, but I did not want to push my luck, so I only indulged in a few sips. I told them all about my experiences in D.C. and how well everything had gone. As I was planning on attending my Russian language class at nine o'clock the next morning, they only stayed for a brief while. Before falling exhausted into bed, I had one last thing to do, and that was to call my mom. I related to her every detail about the day—a day that we both agreed had been, without a doubt, the greatest day of my life.

Next Year in Jerusalem

> Gradually it was disclosed to me that
> the line separating good and evil
> passes not through states, nor between classes,
> not between political parties either—but
> right through every human heart.
> —Alexander Solzhenitsyn

Nine hours later, I jumped right back into student life, starting with my 9:15 AM Russian language class. As I went up the stairs to my classroom, a student stopped me and asked if I was the one who had just finished the hunger strike. I answered affirmatively.

"I'm Jewish, and I want to thank you for what you did," he said.

I had an hour break after my Russian class and took the opportunity to eat! On the way to an on-campus café, I picked up both the Minneapolis and St. Paul papers. My roommate had saved the *Minnesota Daily* paper for me from the day before, which I had also brought to read. The article about my hunger strike was the front-page story on the *Daily* and was titled, "Lisa Paul's Protest Calls Attention to Oppression of All Soviet Jews." I was very proud of that characterization because it was consistent with the message that Inna asked me to convey.

I peeled and started to eat a banana as I read the article about my press conference in the *St. Paul Pioneer Press* when a woman sitting at the table next to me said, "Hey, are you the one that just did a hunger strike?"

"Yes, I ended it yesterday," I said, making it clear while chewing that my strike had ended.

"That was a really great thing."

On January 9, I received a note from Steve Feinstein in the mail, congratulating me on the success of my hunger strike. He included a copy of the following telegram the Minnesota Action Committee sent to Inna, dated January 8:

> Dear Inna:
> Please know that the action taken by your friend Lisa Paul has gained much admiration here. Lisa's interviews on several television and radio stations have made your situation known to thousands of people. We pray your health will improve.

Steve also noted that the committee activated their telegram bank for Inna which, he explained, meant that it had requested in its newsletter that people send telegrams to Inna or on her behalf to U.S. officials, urging them to contact Gorbachev and demand Inna's release.

On January 10, I wrote Steve a letter, thanking him for the committee's support and interest in Inna's case. I enclosed some articles about my hunger strike and a copy of the speech I gave at my press conference. He had previously told me to keep track of my expenses because the committee would reimburse me, so I also enclosed the following itemization:

Tape cassettes: audio of KSTP interview	$25.00
Post Office: stamps and 3 express mailings	$40.00
Photocopies	$15.00
Telex	$10.00
Phone, including 2 calls to Moscow	$140.00
Total:	$230.00

I thanked him for the committee's financial assistance, explaining that it allowed me to do things without worrying about how I would pay for them.

I also informed him that I had set up several speaking engagements, including January 18 at Beth El Women's League in Minneapolis; January 22 at the Jewish Student Center on campus; January 25 at Temple Israel in Minneapolis; and January 29 at University of Wisconsin–River Falls.

The next day, my effort to divert my energy from Inna and to focus on my studies was interrupted by a telephone call from Sister Ann Gillen, Executive Director of the National Inter-Religious Task Force for Soviet Jewry, located in New York. She had just been to Moscow and visited Inna. Sister Ann told me that Inna was energized by my fast. "It gave her fresh hope and a new lease on life, literally," she told me. "Inna told us, 'Leeza is not Jewish; she is not related to my family, yet did this for me.' Inna talked about how desperate her situation is and concluded by saying, 'They may have conquered me, but they have not conquered Lisa Paul.'"

Sister Ann also told me that Inna suggested that I write to First Lady Nancy Reagan and ask her to intervene. I thought it was a good idea and along with my letter included copies of press clippings from my hunger strike. I wanted to be urgent in my appeal to her, so I began the letter: "This letter to you is the last chance I feel that I have to try to help my friend Inna Meiman. Her life might depend on it." Then I provided background information about Inna and explained the purpose of my hunger strike on her behalf. I ended the letter with a plea that the first lady please hurry with any effort she could make on Inna's behalf as time was running short. I sent the letter to Mrs. Reagan through Senator Simon's office, but unfortunately never received a response from her.

The next night, I wrote Inna about my hunger strike and included copies of newspaper articles and the speech I gave at my press conference in D.C.:

January 12, 1986

Dear Inna:

As you will see by the enclosed letter, I followed your suggestion and wrote to Mrs. Reagan. I also sent her most of the enclosed articles that I am sending you. I decided to be dramatic and personal in my approach. I guess I felt like I should sound desperate. I hope you are pleased with it. I spoke to my contact at Senator Simon's office and they said they would try to get it to the president.

Inna, I am feeling very healthy and am no longer the frustrated person I was three or four months ago. I wish I was able to do more for you, but in the short run I feel a lot of good resulted from my hunger strike. At least I have peace of mind now. I feel like I will able to better accept whatever happens because in my heart I know I was true to our friendship, to my feelings, and to my commitment to you. And I know, too, that is enough for you. Now I will put my energy into hoping, praying, and being optimistic.

Inna, one cold, spring day, in the midst of all that I was experiencing in Moscow, I questioned God about the good and evil in the world. I was angry because the evil of the Kremlin is so dominating and ruthless with peoples' lives. I still don't understand why; perhaps it is not within human capacity to understand. But, I know that when I asked God to let me help you and asked and asked, He finally answered me by calling on me to fast for you. My fast was a time when I was inspired by the good of this world, when I committed myself to that which is right. I was able to give a little bit more attention to that force—the good—by standing up for it. Maybe that is all one can do because there is so much that is wrong in our world, so much injustice. But maybe change can take place by individuals taking a stand against the evil, the injustice, and not by just sitting back and tolerating it.

Maybe it won't change the world overnight, but it is a step in the right direction.

Inna, since I do have the time and the chance to tell you, I will try. I know there are several reasons you have touched my life and I also know that I need not explain them. But you are a part of my soul and I will never forget you. I want you to know, and you will know in a special place that hears and feels these things and understands, Inna, I want you to know that whatever your future and for however long it is for, it will not all end when you die. That is, a part of you is free within me and will continue to live. Part of my life will always be a celebration, appreciation, and joy for you and because of you. I have never felt or tried to express myself at this depth, but I am being very sincere and trust that you will understand what I am telling you.

Let us hope that my first lady will act promptly to the letter I wrote her. I will continue to hope to see you sometime, somewhere, soon. I will continue to pray that your pain may not be so difficult and that you may have the spirit to continue your courageous fight.

I don't know what else to say.

God bless you, Inna.

Love,

Leeza, your Leeza

I put down my pen and wept in a way I had never wept before.

⁓

All was going smoothly with my transition back to my regular diet until I went out to dinner with my friend Jenny on January 24. I was having so much fun at dinner, being out again and socializing, that I overestimated my level of tolerance for alcohol. I was very drunk after only a few beers. The next morning I woke up dizzy, nauseated, and completely unable to speak as scheduled at the 10:30 service at Temple Israel. I tried to call my contact at the synagogue, Barbara Cohen, to tell her I was sick and could not make it. But she was not home. Then I threw up. Then I called Jenny and, jokingly, scolded her for letting me drink too much.

"Drink some water and try to get yourself together. I'll be over at ten."

I tried to drink water, but it refused to stay in my system. I managed to get dressed, put some blush on my cheeks so I would not look ghostly white, and waited outside in the cold for Jenny, hoping a little fresh air would help, but it didn't.

My plan, at that point, was to find Barbara as soon as I arrived at the synagogue and tell her I was ill with the flu and unable to give the speech.

There were only a few people in the lobby when we walked into the synagogue. I asked a man if he knew where Barbara was, and he led me to the doorway of the sanctuary. As I stood in the doorway, I heard a woman on the altar at the podium proclaiming, "Our speaker, Lisa Paul, should be here any minute. She, as most of you know, recently waged a hunger strike for a Soviet refusenik. . . ." Then she stopped, recognizing me in the doorway. Before I could do anything she enthusiastically announced, "Ladies and gentlemen, it is my pleasure to say Lisa is here." The entire congregation turned around, looked at me, and broke out in applause.

As Barbara motioned for me to come forward, I had no choice but to walk down the aisle and take my place at the podium. I started out a little shaky, but soon the words I had spoken over and over during the hunger strike began to flow and I did just fine.

The first week of February, I received a call from Rabbi Alan Mittleman, who was with the American Jewish Committee in New York City. He had visited Inna in December with Sister Ann Gillen and told me he was very interested in working with me to do something for the Meimans. He asked whether I had any other plans under way, and I explained that I was settling into my studies and did not have anything planned at that time. He encouraged me to use the momentum I had generated by my hunger strike to take more action on Inna's behalf. I told him that I would think it over, but that any action would have to wait until my spring break.

While it was tempting to drop everything and go on an all-out crusade for Inna, I knew she would want me to continue with my classes and graduate in the spring. So, while I set out to make my classes a priority, it wasn't easy. Soon I received a letter from Inna that made concentrating on school even more difficult:

February 7, 1986
Dearest Leeza:
I have received your warm and loving letter and I want to write to you what I think on all those important and crucial you and me points. I think I'll write in Russian, not to be hampered by your "foreign for me" tongue.

I very attentively and several times read and reread all that you sent me. And not because reading about my own personal tragedy (and on paper, of course, it all sounds so awful) causes me pleasure, by no means, no. I wanted to see how you were able to display everything and you did so with such character and intelligence and conveyed everything on such a humane, yet business level. Leeza, you're remarkable, and believe me that is not a compliment, but my joy. I am sure that if you did all of that, then you will be able to do many other things. I want to be witness to your success in life. However, Leeza, you must hurry so that this will be possible.

Now a few words about me. Honestly, my situation is not good. The tumor is big and it is hard to hold my head up. Sometimes there are very hard moments but this happens even with healthy people, right? I am taking herbs and some poison extracted from herbs but there is no improvement seen. On the contrary, the tumor continues to grow. The doctors here categorically reject surgery and suggest chemotherapy instead. I don't know what to do. Should I go to chemotherapy? First, I feel sorry for Naum, my sister Olya, and Lev. Second, I fear the future; the fear of what to expect in the future because if now there is so much pain, what will the future be? Leeza, dear, I am certainly not afraid of death and consider that every person has his time. In that sense, I am a lucky person, and to die will also be without tragedy. I have thought about that very much and so, I write it to you, it is not my bravado, but my reconciliation. However, I still have not lost hope for my visa and treatment. Yes, I wrote you about death, not because I am ready for the "final road" no, no, no!!!

Leeza, I was not able to read your letter without tears. I am lucky that I have such a remarkable friend like you and very lucky that we are together. If I survive, we will be together; if not, then we will also be together—I will always be with you, believe me. I don't know if I am worthy of your love and devotion, but I will try to be.

Now it is difficult to live, I am often in a stupor of pain and illness. My brain is not nourished, it is difficult to read. However, I started to record some stories about Anuta from my village, "Anuta's Stories," and I hope to be able to finish this and send it to you. This will be my gift to you. You could do whatever you want with it.

Lisa: would you like me to send you some Russian books? Could I possibly help you in your studies? I am very curious about what you are studying. What is your main interest? If I could be useful in your studies, I will feel great.

This is it for now. I'll write you soon. I will be able to send this letter now.

My very best and kind regards to your family.

I kiss you.

Yours,

Inna

The letter evoked so much emotion in me that I immediately called Rabbi Mittleman. I told him I was very interested in arranging some type of event for Inna, explaining I had just received a letter from her and there was really no time to waste. I also explained that because of my studies, I did not have the time to take the lead on planning anything but would participate and do whatever needed to be done. He said he would talk to some of his colleagues and his contacts in Washington and get back to me. We agreed that any event would take place during my spring break, during the second week in April.

At the end of January, the Minnesota Action Committee honored me with a human rights award. They presented it at a synagogue, after a well-known professor gave a presentation about the plight of Soviet refuseniks. The plaque is inscribed with the following quote by Anatoly Sharansky: "For more than 2,000 years the Jewish people, my people, have been dispersed. But wherever they are—wherever Jews are found—every year they have repeated, 'Next year in Jerusalem.'" As Steve Feinstein read the quote, I remembered that the first time I heard that statement was at the Meimans' apartment, as it is a common New Year's toast among Soviet Jews.

I accepted the award and thanked the Committee for their support. I wanted to share what Inna said to Sister Ann Gillen. So I explained:

I recently received a call from someone who had recently been in Moscow and visited Inna and her husband, Naum. Inna told her, and I quote, "They have conquered me, but they have not conquered Lisa Paul." Physically, perhaps Inna has been conquered. Her words have personal meaning to me, but I think they can be meaningful to all of us. They remind us that we cannot be stopped in our efforts to keep this issue very prominent and that we must constantly remind the Soviet government that we demand basic human rights for Soviet Jews and other Soviet citizens. Maybe our success cannot be measured by what we accomplish today, but rather by the difference we make over a period of time. We should also be encouraged by how the individual people survive amid their struggle. This was especially evident in Anatoly Sharansky, who was recently released after serving nine years in a Soviet prison. He demonstrated that the Soviet government can take and control many things, but it cannot control a man's soul.

At the end of January, I received a letter from Congressman Gerry Sikorski. He wrote:

Prompted by your twenty-five-day hunger strike, I have recently written a letter to General Secretary Gorbachev urging him to reconsider Mrs. Meiman's case. The letter, a copy of which I have enclosed, received strong bi-partisan co-sponsorship from forty-five members of the House of Representatives. Also enclosed is a letter being mailed to 1,500 of my constituents urging them to write Mrs. Meiman directly.

   Your efforts have been inspirational for many of us here in Washington. I will continue to monitor Inna's case and do whatever possible to help with its resolution.

I also received letters from people near and far who told me they had heard about my hunger strike and supported it. One letter arrived from a rabbi in California:

I came across your story in one of the newspapers and shared it with my congregation in our synagogue's monthly bulletin. You were also featured in my sermon on the Friday evening before Martin Luther King's birthday celebration. I thought you would enjoy reading what I wrote.

   With all my affection and every good wish,
   Rabbi M. L. Rubenstein

Numerous letters followed suit:

Minneapolis, February 1, 1986:
As a woman, a Jew, a University of Minnesota graduate and as a sixty-one year old who becomes more conscious of death as well as life daily, I feel humanity and pride in your fast.
   Margaret R. Hunegs

Ontario, February 6, 1986:
I saw a copy of the article about what you have done for Inna Meiman, and wish to express my deep admiration for your actions. We cannot invite you to speak in Toronto because, as you know, we are all strapped for funds; but I shall be delighted to tell the Meiman story and what you have done for them. I would like to get the family adopted here and get a lobby going for them in Parliament. We would like to purchase a copy of the CBS videotape to show it to groups here.
   Sincerely,
   Genya Intrator
   Inter-Religious Task Force, Canada

Paris, March 10, 1986:
I have just visited with Inna and Naum Meiman. Professor Meiman spoke very warmly of you and of his appreciation

for your hunger strike on their behalf, and I want to add my gratitude to theirs.

I am a Professor at Brandeis University, on sabbatical in Paris until the end of April. Could you please send me information about your hunger strike, and other pertinent material, for I want to be able to write something that would help the Meimans.

Edward Kaplan

My mom called me at the end of February, thrilled because she had received a letter from Inna. She read it to me over the phone:

Dear Helen:

Thank you very much for writing. Naum and I are so touched and proud by the attitude your family has taken toward us and toward what Leeza has done for us! My words are not the words of compliment or praise—they are the sincerest expression of my admiration for you and your family. Please believe me!

Stay well and I hope Leeza will always have your support and encouragement in whatever she thinks to do best.

Love to all of your family.

Most heartiest greetings from Naum.

Lots of love from me,

Inna

Rabbi Mittleman contacted me the first week of March and said he had joined efforts with the National Conference on Soviet Jewry in D.C. and they would like my help in planning a press conference in April. His idea was to bring together a high-profile group of people in the Capitol to demand Inna's and Naum's immediate release. Together we came up with the following list: Naum's daughter Olga, Senator Gary Hart, Senator Paul Simon, Congressman

Timothy Wirth from Colorado, Senator Rudy Boschwitz from Minnesota, and Congressman Gerry Sikorski. Rabbi Mittleman also mentioned Dr. Douglas Zipes, a cardiologist at Indiana University School of Medicine. He explained Dr. Zipes had visited Inna in Moscow and made a personal appeal to Gorbachev explaining why Inna needed treatment in the West.

I arrived in Washington on April 14, the day before the press conference. Rabbi Mittleman arranged to meet me at the office of the National Conference on Soviet Jewry's office before the press conference. It was there that I met Naum's daughter, Olga, for the first time. She did not look at all like her father. Her hair was black and short, parted to the side; her bangs fell neatly in place above her eyebrows. She spoke English well—soft-spoken with a noticeable Russian accent—and was very pleasant and kind. I enjoyed spending time with her before the press conference began at 11:30 AM in the Russell Senate Office Building. There was a podium at the front of the room with several chairs on the right and left. Propped against the podium was a recent photograph of Inna that horrified me. Her hair was brushed off her forehead, her skin was pale and puffy, and she had dark circles under her eyes. The tumor was visible, protruding slightly off the side of her neck. The sight of her, so ill, made me cry.

The panel of speakers assembled in the room, and we introduced ourselves. I was greeted warmly by everyone, especially Senator Hart and Congressman Wirth. The room was full of congressional aides and about twenty reporters, with cameras and microphones. We all took our places in the chairs, in no particular order. I sat at the end next to Olga.

I listened attentively as each politician spoke about what I knew so well—the grave state of Inna's health and the inhumanity of the Soviet government's refusal to let her leave the country for medical treatment. Senator Hart acknowledged my hunger strike, saying that "much admiration and support is due to University of Minnesota student Lisa Paul." He then made the point that "all efforts are of vital importance in ensuring continued attention to the plight of the Meimans and other Soviet Jews denied their basic human rights." Congressman Wirth said that he and Senator Hart were sponsoring a co-resolution to be introduced to the Senate and House calling for the Meimans' immediate release. Dr. Zipes added his medical perspective, noting it was not too late for Inna to receive treatment in the West that could save her life. Olga spoke eloquently about the absence of her father in her life and about her wish to meet Inna. She also said she would like Naum to meet his grandson, her only child. Congressman Sikorski spoke briefly about my hunger strike and how much interest about Inna's case it had generated in Minnesota. He echoed the demand for Inna's immediate release and then introduced me.

As I walked up to the podium, I knew I couldn't say anything that hadn't already been said, so I chose to be brief. I held up a photograph I had of Inna that was taken in the fall of 1985. I noted the obvious contrast in that photograph to the one on the podium and made the point that the photographs demonstrate how each day that passed was one too many and only made Inna's situation more desperate. I thanked everyone on the panel for their efforts to free Inna and Naum and urged them to continue the fight.

After the press conference, the group of speakers went to Senator Hart's office, where we called Naum. Senator Hart told me that the Soviet authorities had disconnected the Meimans' phone, so someone in the American Embassy in Moscow had gotten a message to Naum instructing him to be at the downtown telegraph office on the evening of April 15. He was not told the reason, just to be there to receive a telephone call. We all waited with Senator Hart as his secretary tried to connect the call and, fortunately, it went right through. Each of us had a chance to talk to Naum. Most touching was hearing Olga say, "Papa, Papa, it is me, Olga. How are you?"

Senators Hart and Simon spoke next and then I had a chance to speak with him.

"Hello, Naum, it's me, Leeza."

"Oh, Leeza, you are also there!" Naum answered in a delighted voice.

"Yes, many of your friends are here today, fighting for you and Inna. Please give my love to her."

"I will, Leeza. She is at a dacha outside of Moscow with her sister, Olga."

After the call ended, I thanked Senator Hart for his help. He put his arm on my shoulder and said convincingly, "Lisa, I am going to do everything I can, and we are going to get them out."

I believed him.

In the afternoon, Rabbi Mittleman, Olga, and I went to the State Department to meet with Richard Schifter, who was then Assistant Secretary of State for Human Rights and Humanitarian Affairs. He seemed well-informed about Inna and Naum's case and expressed his commitment to doing what he could to keep the pressure on the Soviet government for their release.

I returned to Minneapolis feeling elated about all that was being done at the highest levels in the U.S. government to help Inna and Naum. Personally, I tried to imagine the scene when Naum told Inna about the press conference and all of us who were in Washington, D.C., fighting for their freedom. I felt triumph in knowing that the significant action we had taken on their behalf was a bright light that flickered all the way to Moscow.

─◦◦─

When classes started after break it was obvious to me that if I was going to graduate in June, I would need to devote all my time and energy to being a student. I was taking four courses and completing my senior thesis. I also had to take two tests to make up the incompletes I had taken during the fall quarter. Even though I had been admitted into a third-year Russian language class, I still had to take a second-year Russian language test as a formality to receive credits for second year. I wondered how I could possibly do it all. As I soon found out, I couldn't. I had received a poor grade in an art history class and spoke with an adviser about retaking it during the summer session, which she approved. So I lightened my course load to only three classes and breathed a little easier.

While my mind was focused on school work, my heart continued to be devoted to Inna. On April 30, I wrote in my journal, "I am accepting a passive role, but my mind is constantly searching, constantly wondering, if there is something more I can give this. The most difficult challenge is to let go and trust that it is in 'God's hands.'"

On May 6, I received a letter from a friend of the Meimans that included material Naum wished to be considered at an upcoming international conference for human rights in Bern, Switzerland. There was a copy of an invitation for Inna to come to the United States for treatment, which she had recently received from Marjorie Kampleman, the wife of the U.S. ambassador to the Soviet Union, and several U.S. senators. There was also a sheet published by "The International Cancer Patients Committee for Solidarity," of which Inna was a member. The preface stated:

> Moscow, U.S.S.R.
> We, Tatyana Bogomolny, Benjamin Charny, Inna Meiman, Rimma Bravve, Leah Maryasi, and members of our families have joined a group to make people of the world aware of our grave situation and to plead with them for help.

Naum included a note asking me to represent Inna on that committee in the United States. He explained that all of the other cancer patients had family in the West, sisters, brothers, or children to represent them on the committee and that Inna wanted me to serve in the role as her family member. I wasn't sure what it would involve, but I felt honored to represent Inna.

In May I also learned that Inna's health had, not surprisingly, continued to deteriorate. She was receiving chemotherapy treatment—an alternative that could only mean that her situation was more desperate than ever because such treatments had previously been ruled out as an option.

But, despite all of it, Inna had not lost hope for a visa, and she stated as much in a letter she mailed to me that late spring. Unlike all of her other letters, this one was typed:

May 15, 1986

Dear Leeza:

I have not written for a long time, forgive me. I did not have the strength, believe me, not moral (emotional) or physical. I was not able to sit and write a letter. And now I am somewhat able. I was given two doses of chemotherapy treatments, very strong, and I am very weak. The doctor considers that there was an effect, in other words, he considers that the tumor had decreased a little. At least it has not gotten bigger. You can see that this is so, but I myself am very weak and the pain, more than before is very strong. I am only able to walk very slowly to and from my bed. Nevertheless, my spirits have not fallen and I have not lost hope. We know that you are with us! We are very lucky to have such wonderful friends. Towards you I have a special feeling! I often think about you and I would very much like for you to have a life full of happiness.

Well, all is still not lost; suddenly they could say, "Here is your visa." I believe that this is still possible.

Leeza, my dear, please do not worry. I still have patience. I will write you a long letter soon. Please give my heartfelt greetings to your mom and dad, and your sister, Therese, who recently wrote me a letter.

I kiss you strongly,

Inna

I cried after I read the letter and felt utterly helpless. More disconcerting news soon followed. The Soviet contact who received chemicals for Inna's chemotherapy treatments from a doctor in France had been discovered by the Soviet authorities, and the chemicals were confiscated.

It was all very depressing. In a sullen mood, I wrote to Ellen Kort, with whom I had been corresponding frequently since first contacting her in December 1985:

May 14, 1986
Dear Ellen,
It has been a month since my trip to Washington, with no changes for the better and no indication to expect any soon. For me, it is now a true challenge of optimism, hope, and prayer, a challenge that drains my energy. It is difficult to deal with this passively and to accept that there is nothing more I can do. I would run around the world for Inna if I thought it could help.

I spoke to someone in Washington today who had just returned from the Soviet Union, and who visited Inna and Naum last Friday. She said that Inna is up and around, but in a great deal of pain. Apparently, the chemotherapy treatments have reduced the size of the tumor. For some reason, the chemicals for those treatments, which were supplied by a French doctor, have been cut off. That is very upsetting, especially when the treatments seemed to be helping.

This is all so frustrating because I am beginning to feel more negative energy than positive. I feel so sad that Inna and Naum are still there, struggling so. I have to continue to hope that I will see Inna again, that Naum and she may leave there someday, soon! Sometimes I ask myself what I will do if that does not happen, if Inna does not leave the Soviet

Union for treatment, but I don't dwell on that scenario. Mostly, I try to continue to believe in the God who I feel Inna's life is being watched over by, who I believe ultimately will grant Inna the justice she has fought for and has dedicated herself to. That belief, based on my faith, is all I have right now. Faith is what I am trying to have plenty of.

Lisa

Time marched on, as it always does, and it was summer before I knew it. In May I had received a call from a lawyer involved in the Minnesota Lawyers Committee for Human Rights. He said the committee wanted to present me with an award at their annual dinner on June 25 and explained that the topic for the evening was Soviet refuseniks because of the attention my hunger strike had brought to that issue. While I considered the recognition an honor, I was more excited because I viewed it as an opportunity to continue to bring attention to Inna's plight. I asked him if it would be possible to show a portion of Inna's CBS interview at the dinner, and he said he would make the arrangements.

My parents attended the dinner with me, and it was thrilling to have them by my side for what I considered a very special occasion. We joined the crowd as it rose with applause after viewing Inna's tape.

By the second week of July, I had finished my two summer classes. Fortunately, I found the art history class less difficult the second time around, and I redeemed myself—I received an A and was finally a college graduate.

PART III

WASHINGTON, D.C.

CHAPTER

The Chautauqua Conference
on U.S.–Soviet Relations

There was no human dimension in the superpower
relationship. Mid-level officers never had the chance
to get to know each other as human beings.
This is a way of sensitizing the debate.
—John Wallach

G reg and Kathie called me at the end of June to offer me a job in
Washington, D.C. Greg was on an executive committee plan-
ning a major conference on U.S.–Soviet relations to take place in
September in Riga, Latvia. John Wallach, the director of the confer-
ence, was hiring an assistant and Greg thought I would be the perfect
candidate. John, he explained, was the foreign editor for Hearst
Newspapers in D.C. and got the idea for the conference a few years
after organizing a summer program at the Chautauqua Institution in
New York state. He recruited the Chautauqua administration and
Susan Eisenhower, president of the Eisenhower World Affairs Insti-
tute (and granddaughter of President Eisenhower), to co-sponsor the
American delegation and program.

The conference, Greg said, would consist of open dialogue
between U.S. and Soviet policymakers and uncensored participa-
tion by citizens of both nations—in the spirit of Gorbachev's new

era of *glasnost*, or "openness." It was to be the first conference of its kind to ever take place in the Soviet Union.

Greg also told me there had been some concern among U.S. officials that by sending a high-ranking American delegation to one of the three Baltic States, the United States would be perceived as acknowledging Latvia's inclusion in the Soviet Union, a position the U.S. government had rejected outright since the end of World War II. However, U.S. officials ultimately concluded the conference would provide them with an opportunity to assert, while in Latvia, that the Soviets' incorporation of the Baltic States into the Soviet Union was illegitimate.

The job paid only a hundred dollars a week, but Greg and Kathie invited me to live with them, with no charge for room and board. I accepted their invitation and the job without hesitation. The week after I finished college, I flew to D.C. to start work on the conference.

Soon I was helping John coordinate every aspect of the conference, from travel plans to organizing the 220 Americans who signed up to participate as citizen delegates to sending updates on agendas and schedules to the executive committee members. I was also responsible for disseminating this same information to the agents of American entertainers who had signed on to attend the conference, including Grover Washington, Jr., dancers from the American Ballet, and jazz pianist Billy Taylor.

Initially my position was not slotted to attend the conference, but in early August, John invited me to come along. While I welcomed the opportunity, the real thrill for me was that the American delegation was going to be in Moscow for a few days after the conference, which meant *in less than a month* I would be able to see Inna again.

The conference plans were moving along smoothly until Nick Daniloff, who was then the American correspondent for *U.S. News & World Report* in Moscow, was arrested on trumped-up spy charges on August 30, just ten days before our charter was to take off from D.C. The speculation was that the Soviets had arrested him in retaliation for the FBI's arrest of a Soviet spy, Gennadiy Zakharov, a week earlier. Zakharov, a Soviet physicist working at the United Nations, was taken into custody by the FBI on August 23 in a New York subway while paying a U.S. defense contractor employee for classified documents.

Daniloff's arrest caused immediate concern among the organizers of the conference. Some U.S. officials immediately withdrew from the trip, including Richard Perle, Assistant Secretary of Defense, and Alan Keyes, Assistant Secretary of State for International Organizations. John and other members of the executive committee met with Secretary of State George Schultz, who was adamant that the White House would prohibit any remaining U.S. government officials from attending the conference and would not endorse it if Daniloff remained in a Soviet jail. John believed, however, that the conference was a significant American negotiating tool because the Soviets had the most to gain from the conference in terms of international public relations.

On Friday, September 5, five days before our scheduled departure date, a State Department official told John that there would be a change in Daniloff's status, possibly as soon as that next Monday. So even though Daniloff was still being held captive, the decision was made to go ahead and bring the American participants to Washington as scheduled the following Tuesday. The hope was that Daniloff would be released to the American Embassy before the charter was to depart on Wednesday afternoon. The executive committee members were all optimistic that the Soviets would be unwilling to sacrifice the conference over Daniloff's arrest.

Late that Friday afternoon, I went to the Soviet Consulate to pick up the visas for members of the American delegation. I returned to the office and went through the entire batch, matching each visa to the names of the conference participants. When I had finished sorting, I discovered that visas had not been issued for several applicants, including three reporters for Voice of America, one Latvian American who was active in the cause for a Latvian state independent of the Soviet Union, and me.

It was my job to contact the Soviet Consulate about the visas that were not issued, and I spoke to a Soviet consulate officer that afternoon, who assured me that all five visas were still being processed and awaiting approval from Moscow. When I told Greg that my visa had been denied, he wasn't surprised and speculated that the reason was my hunger strike: "Soviet officials apparently heard the message you were trying to send loud and clear."

"It would be great if they did, even if it means I can't go on this trip," I replied.

Greg said he suspected that the Soviets were withholding their decision on the "controversial" visas until the fate of the conference was known. He told me he would call the Soviet Consulate and try to move the visas along.

All members of the American delegation arrived in D.C. on Tuesday, September 9. The charter to Latvia was scheduled to depart from Dulles Airport at six o'clock the next evening. Unfortunately, as of Wednesday morning, there were no new developments in the Daniloff case. The executive committee members met that morning and decided to cancel our departure and wait things out until Friday. The consensus remained that we could not attend a conference hosted by the Soviets while they were detaining an innocent American journalist.

Meanwhile, there continued to be no word from the Soviets on my or the four other visas. The situation deteriorated for me when the Soviet Consulate would no longer accept my telephone calls. When I asked for my contact there—the man with whom I had worked closely over the last few weeks and who had always been pleasant with me—he refused to take my calls.

On Friday morning, members of the executive committee gathered at the Grand Hotel, where many of the Americans were staying and where the committee had been operating all week. I learned from John and Greg that the chances were very good that Daniloff was going to be released to the custody of the American Embassy by the end of the day. A press conference was scheduled for two o'clock that afternoon in the hotel ballroom to announce both the fate of Daniloff and the conference. I knew going into the press conference that the Pan Am charter had been rescheduled for Saturday morning, so I was optimistic Daniloff had been released.

Dr. Daniel Bratton, President of the Chautauqua Institute, began the conference promptly at two o'clock. The room was packed with members of the press, the executive committee, and as many of the Chautauquans who could fit into it. I sat up front next to Greg and Kathie. Dr. Bratton began by thanking everyone for their patience, then smiled and announced that Daniloff was in the U.S. Embassy in Moscow and that the American delegation would be leaving for Latvia the next morning. The crowd roared with applause. Then John enthusiastically announced that the two Voice of America reporters had been issued visas, the first time the Soviets had ever granted permission to Voice of America reporters to enter their country. The crowd applauded again. As John began talking about the logistics of getting to the airport on Saturday, I felt Greg's hand squeeze my shoulder. I looked at him and, with a very sad expression he moved his head from left to right.

"I didn't get a visa?" I asked him.

"No, I am sorry, Lisa. You didn't," he replied.

I was about to burst into tears, so I got up, not wanting to make a scene, and made my way to the aisle. I walked out of the room, down the hallway, and entered a bathroom. I stood at the sink and ran the cold water, cupped it in my hands, and splashed it on my face, realizing what I had accomplished by getting my visa denied by the Soviet government. Greg was right—the Soviets *had* heard the protest I was trying to make by my hunger strike. Looking at myself in the mirror, I felt absolutely triumphant. I dried my face off with a paper towel and composed myself. As I walked out of the bathroom, I was greeted by Kathie.

"Lisa, I wondered where you went. I am so sorry you can't come with us tomorrow, but both Greg and I are proud of you," she said as she gave me a hug.

Only two other visas had been denied to the American delegation. One was denied to a Voice of America reporter who was a specialist on Soviet affairs. Greg told me the Soviets explained that she was denied because she had reported on something in the past that was anti-Soviet. The other was denied to Vita Terraudis, President of the Latvian American Youth Association, even though the Soviets had issued visas to other Latvian American activists. At the Guroffs' later that evening, Greg told me he had contacted the Soviet Consulate to officially protest the denial of my visa. He even spoke to the Soviet Ambassador to the United States, Anatoly Dobrynin, and personally guaranteed that I would not cause any trouble if I were issued a visa. Ambassador Dobrynin told Greg he would immediately send a telegram to Moscow requesting reconsideration and that he would call Greg at home if there were any changes.

As there was a slight chance I could still go, I packed a suitcase. I finally got into bed around midnight, feeling anxious as I tried to sleep. I drifted off imagining Kathie knocking on my door, telling me that my visa would be waiting for me at the airport. But my alarm went off at seven o'clock the next morning, and there had been no call.

I drove Kathie and Greg to the airport and said good-bye to the many people I had come to know during those few days in

Washington. It was obvious that word had spread among the group as to why the Soviets denied my visa and I received many compliments about my activism for Inna. One woman observed that I must have felt great accomplishment in having the Soviets deny me permission to visit the country. Another, Florence Ross, gave me a kiss on the cheek, then handed me a note and told me to read it when I got home, which I did:

> Please know that we sincerely regret you could not join us, but we feel keenly that the courage you displayed on behalf of your friends is being picked up and will become a fresh breeze that will permit them to breathe more freely in the days ahead.

Uvidimsya—We Will See Each Other Again

> Both now and for always, I intend to hold
> fast to my belief in the hidden
> strength of the human spirit.
> —Andrei Sakharov

On Monday I received a letter from Inna:

September 5, 1986
Leeza, dear!
Please forgive me for not writing. I received all of your letters, but have not been able to answer them. All summer I
was in bed and barely alive. I had pneumonia and so on. In
short, every three months I have chemotherapy. I mostly
stay in bed, and have some limited walking. But spiritually I
am all right and my friends, as always, support me.

The list of my health problems would take all the space
of this letter, but I wish to use it differently.

Leeza, although I have not written, I often think of your
love and work for me. I feel your love and care almost physically—that is the truth. Do not worry if I do not answer
your letters right away. I will. I congratulate you on gradu-
ating from college. Through my friend I am going to send
you a small gift, a book by Pushkin. I very much love the
book and therefore, want you to have it. Of course, it is hard

to understand it but a talented artist did beautiful illustrations. Naum and I are happy for you, I am very glad that you are in Washington and that you have a job. Leez, dear, I have not lost hope, all could be changed any time, but without my visa it looks hopeless. Of course, in life there is much to do, but not when you are in bed and can't even write a letter. This is really a tragedy.

Here it is everything the same: endless chatter about the humanism of our state and government. But what could be said about a state, which does not provide needed drugs for cancer patients?

I recall you very often and think it was wonderful to have you here.

I am always with you even if I do not reply to your letters.

Best regards to your family and friends,

Inna

After reading the letter, I couldn't help but think I had been spared going to Moscow and seeing Inna so ill, only to have to go through the pain of leaving her behind. My dream that I would see her again would have to materialize in a country outside the Soviet Union, and I prayed like never before that our reunion would happen soon.

A week later, I drove to Dulles Airport to greet the American delegation when it returned from the Soviet Union. One couple, the Levins, who had been delegates from Chautauqua, rushed up to me after they cleared customs and happily informed me they had visited Inna just the day before in Moscow. I cried in Mrs. Levin's arms because I was so happy she had seen Inna. They explained to me that her spirit seemed strong but that she was obviously very ill. They gave me a letter from her:

Dear Leeza!

I cannot tell you how disappointed we were to have heard on Voice of America that you are not allowed to come here. I don't want to sound like a sage, but I expected it. I just could not believe that after your open and heroic fight for my freedom, or to be more fair, for my survival, they would allow you to come and see us! Well, Leez, I only hope that you were not terribly upset and this does not affect your career in any adverse way.

We were visited by Warren Zimmerman [who was at that time the head of the U.S. delegation at the Conference on Security and Cooperation in Europe in Vienna] a few days ago and Naum talked to him about you. He told Warren that, in his opinion, you would be a credit to the American team in Vienna, to which Warren, as you might know, is the head of now. Warren agreed with Naum most heartily, so take the tip and act as you see fit. We, on our part, would be happy to have you near us, and I am sure you will be able to prove yourself to your best.

Leeza, I am happy to tell you the last five days I have been up most of the time. True, I take an enormous amount of medication, hormones among them, but never mind as long as I can get up and write you a letter then everything is okay, isn't it?

I had my last chemotherapy three weeks ago; the two weeks that followed were horrible. I was literally half-dead, the last five days alive again. But the doctor is coming tomorrow possibly to start a new course of chemotherapy. I will be asking him on my bended knees to postpone the injection for at least ten days so that my brother and I can go to my village for a few days.

I am sending you a few modest presents, a pendant and a piece of lace for you that Anuta made, a book for your niece, a piece of lace for your mother and for your sister. Also for you, an amateur watercolor of Anuta's hut. Do you know that I have bought this hut for 100 rubles?

Leeza, stay well and optimistic. I need your strength very badly now.

Lots of love from me and Naum,

Inna

After I read the letter, I felt for the first time since I'd started fighting for Inna's freedom that she might die in the Soviet Union, which terrified me. I reread her letter and realized that she was not feeling defeated yet, so I would do exactly as she asked and stay optimistic and strong.

During the first week of October, Steve Feinstein called to inform me that he had read a press release by the Union of Councils for Soviet Jewry that the Soviets agreed to release a Soviet cancer patient, Tatyana Bogomolny. There was also an unconfirmed report that Inna was one of two other cancer patients who were being moved forward in the process. He cautioned me not to get my hopes up, because he had no other information. How could I not get my hopes up? The Reykjavik Summit between Reagan and Gorbachev was scheduled to begin October 11. Previous patterns showed that the Soviet government would release a high-profile dissident either before or after such a high-level summit meeting. I was extremely optimistic that the summit would trigger Inna's release. But the summit came and went, and there was no news of a change in Inna's status.

As November began, I became distracted by the instability in my own life. My efforts to find a full-time job after the Chautauqua Conference were unsuccessful. I did accept a job with a temp agency, which placed me at a different office each day or week, usually as a receptionist or office assistant. The work brought in enough money for me to live on and to save money for an apartment. The Guroffs did not give me any indication that they wanted me to move out, but I didn't want to overstay my welcome.

As far as Inna's situation was concerned, I continued to write letters to my contacts in the Senate, Congress, and to other influential people, such as Richard Schifter and Armand Hammer, a prominent American businessman whose contact with Soviet leaders went as far back as Vladimir Lenin. I asked that they continue to pressure the Soviets to grant Inna a visa. I also continued to hope and pray. One day, I entered the cavernous and grand interior of the National Cathedral. The grandeur of the building was the perfect place to hold the enormity of my single prayer, which I repeated over and over again: "Please God, let her go before it's too late."

At the end of November, I moved into a three-bedroom apartment with two American friends whom I met in Moscow—Michelle Lynch and Suzy Crow.

The second week of December I had a weeklong assignment organizing files in a law firm. There I would sit from 9:00 AM to 5:00 PM every day, alphabetizing files. During my afternoon break on December 17, I called a friend of Steve Feinstein's—a lawyer who worked in D.C. and who Steve suggested could help me in my job search. I introduced myself, explaining that I met Steve through my work on behalf of a Soviet refusenik named Inna Meiman.

He answered, "Oh yes, Inna Meiman, she has been trying to leave the Soviet Union for medical treatment."

"Yes, she has."

"That's great she is finally getting permission to leave."

"What?"

"She has received permission to leave," he repeated.

"Are you sure?"

"Yes. I read an article about it this morning in *The New York Times*," he responded.

"This is incredible news! I have to go. I will call you back later."

I ran out of the file room and then impatiently waited for the elevator, wanting to fully believe what he said. I knew that Senator Hart was in Moscow and had secured the release of Rimma Bravve, another Soviet cancer patient, earlier that week after meeting with Gorbachev. (I would learn a few weeks later, in a letter I received from Naum, that Hart stopped to see him and Inna before meeting Gorbachev at the Kremlin.)

As soon as the elevator reached the ground floor and the doors opened, I ran to a newsstand in the building next door. I grabbed the *Times* and dug in my purse for some change.

"What is your rush, lady?" the cashier asked. "There's no fire." *Oh yes, there certainly is,* I wanted to shout at him, but instead I took the paper, sat down on a bench in the lobby of the building, and scanned through each page looking for a headline with Inna's name in it. On page A-14, I saw a photograph of Senator Hart with Bravve at the airport in Vienna, and my heart sank—maybe that's who Steve's friend meant, Rimma Bravve, not Inna. I read the headline, "Dissident Sees Soviets Letting Wife Leave for Cancer Treatment," and anxiously continued reading:

> The Soviet Union was reported today to have decided to allow the wife of a human rights campaigner to leave the country for experimental cancer treatment in New York.
>
> The campaigner, Naum Meiman, said today that Senator Gary Hart, in a meeting with Foreign Minister Eduard Shevardnadze on Tuesday, was informed his wife, Inna Kitrosskaya Meiman, would be allowed to leave. Mr. Shevardnadze reportedly did not say how soon she would be given an exit visa.
>
> Mrs. Meiman suffers from an inoperable tumor on her neck. Despite years of appeals from prominent scientists and political figures in the West, she has been denied

permission to seek the specialized radiation therapy she believes is her only hope of survival.

Mr. Meiman said that the Foreign Minister told Senator Hart that the Soviet government was "reconsidering" her case. He said that he had discussed the matter with his wife and that they had agreed that she would leave without him if necessary.

"It is inhuman to make her go alone," Mr. Meiman said today in an interview in his apartment. "But we have no other choice. Every day is valuable."

Mr. Hart said in Moscow this week that he had made a special plea for the Meimans when he met on Monday with Mikhail S. Gorbachev, the Soviet leader.

There was no way I could return to work, as I was bursting with emotion, so I went back to the file room, got my things, and told my supervisor I had a personal emergency and had to leave.

I called Greg from a pay phone before taking the metro to my apartment. He said he had been trying to reach me all day and confirmed the facts in the article, but had no other information.

The next few nights I placed phone calls to Moscow to talk to Inna and, finally, on the third night, my call went through to her at three o'clock in the morning my time.

"Hello," Naum answered.

"Hello, Naum. This is Leeza."

"Oh, Leeza, hello," he responded in Russian, and then began speaking in English, "It is very good to hear your voice. Ahh, Inna not here now . . . at dacha with her sister."

"I have heard the news about her visa. How is she? "

"Very weak, She, ah, will not leave without me."

"What are you going to do?"

"I told her she must leave without me. Ahh but she will not. So I accept her wishes. She hopes we both get visa if she refuses to leave alone."

After I hung up the phone, I felt sick to my stomach. All the refusenik cases that had been resolved during the last year appeared to be hassle-free. But things were not falling into place so easily for Inna and Naum.

⎯ↄ.ↄ⎯

I went home to Appleton for Christmas. Before leaving, I spoke with Greg, and he promised to call me if he heard any news about Inna. He also told me I could call Kathleen Lang at the Soviet desk at the U.S. State Department for more information. When I called a few minutes later, Kathleen cordially told me she had read about me in several newspaper articles, which were in the State Department's file on the Meimans. She promised to call me at home if she heard anything about Inna's visa during the holidays.

But all was agonizingly quiet while I was in Appleton. There had been absolutely no news about Inna. Once my vacation ended and I returned to D.C., I called Kathleen to find out if anything had changed. She told me Senator Hart was continuing to pressure the Soviets for the Meimans' release and was asking leaders of other foreign governments to do the same. Other than that, she had no new information.

I kept trying to move forward with my life, sending out résumés and continuing my work for the temp agency, but it was very difficult to think about anything but Inna and Naum. I was assigned to work as a receptionist at an engineering association the first week of January and apparently did such a good job that I was invited to stay on there for as long as I wanted. I welcomed the stability of a consistent assignment while I continued to search for a full-time job.

The next week I had a second interview with a nonprofit group called The American Committee on U.S.-Soviet Relations, which was a membership organization consisting of leading U.S. experts on the Soviet Union. The committee's main effort was preparing an overall analysis of the status of U.S.-Soviet relations. The job called for an executive assistant, which would involve primarily administrative duties. This was not exactly what I had in mind, but I thought if I could get my foot in the door, I might have an opportunity to move into a more challenging position in the future.

Kathleen called me at the end of the week to report that the Soviet government would issue a visa to Inna in the next day or two. However, there continued to be no indication that the Soviets would issue Naum's visa, so the news I had been waiting to receive for so long was bittersweet. *How*, I wondered, *could Inna leave Moscow without Naum?*

I was also in contact with Teeny Zimmerman during this time. Her husband, Warren, was the U.S. ambassador to the talks in Vienna on "Security and Cooperation in Europe." Teeny had studied Russian with Inna, and they were very good friends. She confirmed that the Soviets were going to issue Inna a visa any day but, like me, was not sure that Inna would leave the Soviet Union without Naum.

On Wednesday, January 14, I was offered the job at the American Committee and was to start on Tuesday, January 20. The next day, I decided I'd better tell my future boss, William Miller, about my activism for Inna. I was concerned that my adversarial stance against the Soviet Union would be in conflict with the mission of the American Committee. When I told him about my friendship with Inna, he replied that what I did for her was admirable and that it would be fine for me to take time when I needed to do so if she did happen to travel to the United States.

On Thursday, January 15, Teeny called me at work.

"Lisa, Inna is leaving Moscow this Sunday. They gave her a visa today."

"Just Inna?" I asked.

"Yes. Lisa, this is good news. It is what we have been fighting for."

"I know. But I just can't believe they are forcing her to leave without Naum."

"Inna said she feels strong enough to make the trip by herself, and she is very hopeful that Naum will be allowed to follow soon," Teeny explained. "She will travel to Vienna and then to Washington Dulles Airport on Monday, the nineteenth. I am making arrangements for her to check into the Lombardi Cancer Center at Georgetown University Hospital. Inna told me she decided to come to Washington because she has many friends here."

"She'll be here on Monday?" I repeated the news out loud, trying to believe it.

"Yes, on Monday," Teeny answered. "I will call you again when I know more details."

After I hung up, I asked a secretary to cover the phones for me. I walked outside into a small park in front of Union Station, sat down on a bench, and sobbed. I didn't know what to do. I saw a pay phone at the end of the block and wanted to call my parents, but I knew they were both still at work. More than anything I wanted to call Inna, but it was impossible to immediately do so. So, I sat for a few minutes more, composing myself, and went back into the office. Somehow I managed to work until the end of the day.

Teeny called me on Friday and gave me the exact details of Inna's arrival information—Pan Am flight number 61, arriving at Dulles Airport at 5:30 PM, Monday, January 19. She had already arranged for Inna to stay at her house that night and for Dr. Jerry Batist (an oncologist from Canada who was an adviser to the International Cancer Patients Solidarity Committee) to also spend the night to render any necessary medical attention to Inna. On Tuesday or Wednesday, Inna would be admitted to Georgetown University Hospital.

I managed to get a call through to Moscow at four o'clock that Saturday morning. The connection was good.

"Inna, this is Leeza."

"Oh, Leeza. I am packing," her voice sang, and then she added, "It has been so difficult for Naum and me the last month. First, they are going to give me a visa. Then, we hear nothing for several days. Then, we think maybe Naum will be allowed to leave with me. You know, at first I thought I would not go without him. But finally I said enough of all this nonsense. I will go. Leeza, Naum and I agreed that the doctors there might be able to help me, and we also know that you will be there with me."

"Yes, Inna, I will be here with you every day."

"Will you be at the airport? You know, you are the first person I want to see when I get off the plane."

"Of course, I will be there."

"Let's not waste your money on this call. We will see each other on Monday. Is there anything else you want to tell me?"

"Just that I will be thinking of you every minute of your journey."

"Thank you, Leeza. *Uvidimsya*."

"*Uvidimsya*, Inna," I said, remembering we said exactly that to each other on my final day in Moscow. Now, it was about to come true—we were going to see each other again in less than seventy-two hours.

Free at Last

Free at last! Thank God Almighty, we Free at last!
—Dr. Martin Luther King, Jr.

The Washington Post, January 19, 1987:
"Soviet Activist's Wife on Way to U.S."
Moscow (UP)—Inna K. Meiman left Moscow on Sunday to undergo cancer treatment in the U.S. Mrs. Meiman was to spend a night in Vienna before flying Monday to Washington, where she will begin treatment at Georgetown University Hospital.

Her husband, Naum, 75, a mathematician and founding member of a group to monitor Soviet compliance with the 1975 Helsinki Accords on human rights, silently hugged his wife, refusing to talk about his own efforts to leave the country. He has been refused permission to emigrate for almost 12 years.

I woke up early Monday morning after finally dozing off for only a few hours. All night I had been thinking about Inna and where she was in her journey—that moment when she left all she had ever known. How had she found the strength to leave all those she loved—Naum, her son, her sister, brothers, and all her friends? How did she feel when the plane landed in Vienna and as she boarded the final flight to the United States?

Once I got out of bed, I had no idea how I was going to pass the time until meeting Inna at the airport. I managed to clean my room, do some laundry, and watch television until a friend picked me up at 3:15 in the afternoon and drove me to Dulles Airport.

Teeny told me to meet her in a FAA conference room at the airport to gather with others before Inna's flight arrived. When I got to the conference room, several people, many whom I recognized, had already gathered—Senator Paul Simon, recently elected Senator Timothy Wirth, Teeny and Warren Zimmerman, and Dr. Batist. Teeny introduced me to Andrea Hart, Senator Hart's daughter, who was standing in for her father since he could not be present. I also met Leon Charny, a friend of Inna and Naum's whose brother, Benjamin, was in Moscow trying to get a visa to travel to the West for medical treatment. Anne Garrels and I exchanged hellos and then I was introduced to Misha Plum, Naum's son-in-law, who had flown in from Colorado to meet Inna for the first time.

Within a few minutes, people began to leave the room to greet the plane. Through the window I watched an airplane come to a stop on the tarmac about fifty yards away. Then I saw a bus pull up to the building where we were all standing. Mark Levin, executive director of the National Conference on Soviet Jewry—the organization that was financially sponsoring Inna's trip—was also waiting by the door. I asked him what was happening. He told me the bus was going to the plane and would bring Inna directly to the airport.

I remembered Inna had told me on the phone that I was the first person she wanted to see, so I approached Mark and asked if it were possible for me to be on the bus. Disappointingly, he told me that seven people had already been chosen and I was not one of them. I was suddenly left behind as he and the others boarded the bus, feeling like the wind had been knocked out of me. I took a few deep breaths and looked back out the window, watching the bus approach the plane, where it stopped for only a few minutes before returning to the terminal.

I was standing next to Senator Simon when the door in front of us opened and I saw Inna sitting on the bus with several people around her helping her step into a wheelchair. She was wearing faded black boots, a very heavy and too-big looking brown fur coat that dropped below her knees, and a neck brace.

There was a ramp about ten feet long connecting the bus to the building.

I turned to Senator Simon and said, "I cannot believe I am really seeing Inna again." He put his arm around my shoulder and said, "Yes, you are really seeing her again." I hugged him and started to cry. Then he turned to Senator Wirth, who was standing right next to him, and said, "Let's let Lisa stand in front of us and greet Inna first." Seconds later, Andrea Hart was behind Inna's wheelchair, pushing her up the ramp, through the airport door, and directly in front of me.

All weekend I had tried to think of the words I would say to Inna when our eyes met, but in the moment they did, I was speechless. Inna looked at me, smiled, and leaned forward as I bent down and gently kissed her cheek.

"Hello, Inna."

"Oh, Leeza, I'm here," she said.

Her head was propped upright by the neck brace. She was holding a full bouquet of red roses, white carnations, and a few stems of baby's breath wrapped in green tissue paper in her lap. Their color burst against her brown fur coat.

Her face was no longer plump and cheery, as I had remembered it. Instead, it looked as if it had been flattened and removed of all color; the skin on her cheek was slack on her jaw. Her hair was no longer thick and black; it was short and thinned-out and a mix of gray and black, with a few streaks of silver around her forehead. It was parted in the middle and completely devoid of the natural wave that had usually lifted it off her face. Her eyes were moist with tears and triumph.

I stepped aside to let Senators Simon and Wirth greet her. Andrea continued to push the wheelchair, and the crowd that had gathered to greet her followed her to the conference room on the lower level.

Once there, I walked up to Inna, who was seated in the wheelchair near the podium, and asked if I could do anything for her.

"Oh, please, Leeza, stay near me. I need you now more than ever."

"Would you like to take your coat off?"

"No, but will you take the flowers for me?"

I took the flowers, and once Inna's hands were free, she reached back and tried to take off her neck brace. "Leez, help me take this off," she asked, and I did.

Andrea Hart stood at the podium and read a statement from her father:

Dear Inna,

Today is a day of great joy, but today is also an incomplete day.

You and Naum have been in our thoughts and prayers for a very long and difficult time. With your arrival in the United States, part of those prayers has been answered. They will all be answered when Naum is free to join you.

You and Naum have friends and supporters all over the world. Several of those friends are with you today, and I know you will join me in expressing gratitude for their support and determination: my former colleagues from the U.S. Senate, Paul Simon, Frank Lautenberg, and Timothy Wirth; Dr. Jerry Batist of Montreal; Mark Levin and the leaders and members of the National Conference on Soviet Jewry; Lisa Paul of the University of Minnesota and the hundreds of students who supported her efforts; Ambassador Arthur Hartman and his colleagues in Moscow; the superb and generous medical staff of the Lombardi Cancer Center at Georgetown University Hospital; and, in particular, Ambassador Warren Zimmerman and his wife Teeny, whom we are proud to call our special friends.

Inna, I know you are tired from your journey and that you look forward to a much-needed rest. But I want you to know that you arrive in Washington on a very special day— a day on which this nation is filled with joy and yet a day that for us, as for you, is incomplete. Today, our nation celebrates the birth of Dr. Martin Luther King, an American hero and statesman whose cause of justice, equality, and freedom is also your cause.

Our work will not be over, and our day of joy will not be complete, until as Martin Luther King said a generation ago, we can all say: "Free at last. Great God Almighty, free at last."

A few others spoke and then, finally, it was Inna's turn.

She stood at the podium, very poised, and began by thanking everyone who had come to greet her: "I'm happy to be here on behalf of all of those who I have left behind." She acknowledged her prognosis was "very grim," then said boldly, "I haven't come to America to die; I have come here to recover!" She paused, moving her head from left and right, as if stretching a stiff neck, and then reflected, "Though if I'd been allowed to come three years ago my chances would have been better.

"When I was leaving Moscow, the custom officials asked me if I had any silver or gold. 'No, I do not have any,' I told them. Then I thought to myself, I have never owned such things in all my life. They asked me again and again I answered 'No.' Then I thought about all of my friends, those to whom I had just said good-bye and those waiting for me in the West, many of you in this room, and I realized that my life has been full of silver and gold."

Inna talked about the many people who had done so much to help her and Naum. Then she paused and looked at me. "Our friend Lisa Paul, as a college student, went on a hunger strike for twenty-five days for me. This meant so very much to Naum and me. Lisa Paul represents the best of America. She represents what America is all about."

I looked at Inna and gulped as I tried to hold back my tears.

She said a few more words and then a reporter asked her how she felt about leaving without her husband. She hesitated, visibly gathering her strength, and then replied, "It was such anguish for me to come alone that I can't even talk about it. What is all this cruelty for? It is not understandable."

After the press conference, Warren Zimmerman helped Inna back into the wheelchair, and Teeny announced that she and Warren were taking Inna to their home for the night. I walked up to Inna and told her I would call Teeny's the next day.

"*Spokoinoi nochi*," I said, wishing her good night in Russian.

Inna grabbed my hand, squeezed it, and said, "*Spokoinoi nochi, Leeza*."

I watched as Warren wheeled Inna down the hallway toward the exit doors, her small travel bag hanging from the handle of the wheel chair. To a stranger walking by, there would have been nothing extraordinary about this man pushing a woman in a wheelchair through the doorway. But for me, watching Warren push Inna through to the car waiting outside for them was no less extraordinary than watching Neil Armstrong's first step on the moon.

Mrs. Meiman, Room 420

V'im lo achshav eimatai? And if not now, when?
—Rabbi Hillel the Elder

United Press International, January 20, 1987:
Refusenik Inna Meiman said Monday her trip to America for cancer treatment is part of "a fight for human rights" and vowed to help all people who stayed behind.

"I haven't come to America to die," said Meiman, who has undergone four operations in the Soviet Union for a malignant tumor on her neck.

Warren Zimmerman, a U.S. official who monitors the Helsinki human rights agreement, said Meiman's arrival for treatment at Georgetown University Hospital "is really only half a gesture" because her husband, Naum, had to stay behind.

"This is a fight for human rights," said Meiman at the Dulles International Airport news conference. "It is a fight for people who survive . . . for their dignity. As far as Jewish immigration is concerned, you can see by my lonely arrival how bad things are."

Forty senators signed a letter Monday asking Soviet leader Mikhail Gorbachev to allow Naum, other Jewish cancer patients, and "divided spouses" to travel to the West.

Inna, whose cancer makes it difficult for her to walk, has spent the last two months in bed. When she recovers, Meiman, fifty-[four] said, "I am going to help all the people who stayed behind."

At Dulles, Meiman was greeted by Lisa Paul, who met the Soviet couple while studying in Moscow; Sens. Timothy Wirth, D-Colo., and Paul Simon, D-Ill; and the daughter of former Sen. Gary Hart, D.-Colo., who raised the Meiman case during meetings with Soviet leaders last month.

Meiman is the third Jewish cancer patient allowed to travel to the West for medical treatment, but two other refuseniks have been denied permission to leave.

I woke up on Tuesday morning as if from a dream; all the unbelievable images of the day before were flashing through my mind. "Inna is in America," I repeated a few times out loud simply because the words were so incredible to say.

I called Teeny in the afternoon and learned that she had taken Inna to the hospital in the morning. "She had a peaceful night here and was resting comfortably in the hospital when I left," Teeny said.

When I called Inna a few minutes later I felt joy in simply dialing her number and being connected to her without worry that her phone had been disconnected, without the challenge of getting a time slot to place the call, and without the frustration of waking to the ringing phone in the early hours of the morning only to be told that no one had answered in Moscow.

"Inna, hi, this is Leeza. How are you?"

"I am feeling very tired. They have already done a series of tests on me. When will I see you?"

"I could come tomorrow after work, but you sound so tired. Why don't I come on Thursday night?

"Thursday would be better. I am very tired."

"Can I bring you anything?"

"No. I am very comfortable."

A major snowstorm on Wednesday night shut D.C. down on Thursday. I set off to take the metro to work but could barely move my legs through the deep snow to get to the station. I returned to my apartment and called the office. Only one person was there, and she told me not to bother to come in, so I decided to go see Inna. I thought I would take a bus, which I could catch in front of my apartment building. That, however, proved to be impossible. The few buses that were running were so crammed with passengers that they did not stop to let me on.

I started walking in the street—in tire tracks where possible—back in the direction of the metro. My plan was to take it to the Dupont Circle stop and then walk to the hospital from there. But, when I surfaced at Dupont Circle and tried to walk, the snow on the sidewalks had not been shoveled, and it was too deep to walk through. I managed to get into a cab with three other people, all headed in the direction of Georgetown University.

I vividly remember the corridors of the hospital leading to Inna's room. I remember the first patient I saw in the Lombardi Cancer Research Center. He was frail, bony, and sat slumped in a wheelchair in a hallway. I remember the slow and weighted motion of my steps as I approached Inna's room, and I remember the handwritten sign on Inna's door that read, "Mrs. Meiman."

Teeny was just saying good-bye to Inna when I arrived. We exchanged greetings and comments about the snowstorm. As Teeny walked by me to the door, she said, "Keep your chin up, kid, because there is a whole lot more for you to do."

Then I was finally with Inna.

"Leeza, you made it through this blizzard? Your cheeks are so red. Pull up that chair and sit next to me," she said, her voice sounding weak.

As I pulled the chair next to her bed, Inna's diminished body shocked me. She was so thin, except for her swollen feet. Her hair was flat around her pasty white face, and her droopy eyes were surrounded by dark, puffy skin. The tumor had forced her neck to widen to the left.

I took her hand and held it in both of mine.

Neither of us spoke for at least a minute. Then a tear rolled down Inna's cheek.

"Leeza, my dear."

"Inna, I can't believe you're really here . . . in Washington, D.C."

"Yes, I am really here. Leeza, you have done so much for Naum and me. Your hunger strike meant so much to both of us. I am sure you know how I feel."

"Yes, Inna. That was such an incredible time for me. I learned so much about myself. I was so strong."

"And, have you gotten wiser?"

"Yes. Very wise," I smiled and nodded my head. We made a transition into lighter conversation. Inna was intrigued that the snow had closed down the city.

"This may be a good day for Mr. Gorbachev to send his troops to Washington," she said jokingly. Then she became serious, asking me if she had come off as too bold at the airport. She repeated her words, "'I have not come here to die; I have come here to recover.' Perhaps I gave people the wrong impression?"

"No, Inna, you did not give people the wrong impression. You expressed your optimism and determination."

"You know, Leeza, before landing in Washington, I had to complete a customs form. I had to answer the question, 'What is the purpose of your visit, business or pleasure?' I did not know what to answer. Finally I chose pleasure and wrote, 'It is a pleasure for me to come for treatment.'"

"It is a pleasure to have you here."

We talked about my new job and then I told Inna about my sisters and parents. I didn't know how to ask her about Naum and her son, but it was such an obvious subject, I couldn't ignore it. "I hope this question does not upset you, but is it difficult for you to think about Naum and the rest of your family?"

"No, it is not so upsetting for me to think about them. That is, I experienced all of the pain I possibly could when I left. I have experienced the worst. It is over. Now I am here and I must help the doctors try to help me. Besides, I really hope that my being here will open the door for my son Lev and his family to come to the West."

I didn't stay long that first visit. Although the words she spoke sounded like the Inna I knew, she looked drastically different than how I remembered her. She was now so weak and sick, and so very exhausted.

"Inna, you better rest this afternoon. Don't let them put too many needles in you before you feel stronger, okay? I will call you tomorrow."

"Okay. Please come and see me again soon, Leeza."

"Sure, I'll be here every day if you'd like." I couldn't stop my tears as I leaned over and kissed her cheek—overcome by how fragile she had become, yet in awe of how heroic and brave she continued to be.

I walked out of the hospital dumbfounded as how to get home. A cab ride was too expensive, and the walk to the Foggy Bottom metro station seemed too far. But I was incapable of deciding because all my mind could do was try to comprehend the reality that Inna was in Georgetown University Hospital, receiving medical care, and was free.

When I called Inna on Friday afternoon, she said her day had been full with doctors, nurses, and a few visitors. So I suggested I come in the morning so she could rest that night, and she agreed that would be best.

I got to the hospital by about ten o'clock the next morning, Saturday, January 24. Inna looked much better than she had on Thursday, rested and with more color in her face.

"How are you feeling today?" I asked.

"I am feeling a little better. I think I have already seen more doctors here than there are in all of Moscow," she joked. She was eager to tell me her initial impressions of Americans: "People are so polite to each other; 'May I take this?' 'Please can I do this?' and always, 'Thank you.' It is so interesting to watch the way Americans interact with each other, they are all so kind; not only the doctors and the nurses toward the patients but all toward each other.

"When I went for a CT scan and the nurse said, 'Please move this way' and 'Please move that way.' I thought it was because we had just started the procedure, but the next thirty minutes was full of pleases. In Moscow it is the opposite, commanding, 'Take your jacket off,' 'Move this way,' 'Go to that doctor.' It is not because the people are worse there than here. They are just on two completely different planets, aren't they, Leez?"

I nodded my head in agreement.

"After the test, a woman custodian standing nearby saw my face grimace with pain as an orderly wheeled me into an elevator. 'Can't you see that every bump causes her pain?' she scolded the orderly. Her reaction was really great, as if my comfort was her only concern, as if I were Raisa Gorbachev. You know, our image of Americans does not include how kind you are or the fact that you like to work.

"When I was last in the hospital in Moscow, I was treated very nicely. There was a doctor there who found out that I am the wife of an important dissident. So he told his colleagues I was important and should be treated with extra care, and I was. I had my own room and was given extra attention. But this logic is funny, isn't it?

"Leeza, when I am feeling better, I want you and me to start a crusade. Before I left Moscow, I collected information about several refusenik cases that I would like to help. After studying several cases, I decided to start with the three I considered most urgent. I feel it is better to be realistic and focus our energy on just a few at first, and not to be too ambitious and end up helping no one.

"One person, a beautiful and kind woman, is Janna Sakuta. She has a terrible eye disease and could end up totally blind if she does not get treatment in the United States. Nothing more can be done to help her in the Soviet Union. I want to think of a way to get the media's attention to her case. I want you and me to work together."

While I was flattered Inna wanted us to work together, in my gut I wondered how she would be able to help others when she had so many medical problems of her own. But the fact that she was already thinking of others completely amazed me.

The medical news Inna received after the first week was not encouraging. One of the very first tests revealed a tumor in her lung, and because of its location and size, it posed a more imminent threat to her health than the tumor on her neck.

"Maybe my doctors in Moscow knew about it," Inna speculated, "but did not want to worry me. After all, they could do nothing more to help me."

A biopsy of the tumor in her lung was scheduled for Monday, January 26. Inna was nervous about it because she would have to be put under general anesthesia. I was concerned she was being rushed into the procedure. Even though I realized her medical needs were urgent, she had not been given any time to just rest and catch her breath from her long journey to freedom.

I visited Inna on Sunday night before the biopsy and, by then, she had fully "Russianized" her room. She turned the temperature down to a chilly sixty-two degrees; on her nightstand she had a few pieces of fruit she had collected from her meal trays; and on the wall at the foot of her bed she hung a watercolor of birch trees that was painted by her friend in Moscow, Flora Litvinov. "Flora also did the painting of Anuta's hut that I sent you last fall," Inna explained, then offered me an apple, asking whether I was hungry and treating me as if I were her guest. "Leeza, would you like some coffee or tea? Please have some of my dinner." And although it was awkward for me to take food from a sick woman's tray, I knew it made Inna feel more at home, so I politely took an apple and had a cup of tea.

Inna always had an observation to make about what she experienced that day. Her favorite one, which she told me each visit as if for the first time, was about how her nurses had such a difficult time taking blood from her arm. "Leeza, with all the advanced medicine and modern equipment here, American nurses have as much difficulty finding my veins as those in Moscow. It is ironic, isn't it?

"Can you believe that on the radio, on Voice of America, I actually heard our ambassador to the United States, Anatoly Dobrynin, say I did not have cancer? I was happy for a split second because I believed him." Then Inna said very seriously, "Not for a full second, just a half."

Then Inna said that she wanted to write a letter to Senator Hart to thank him for all he did for her. So I took dictation as she struggled to express her gratitude. She began, "I know you are very busy, but I hope this letter will reach you and you will know of someone who you've rescued in the most direct and unsophisticated meaning of the word. Leeza, let me start again," and she did, this time able to express her thoughts more poignantly:

I know my letter ought to be a letter of thanks. Do believe me, please, I am extremely grateful, but mere words cannot express the depth of my gratitude and feeling. Your daughter, Andrea, was most kind and warm; she was also so charming and efficient. Please, pass my warmest regards on to her.

My medical news so far has not been encouraging, but, of course, I am determined to do my best to help the doctors help me. The hospital is just beautiful, but that is not the most important thing. The most important thing is the sensation of being among friends, of being cared for and about. I have read a lot about your country and your people, but what I have seen and heard even from the door of my hospital room have surpassed all my expectations. Yours is a country of beautiful people—I have no doubt about it whatsoever.

When you came to Moscow, I was in such bad form that I could hardly talk to you. I am sure you were aware of that.

"Leeza," Inna paused for a moment, "the last couple of months in Moscow were horrible. Naum and I were like yo-yos on as string—'yes you can go; no you can't go.' We could not take it anymore. OVIR [the Soviet visa department] would call and tell Naum to come to their office. He would go all the way there only to be told there was no change in our case. I told Naum, 'Okay, then, let them have their way. It is not worth it anymore. Let's just forget about it all together and live a quiet and peaceful life here without playing their games.' But Naum insisted that if I had the chance, I must take it. He could not tolerate watching me die any longer. It was too much for him. It would be too much for any man. When they finally said that my visa was ready, we had already decided I would go."

On Monday night I called Inna and learned that the biopsy had been postponed until Wednesday, so we agreed I would visit her on Tuesday night. When I arrived, she was energetic and in a good mood. I gave her a loaf of Russian bread I bought at a market near my office that morning. Inna was delighted and enthusiastically announced that she would like to prepare a Russian meal for me.

"Leeza, in the nurses' station there is a refrigerator where I have some food. There is kolbasa, cheese, and an apple. Go get it and we will eat it with this beautiful bread."

As I gathered the food from the refrigerator, Inna instructed me from her doorway, smiling, "The cheese is in the white bag, on the lower shelf."

As I turned around to go back to her room, with the items from the refrigerator in my hands, Inna had also turned around to go back in the room. When I got nearer to her I saw, for the first time, the total disfiguration of her neck from the multiple surgeries she'd had to remove the tumor. The muscle tissue had been carved away; there were several scars and protruding out from the side in the shape of a half circle the size of a baseball was the tumor. Looking at Inna straight on, I had only noticed a slight bump on the side of her neck, but the posterior view revealed how maimed she really was. I was absolutely shocked.

I joined her by the table next to the sink and we stood side by side making dinner. The flavor of the food was the flavor of Russia.

"Inna, it's just like we are in Moscow," I commented.

"Yes, like we are at the train station or on a picnic. Quick, open the curtain so I can see that I am here in Georgetown!" she said playfully.

"Where did you get this sausage? It looks like it came from a Russian market."

"When I was young, I played all the time with a neighbor boy across the hall from me. Ten years ago he left Moscow, and there was no hope we would ever see each other again," her eyes glowed, "and he was here today from Philadelphia and brought me this kolbasa."

She sat down on the bed and I pulled the meal tray over to her. She asked me what time it was and when I told her 6:30 she asked me to hurry and turn the television to NBC. "I want to see Anne Garrels," she said, explaining her frustration that she had been unable to find the channel the night before: "It is such a luxury and an expense to spend three dollars a day on this TV box, so I ought to be able to figure out how to use it.

"Your American commercials are so funny," she added. "I was so interested in one that was on earlier today. It was promoting the reasons to buy a certain automobile: 'Reason one, save money; reason number two, save money,' and then they said, 'reason number three, save more money.' It was a disappointment. I thought they would be cleverer than that."

"Inna, have I really seen the day that you can imitate American commercials?" I laughed, and she laughed with me, responding, "Yes, you have really seen the day!"

Then Inna became serious and told me she wanted to try to get an article published in the "My Turn" column of *Newsweek*. I cleared the plates and put the food back in the refrigerator, while she got comfortable in bed. She said she had written some notes and asked me if I would help her with it. I agreed and she began dictating her article to me:

> I want to tell my story just to answer the questions Americans have been asking me, "How are things in Moscow?" How can you answer the question when a group of cancer patients form a solidarity committee?
>
> There is talk about the Soviet bureaucratic machine working better. If this is true my article should serve a good purpose. Maybe it will speed up visas—for those in prison camps, for those who are physically sick and who can be treated elsewhere, and for those who wish to emigrate.
>
> They let me go in a manner that was disgraceful. They threw me as if a bone to the West. The clerk who gave my husband my visa told him, "We know that your wife is not going to return." Did he mean I would not survive the trip? Without the help of the Americans who accompanied me and without the wheelchairs that took me to and from every plane, I might not have made it this far.
>
> And so here, in Georgetown University Hospital, I am asked every day, "How are things in the Soviet Union?" I am not sure that I know the answer; perhaps it is not there; you cannot find it. But if my family, my friends, my people are being treated better, I would be the first to say, "Hello, Mr. Gorbachev, thank you very much!"

The Rainbow-colored Potholder

> And now these three
> remain: faith, hope, and love.
> But the greatest of these is love.
> —Corinthians 13: 4–13

I called Inna the day after her biopsy. "Leeza, it was awful." Her voice sounded so weak. "The biopsy was horrible. I thought I was going to die. . . . That's it. I can't talk about it anymore." I had never heard her sound so depressed and defeated. I suggested she rest and that I would come the next day.

She surprised me by saying firmly, "After my awful day yesterday, today I thought, where is my Leeza? I want to see her. So, please come tonight."

I went to the hospital immediately after work. When I got to Inna's room, the lights were off, and I thought she was sleeping. I walked quietly over to a chair next to her bed, and as I sat down, her eyes opened up a sliver to look at me. For the first time in my life, I understood what it meant when someone "looked on her deathbed." Her skin was ashen, her face deflated and flabby, her lips colorless, and her hand, when I held it, limp and cold.

I told her I was so sorry the biopsy procedure had been so horrible.

She explained that the anesthesiologist was not aware of a medication she was taking, which caused quite a desperate situation in the operating room since the medication interfered with the anesthesia, causing her pulse to decrease rapidly. For several moments they thought they were going to lose her. They were eventually able to stabilize her but had to leave her semi-conscious during the biopsy, which was an extremely painful experience.

"You know, Leeza, I felt a moment of weakness while I was lying there on the table. I thought to myself, is it even worth it anymore? I have suffered enough." Tears welled in her eyes. "It was only a moment, and everyone has their moment," she concluded.

Tears welled up in my eyes, but I managed to stay composed. "At least it is over," I said, and tried to encourage her: "Now we have to hope for good results." But her spirits were not so easily lifted.

"It bothers me that my eyes are swollen with pain and that I have lost my beauty. Not that I was ever a beautiful woman, but I was attractive and men liked me; not all men, of course. And I wasn't interested in all men, either, just a few," she revealed to me.

"Inna, you're still beautiful," I told her.

"Oh, Leeza, when you go into your next life, you should be old and gray and ready to start over," she refuted.

"So you will get old and gray."

"No, I am sick and dying," she stated.

"Oh Inna," I said, tears welling up again, "You're very much alive."

"No, only a little."

She was also disheartened that her doctor had not been to see her since her botched biopsy. "This is both funny and tragic. I am sure he does not feel good about his mistake, but to stop visiting me? He had been in to see me each day before the biopsy. So the man is a coward, and I will not try to reform him. It does not matter where you live after all; people can act poorly."

As our visit continued, I remembered I had brought a gift for Inna from my sister Therese. I showed it to Inna, hoping it would cheer her up.

"There is a note with it," I told her.

"Read it to me right away," she insisted, perking up a little bit:

Dear Inna,

Welcome to the United States! We are very proud to have you as a guest in our country and hope you can soon be joined by your husband and that your stay will be a very long one. We are truly honored to have such a brave lady as you among us. Please know there are many people like me who hold you dear in their thoughts and hope every day for the improvement of your condition.

I am planning to meet you sometime this spring when I come to D.C. for a visit. It would be a great honor for me to meet you, yes indeed. I have enclosed a little gift for you.

I wish you the strength, that by your example, you have given to me.

My very best to you always,

Love,

Therese (Lisa's sister)

"She is so caring," Inna commented and then asked, "What is the gift? Please, show it to me."

I handed her the box and helped her open it. She removed the tissue paper and held up a hand-knitted, rainbow-patterned pot-holder. There was a short note from Therese in the box explaining that it was knitted by her husband's grandmother, who was in her late eighties. Inna held it in her hands and exclaimed, "It is beautiful."

"You can put one of your plants on it," I explained.

"And get it soiled and dirty? No. It is too nice for that. The colors are so bright. I will keep it near me, and when I see it, Leez, I will think of you."

Later, when I was getting my coat to leave, Inna looked puzzled.

"Is something the matter, Inna?"

"Where is it? I can't see it."

"Where is what?"

"The potholder."

"Right there," I said pointing to the nightstand.

"I can't see it. Please give it to me," she asked.

I handed it to her and she tucked it behind her head. Then I leaned over and gave her a kiss on the cheek. "Sleep well. I hope you feel better in the morning."

As I was about to walk out the door, I looked back at Inna. Only the light above her bed lit the room. She smiled feebly. Radiating above her shoulder were the bright colors of the rainbow potholder.

I walked out of the hospital in a daze, incredibly upset about the biopsy. That she almost died from an American doctor's mistake was incomprehensible and exasperating to me. I was afraid to cry for her, afraid that if I did I would be giving up at a time when she needed me most.

A light snow was falling as I walked the narrow street from the hospital to Wisconsin Avenue, the main street in Georgetown. My mind was swirling like the snowflakes around me. For so long, all of my energy had been focused on the fight against the Soviet government to grant Inna a visa. Now she was here, and my only focus was on her fight to live. All the medical reports had been so discouraging. It was difficult to for me to imagine that she would, as she declared at the airport, recover, and the reality that she might not caused tears to fall on my face.

I continued to walk south, feeling completely separate from the hustle and bustle of the traffic and pedestrians as I approached the intersection of Wisconsin Avenue and M Street—the heart of Georgetown.

Then I walked east on Pennsylvania Avenue about two miles to the corner of the Old Executive Office Building, which stands just to the west of the White House. The cold air and snowflakes felt refreshing hitting my face as I waited for a bus to take me home.

The street was desolate, and a white dusting of snow on the buildings, street lamps, and tree branches around me created a winter wonderland and lifted, ever so slightly, my heavy heart. I wanted to sit down, but there was no bench, only a huge snowbank piled high along the curb. I turned my backside to it, then jumped up and plopped down like I was a kid again, goofing off in the snow on my way to school.

I sat there comfortably, feeling a wave of exhaustion overcome me. I hadn't really slowed down since Inna's arrival. *So much has changed in the last few weeks*, I thought. Yet, as I sat there in the snow, it occurred to me that so much had also stayed the same, because what had been guiding me all along—and what I needed more than ever before—was faith, hope, and love.

CHAPTER

Human Dignity

Friendship marks a life
even more deeply than love.
—Elie Wiesel

The news at the end of the second week, after the biopsy, was not positive. The doctor told Inna the preliminary tests indicated she likely had only six months to live. Inna was not surprised. In fact, she felt the doctor was being optimistic in his prognosis, and, as much as I wanted to, I couldn't disagree with her.

"I realize my time here might not be long, but I do not want to die a pathetic death," Inna told me the next time I saw her. She looked much better than she had after the biopsy, and her voice was stronger. "There are things I would like to do, writing perhaps. I want to get better, or at least stronger, so I can help the people I left behind."

Inna told me she and Teeny were already discussing where she should live once she was released from the hospital. One option was that she could move to an apartment near the hospital. However, there was concern that she would be unable to care for herself, especially if she was undergoing chemotherapy for the tumor in her lung. "First, I must get stronger so that I can help the treatments work for me," she said. "I know that I must be able to fight with the chemotherapy in order for it to be effective at all, but I'm not sure how much I have left to fight with."

The second option was moving her to a retirement home in Georgetown, about eight blocks from the hospital, which provided twenty-four-hour medical care. There was some discussion about me living with her in an apartment, but she knew, as did I, that she was too sick at that time to live in private housing. Ultimately she chose the retirement home, where she knew she could get the medical care she needed while enjoying as much independence as possible.

I agreed with her decision, because it was obvious to me that Inna was too ill to live independently. In fact, I was surprised that she was even being asked to consider leaving the hospital; I thought she still seemed to need time to recover from the physical and emotional strain of her trip to the United States.

Even though her medical diagnosis was bleak, she spoke to me about her hope to gain enough strength to work and earn some money of her own. We talked lightheartedly about her career opportunities. "I am not sure if I would prefer teaching or doing translation work. Or maybe I should try something different," she said.

"Inna, I wish I had your worries," I told her.

"Ah, that's right! 'I wish I had your worries,'" she said smiling. "Leeza, did I tell you in September we had a visitor from the State Department? She asked about you. She said she received many letters about me that referred to you—that they knew of my case because of you. Naum said, and it is true, your hunger strike brought our case to a whole new level of awareness at a time when politicians and friends who were fighting for us had grown tired because nothing was changing. You gave us all energy. You gave us hope."

Had I not seen Inna again and had she not told me that, I might never have realized the personal impact of my hunger strike on her—that at a time when all was so desperate and gloomy in her life, my actions were a positive diversion for her. That I gave her hope is something for which I will always be grateful.

"Leez, let's talk about you. Tell me, do you have anyone special in your life?"

"I have been seeing someone for the past two months. He brought me to the airport the night you arrived."

"Is he romantic?"

"Not so much."

"Neither are our Russian men. They are more worried about their jobs and about such things as where they will be able to buy two kilos of potatoes or carrots.

"People can try very hard to find each other and can go in circles if they are not meant for each other. But Naum and I did not have to go in circles. I was attracted to him because he was so brave, and when I met him, I was only beginning to be brave. I was enamored by him but soon I realized that he was alone like me.

"Did I ever tell you about my first date when I was a student in the 1950s? I came home after a long day of studies to prepare for him to arrive. My face was very pale when I looked in the mirror, but all I could find to use for blush was a red pencil. So I put a streak on each cheek. The first thing my date said when he saw me was, 'What are those red marks on your face?' I was so humiliated. I never bothered with blush again!

"It is getting late, and you'd better get going. But before you go, I have a favor to ask of you. Next time you come, will you bring me two or three apples?"

"Sure."

"How much will they cost?"

"Less than a dollar."

"I only have a fifty-dollar bill. Let's try to get change so I can give you the money."

"Inna, the gift shop is closed."

"Maybe you could ask a nurse."

"I doubt they would have that much change. Don't worry, I'll buy the apples."

"Are you sure? Can you afford it?"

"Yes, Inna, I can afford it."

My next visit I brought Inna the apples, and she gave me the dollar. I felt silly taking it, but she insisted.

"Can I buy *you* anything?" Inna offered. "Do you need anything? I have lots of money."

"From where?" I asked.

"I changed rubles before I left, and I brought six hundred dollars with me. I also have a monthly spending allowance from the Jewish group who is sponsoring my stay. I can't wait to go to a bookstore and buy any book I want! Can you imagine that I will be able to browse through the shelves without worry and choose any book? Ah, I am sure the feeling will be as if I am rid of the cancer."

Inna's time in the hospital was filled with visitors and telephone calls from friends. She told me that many friends from her childhood, who had immigrated to the States many years ago, had called and a few even traveled to D.C. to visit her. She received one call from a woman who had been her English professor in Moscow and now lived in Chicago. "It was incredible—to think it is possible to hear from someone I knew thirty years ago? I can't describe it, really." Russian dissidents who had emigrated from the Soviet Union also visited her, some who didn't know her personally but knew of her case, or had known and worked with Naum. She was also very touched to receive visits from Americans who worked for her release, some from the State Department and some from Capitol Hill. She received mail each day from complete strangers who extended their best wishes. All of this outpouring of affection and support amazed her.

Inna told me that one of her nurses, who noticed her many visitors and phone calls, commented about all the friends she had. Inna replied, "I don't know if I have so many friends, but if

I do, it is because each friend I have made in my life I have tried to keep."

When I overlapped with other visitors, Inna introduced me to them with pride. And each of her friends would greet me with a familiarity and warmth. One of Inna's Russian friends shook my hand and said, "Very nice to meet you. You are my hero."

One afternoon I came in about an hour after Anatoly ("Natan") Sharansky had been to visit her. I had a photograph of Sharansky from *Newsweek* on my bulletin board in my bedroom that captured the moment on February 11, 1986, when he walked to freedom over the Glienicke Bridge to West Berlin. He had been flown to East Berlin that day directly from a Siberian labor camp, where he spent eight years, and was exchanged for two Soviet spies who were being held in the West. Ever defiant toward the Soviet authorities, he walked in a zigzag pattern over the bridge to West Berlin because his Soviet guard had told him to walk in a straight line.

"Of course, I never met Anatoly in Moscow because he was arrested in 1977 before I became a refusenik," Inna told me. "But Naum knew him from their work together in the Helsinki Watch Group. He visited with me for an hour and a half and talked as if he was in no hurry. He is a very nice and very strong man. He said when he visits again he will bring his wife and daughter. Isn't it great that they have a baby?"[1]

Early in the third week, there was a young woman visiting Inna when I arrived. I excused myself for interrupting and offered to come back later.

"No, please stay," Inna said. "I want you to meet my friend, Joy Weber."

---

[1] Sharansky would later become very active in Israeli politics, serving as the deputy prime minister of Israel, interior minister, and minister of industry and trade. He was awarded the U.S. Congressional Gold Medal in 1986 and, in 2006, the Presidential Medal of Freedom, by George W. Bush. His memoir, *Fear No Evil*, was published in 1998.

The woman walked over and warmly shook my hand. "So you are Lisa."

"Joy visited me in Moscow in September," Inna explained.

"It is nice to meet you."

"It is my pleasure to meet you," Joy said enthusiastically. "Inna talked so much about you when I was with her in Moscow that I feel like I know you."

We chatted briefly and then Joy gathered her things and told Inna she would call her soon. After she left, Inna explained that Joy had leukemia, which was in remission. "The doctors have decreased the level of hormones I take, and this has been an awful experience for me. Joy understands this because she, herself, has been through hormone adjustments. She assured me that it is normal to feel very depressed when your body has to adjust to a reduction in hormones, and this was very helpful for me to hear."

Later, Inna told me that Teeny had arranged for her to move to the retirement home on February 4, the day before Teeny was to return to Vienna. I visited Inna there the next evening—Thursday, February 5. She had her own small one-bedroom apartment. The main room was both a living room, with a couch and chair on one end, and a kitchen with a small table and refrigerator at the other. The bedroom was directly behind the kitchen area and had a closet and small bathroom.

She was resting comfortably in her bed, and I pulled up a chair next to her side. She told me how much she enjoyed the ride from the hospital in a limousine through Georgetown to the retirement home: "It felt so good to be out of the hospital and see some of Washington." She explained the retirement home was "just how American writers had described it—softly lit hallways, paintings of country scenes on the wall, and people sitting around in no hurry at all. Of course, I am not as old as the people I have seen here—I am only fifty-four. But that is fine, I am comfortable.

"After I got settled here today, I started to read a book and immediately realized that, for the first time in my life, I did not have to look over my shoulder with worry the KGB might barge in. It was a great feeling!

"It might sound strange and be difficult for you to understand, but maybe you can. Considering what I have been through and the worry I have about the chemotherapy treatments that await me, I am happy here. Yes, I am happy to be in Washington, D.C."

"I understand and I am happy, too. You have what you fought so hard for—you have human dignity," I told her.

Inna was taken aback by my remark, nodding her head up and down for a moment and then said, "Yes, Leeza, I have dignity," her eyes filling with tears.

"Look at all those clothes hanging in my closet. I have more now than I have ever had in my entire life," she chuckled. "Can you believe when I was a student at the Institute I had one skirt and two blouses and that was all?"

I looked in the closet and noticed it was about a third full. I recognized my winter coat, the one I gave to her when I left Moscow.

"I'm glad to see that you have taken good care of my coat," I commented.

"Leeza, I wanted to leave it in Moscow with my sister, but Naum insisted I might need it here. Can you imagine us arguing about such a thing while I was packing? Finally I said to Naum, 'All right, let's not fuss about it, I will bring it.' So I wore it on the plane when I left Moscow."

On the floor of the closet was a pair of Adidas tennis shoes.

"I see you brought your walking shoes," I told her.

"You know, there is a funny story about those shoes. Last summer, two teenagers approached me in the middle of the day when I was on the small bridge that goes over the canal near my apartment. Remember, Leez, near where I first met you? Anyway, I was wearing those Adidas shoes, and the boys ordered me to take them off right there and hand them over to them. I replied, 'You may think I am old and not as strong as you, but you may not have these shoes. I would rather jump off this bridge and into the river before I would give them to you.' They were so surprised by my response and determination that they ran off. So you see I had to bring them with me."

There was an oxygen tank next to her bed, and I asked when she was supposed to use it.

"The doctors said that I should sleep with it on, but I don't think I should. I do not want to come to depend on it, because I am afraid if I do, I will get too used to it and become too weak to breathe without it."

Then she told me she was going to have very special visitors on Saturday. "Friends of mine, Al and Cynthia Cotcher, called from England, and they are flying here this Saturday just to see me," she said happily. "They will return to England on Sunday. It is incredible, isn't it? A friend introduced me to them when I worked at the Institute. Al was a businessman in Moscow, and we managed to become friends in the 1970s. He was the first native English speaker I really knew, and he helped me tremendously with my conversational English."

"Is there anything I can bring you for their visit?"

"No, I think we will just have tea. But I would like to get another pair of these slippers," she said, pointing to a pair of fluffy flannel slippers on the end of her bed. "Can you imagine that these were less than five dollars? I would like to send a couple of pairs to my friends in Moscow. Leeza, if I make a list of the things I need and presents for my friends, would you like to go shopping for me?"

"Of course, I would be happy to."

"I've noticed the nurses wear such nice cotton turtlenecks. Do you think you could find one for me?"

"Yes, Inna. You are in America. You can have anything you want."

"I am in America; I can have anything I want," she said, repeating my words her eyes wide and bright. "Leeza, it's really true, isn't it? I am in America. Anyway, if you can find me a close-fitting sweater vest to cover the turtleneck, that would be more comfortable for me. Hand me my purse. How much money do you need?"

"I think fifty dollars is plenty."

I told Inna that I would try to stop by Friday night or Saturday morning. "When are your visitors arriving?"

"I am not sure, I think at one o'clock. Why don't you come by so you can meet them? Come around two."

"Okay, I'll stop by on Saturday," I agreed. It was close to ten o'clock, and I had been there four hours—my longest visit with Inna since her arrival. I left feeling upbeat and happy that she was so excited about her upcoming visitors.

I met the Cotchers on Saturday. It was a beautiful sunny and unseasonably warm February day. The mood was very festive. Inna and the Cotchers were so obviously enjoying their time together that I stayed for only twenty minutes, not wanting to intrude on their reunion.

I informed Inna that I was on my way to the store to shop for her. She smiled at me, and as she did, her expression froze for a moment, as if allowing my memory to take an instant photograph of her. She was standing in her living room, the sun shining through the window on her flannel robe and her cheeks rosy from the excitement of seeing such dear friends again. Her hair was brushed nicely and she looked rested. And from my angle, I could not see the tumor on her neck.

"You look good, Inna, the best you have since you arrived," I told her. "You have color in your cheeks today."

Inna looked at me and slowly nodded her head up and down. Then the expression on her face changed, becoming serious—as if to tell me not to be fooled, that although she might have looked much better, she was, in fact, very ill. I gently hugged her, choking back tears. Then I kissed her cheek, turned around, said good-bye to the Cotchers, and left.

I went directly to Hecht's department store. I found a soft velour turtleneck that zipped up the back, which was perfect because she could slip it loosely over her head. Then I saw a hunter green knitted vest on sale. I was excited with my purchases and could not wait to bring them to her.

I called her Sunday afternoon. She said she had a wonderful visit with the Cotchers and they had stopped by briefly that morning before going to the airport. I told her I was successful in my shopping and briefly described the items. "You sound tired. Should I come tomorrow instead of today?" I asked.

"Yes, I am feeling quite tired. Tomorrow will be better. I am going to the hospital for some tests in the morning, but I will be back in the afternoon. Can you come after work?"

"Sure. I'll call you in the afternoon to see how things went at the hospital before I come, okay?"

"Yes, very good, Leeza. Good night."

"Good night, Inna."

CHAPTER

"Babushka, Are We Going
to Israel Today?"

Courage: Great Russian word, fit for
the songs of our children's children,
pure on their tongues, and free.
—Anna Akhmatova

I called Inna a few minutes after three o'clock on Monday afternoon, February 9, thinking she would certainly be back from the hospital by then. There was no answer. I tried again in thirty minutes, and this time the line was busy. When I called a minute later and no one answered, I became very worried. Then I called the front desk to find out if Inna had returned.

"I'm trying to reach Inna Meiman," I told the receptionist, "I have her private number and I am not getting an answer."

"One moment, please."

I heard the woman talk to someone in a muffled voice, as if she was covering the receiver with her hand.

"Who is calling?"

"My name is Lisa Paul. I am a friend of Inna's. I know she went to the hospital for tests this morning and was supposed to be back by this afteroon. Did she come back?"

"Yes," the woman answered tentatively.

"Good. Is everything okay?"

"Well, she did come back to her apartment, but then had to be taken back to the hospital this afternoon."

"She had to be taken? What do you mean? Was it an emergency?"

"I'm not permitted to disclose that information."

Her words echoed loudly through my head and I started to think the worst. I asked, "What information? What's going on?"

"I'm sorry. I cannot disclose any information to you."

At that moment I could only conclude that the worst had happened. "Is she dead?"

"I can't confirm that until we notify her husband."

"Oh my God," I gasped, realizing the only reason they would need to notify Naum would be if Inna had passed away.

"Lisa," a man's voice came over the phone, "my name is David Zelikovich. I was visiting Inna this afternoon." He explained he was an American but he had been living in France the last few years and was involved in a group actively fighting for the release of Soviet Jews. He had been particularly involved in Inna's case and met her the year before in Moscow. "I know all about what you did for her and recognized your name when the receptionist was talking to you."

"Where is she?" I was crying.

"At the hospital. Why don't you come over here and I will explain everything to you?"

"Can't you just tell me if she's okay?"

"I think it would be better if you came here so I can tell you what happened in person." As I hung up the phone my face became hot and my stomach cramped. *Inna must be dead*, I thought, *why else would he need to talk to me in person?*

My boss, Bill Miller, came over and asked me what happened. "I think Inna died this afternoon," I said, my voice shaking. He walked over and put his hand on my shoulder. I told him that I needed to go to Inna's apartment right away. He offered to drive me, but

I preferred to be by myself and take a cab. He went outside to hail one for me. It was after four o'clock and already getting dark. Someone brought me my coat, and, as I was gathering my things, I saw the Hecht's bag under my desk with the clothes I intended to bring to Inna after work. A stabbing pain pierced my heart as I left without it.

The cab ride was miserably long, from southeast to northwest D.C., through rush hour traffic. As soon as the cab stopped in front of the retirement home, I got out and ran up the sidewalk and through the front door, straight to the reception desk. I told the woman sitting there who I was and that we had just spoken on the telephone. She said I should go up to Mrs. Meiman's room. I took the elevator up one floor and slowly approached Inna's door, hoping I had misunderstood everything and that she would be there when I knocked. But she wasn't. Instead, a tall, dark-haired man about thirty-five years old opened the door.

"Lisa, I am David. I'm so sorry."

"Is Inna dead?"

"I was with her this afternoon and . . ."

"Please, just please tell me whether or not she is dead."

"I want to tell you what happened." He insisted on not answering my question.

"Please, just yes or no, is Inna dead?" I couldn't bear to hear another word until he confirmed what seemed to be so obvious.

"Yes. I am sorry."

I sat in a chair and sobbed. "Inna, oh my God, Inna," I repeated to myself. David tried to console me.

I looked up through my tears and noticed the oxygen tank on the other side of the room by the couch. There were papers on the floor, and the coffee table in front of the couch had been moved out on an angle. David started to explain what happened.

"I had been sitting on the couch with her for about an hour talking when the phone rang. Inna got up, walked into the bed-room, and answered it. She returned a few minutes later and told me it was Teeny calling from Vienna. She told me Teeny asked if she had heard any news yet. Inna asked, 'What news?' Teeny responded that Cyrus Vance and Henry Kissinger had just returned to the United States from the Soviet Union. While there they met with Gorbachev specifically to discuss Naum and Inna's son, Lev, and Vance was going to call her today to tell her the best news of all. Teeny offered to tell Inna the news, but she said she would wait for him to call and they agreed Teeny would call her back in an hour.

"Inna told me she clearly understood the implication of what Teeny was telling her—that her son was being allowed to leave the Soviet Union. Then Inna got up and walked to the bathroom," David said. "When she returned and sat on the couch she was out of breath. She asked me to open the window and help her move to the end of the couch so she could get some fresh air. Her breathing became more difficult after I helped her move, so I offered to call a nurse. She told me no and asked me to just stay with her. A few moments later she began to gasp for air so I got up and called the nurse and then went back over to Inna and held her hand. The nurse got here right away and tried to give the oxygen mask to Inna, but she refused it and asked the nurse to just sit with her and hold her hand. When the paramedics got here, it was too late."

Just as David finished talking, Anne Garrels walked in.

"Anne, did you hear about Inna?" I asked her.

Tears were flowing down her cheeks as she nodded her head yes, and then hugged me.

David starting telling Anne what he had just told me, and I couldn't bear to listen again. I wanted to talk to my mom, so I went into the bedroom and called her from the phone on Inna's nightstand.

"Mom, I don't know how to tell you this, but . . . ," my voice quivered.

"What's wrong, Lisa?"

"Inna died this afternoon," I blurted out and started crying.

"Oh, oh, Lisa," I heard her tell my dad, "It's Lisa, Jerry. Inna died." Then she asked me, "Where are you?"

"I'm at her apartment. I tried to call her this afternoon, and one thing led to another. Finally a man who had been with her when it happened recognized my name and told me to come over here. Oh God, Mom, she's gone."

"Lisa, is someone with you?"

"A friend of Inna's, Anne Garrels, is here, and the man who was with Inna when she died. Oh Mom, I wish you were here."

"I know, Lisa, I wish I was there too." She suggested I call Greg. I told her I would and then call her again that night. I then called Greg at work, crying as I told him Inna died.

"Take a few breaths, Lisa," he said, trying to calm me. "Where are you?"

"I'm at Inna's apartment."

Greg, who met Anne when they were both in Moscow in the early 1980s, asked to talk to her. I called Anne into the bedroom and handed her the phone. Then I heard her tell Greg she would be happy to take me home. Anne handed the phone back to me. Greg reassuringly said, "If you need anything, Kathie and I will be home tonight. She will be so sorry to hear this news."

Anne told me we could leave when I was ready, and then walked back in the living room. I continued sitting on the bed, unable to move. Then I put my head in my hands and sobbed. A nurse came into the room and sat next to me, putting her arm around my shoulder. I asked her if she had known Inna.

"Yes, I have been her night nurse since she moved in. I was with her when she died."

"Was she in pain?"

"No, there was no pain. Her breathing had started to calm down, and she asked me to hold her hand."

"Didn't she want the oxygen mask?"

"No, she just wanted me to sit with her. It was very peaceful."

I hugged the nurse and cried some more. I felt triumphant for Inna because it seemed like she knew she was dying and decided not to fight anymore. And she died with the peace of knowing she had accomplished, in large part, what she set out to do in coming to the States, fully aware she was very advanced in her illness. Her son Lev was going be allowed to leave the Soviet Union. When I spoke to Teeny later about the conversation she'd had with Inna before she died, Teeny confirmed that Inna understood with certainty that Lev was being issued a visa. That is what "the best news" meant. While, of course, Inna yearned to see Naum again, it was Lev who had so many years ahead of him and a young family to raise. It was Lev and her grandchildren to whom she wanted to give a future full of promise and freedom.

Joan Paris, a good friend of Teeny's, called me the next day. Her husband, Mark, was the head of the Soviet Desk at the U.S. State Department at that time, but both he and Joan knew the Meimans when Mark worked at the American Embassy in Moscow. Joan explained she had been in contact with Teeny after Inna died, and Teeny suggested she call me and ask if I would help pack Inna's belongings.

When I arrived at Inna's apartment the next day, Joan asked me to start with a desk in the living room. I found a collection of papers with handwritten pages of an English-language book Inna was working on. I also found a large envelope full of her photographs, so I took a pictorial tour of Inna's life. For the first time, I saw what Inna looked like as a young woman. There was one black-and-white photo of Inna with a group of men, dressed in suits and a few wore fedora-like hats. Inna was carrying flowers. On the back of the photo was written, "Parade, May 7, 1962." I loved the image of Inna—so young and healthy and confident—so I told Joan I would like to keep it and she said she was sure that would be fine.

There were also recent photographs of Naum and his family, and her sister Olga and her family. Then I saw a photo of me. It was the one I sent her after I ended my hunger strike in January 1986. I was posing in front of an ice castle built for the St. Paul winter carnival. I held the picture for a moment and then put it back with the others.

In another drawer, I found a notebook. On the first page Inna had written about her departure from the airport in Moscow:

Sheremetyevo
Empty place, young guards with wolfish eyes, trying to be indifferent and appeasing. Donna [the American ambassador's wife] and Kathy [a nurse from the American embassy who traveled with Inna to Vienna] near me all the time, trying to protect me from any casualty, but doing it in such a graceful, gentle way that I don't feel frightened at all.

Young friends, Lenya, Katya, Zhanna, and Marina; good friends, Flora and Misha Litvinov; and my closest ones: Lev, Marina, Vova. Naum. All the faces are blurred, everyone close to tears.

I break down behind the barrier, looking back is unbearable. Seeing them all is more than a human heart can really stand. All my life behind me.

I went to the bedroom and looked in the closet. I searched the pockets of the coat I had given her. There were a few Soviet coins in one and a guest booklet from the hotel where she stayed in Vienna. In the other, there were three bookmark-sized pieces of paper. On each was a drawing of a little girl with long, black hair, the sun shining above her. (Years later I learned the artist was one of Inna's granddaughters, then-five-year-old Leah Kitrossky.) I remembered Inna telling me that whenever she took a cab with her three grandchildren, they would always ask, "Babushka, are we going to Israel today?" And she had finally been able to answer, "Yes, I am leaving the Soviet Union today."

I turned around and saw a bag of saltlike mineral that Inna told me came from a man from Siberia. He said it cured him of cancer, so she tried it and deemed it worthy to bring to the United States. "Joan, what are we going to do with that? She brought it all the way her with her, we shouldn't just throw it away," I said.

"I know, Lisa, I will send it to Rimma Bravve in New York."

On the end of the couch, opposite the end where Inna sat when she died, was the rainbow-colored potholder. I picked it up and held it to my face, breathing in the pungent smell of medicinal oint-ment—breathing in the smell of Inna.

"Lisa," Joan said, noticing I was holding the potholder, "Teeny and I couldn't figure out what that was. Inna always had it near her. When Teeny asked her where she got it, her face beamed with a smile, and she answered, 'Lisa gave me this from her sister.'"

"What should we do with it now?" I asked.

"I think you should keep it."

So I did.

CHAPTER

The Ring

> Be happy and content
> and full of the joy of life.
> —Inna Meiman

There was a lot of media coverage surrounding Inna's death. A lengthy obituary and photograph of her was published in *The New York Times*. United Press International ran a story by Henry David Rosso on February 11, "Soviet Dissident Dies in U.S., Mate in U.S.S.R." It noted that the U.S. State Department had called on the Soviet government to allow Naum to attend her funeral and quoted State Department spokesman Charles Redman: "Her death thousands of miles from her loved ones makes it all the more fitting that her next of kin be allowed to leave the Soviet Union to attend her funeral. Her passing is mourned by the many department employees who came to know her through her valiant struggles against the ultimately incurable illness that gripped her body and through her equally courageous efforts on behalf of human rights in the Soviet Union." The article also quoted Warren Zimmerman: "On the phone with my wife, Inna seemed as usual, cheerful, but short of breath. Minutes later she died." He explained the cause of death was a blood clot formed by the cancerous tumor in her lungs.

Senator Simon gave this tribute: "Inna Meiman was admired throughout the world as a courageous woman with a noble spirit. She was a remarkable person, and she was my friend." It also noted that Simon sent a telegram to Naum in which he said, "Inna's death will not be ignored. The Soviet government cannot hold you any longer. The cruelty of separation and of Inna's passing can only be mitigated by permission for you to come to the West. Try to be strong and remember how many friends you have."

Senator Hart also paid his respects, saying, "Inna Meiman was a woman of intelligence and courage. Above all, she was a woman of great inner strength. That she died is tragic. That her husband and friends were not permitted by her side is outrageous. Inna Meiman lost a personal battle to cancer, but she won many more battles than she lost, and those she left unfinished we are determined to win in her memory."

There was also an editorial tribute to Inna titled, "And Force Unwilling Jews to Stay," published in the *Washington Post* on Sunday, February 15, and written by Marjorie Loory. Marjorie called me on Monday and explained she became friends with Inna when living with her husband Stu in Moscow from 1983–1986. Stu was the Moscow bureau chief for CNN during that time, and she informed me that Stu would like to interview me later that afternoon about Inna on *CNN World Report*, which I readily agreed to do.

Big plans were under way for the funeral service, which was going to be held at the Ohr Kodesh Congregation in Chevy Chase, Maryland on Tuesday, Febuary 17. There was speculation that Vice President George Bush was planning to attend, although he did not. I was very much removed from the events unfolding. The National Conference on Soviet Jewry and the Washington Jewish Community Relations Council were making all the arrangements. The director of the National Conference, Jerry Goodman, was selected to give the formal eulogy for Inna, and he asked Anne Garrels to say a few personal words about Inna. Jerry also asked me to be an honorary pallbearer, which I agreed to do.

Anne called me on Monday and asked if there was anything I would like her to say about Inna. I asked if Inna had ever told her the story about the little fish who dreamed of swimming freely in the daylight and she responded that Inna had and agreed it would be a perfect story for the memorial service.

I rode the metro to Bethesda and then rode in a cab through an affluent neighborhood to the synagogue. As I walked into the foyer, I immediately saw a simple wooden casket, with the Star of David carved into the front panel. It was so simple yet so beautiful. I wanted to stop and touch it, but did not know if that was permitted by Jewish custom, so I walked into the synagogue instead. There were a few television reporters and cameramen standing about, waiting for the service to begin. The chatter of people's voices and classical music coming from a harpist filled the air. There were at least one hundred people there, most dressed in black, and many of the men wore yarmulkes. While the atmosphere was somber and respectful, it was also filled with a social energy, which impressed me. After all, we mourners were not connected through common bonds to Inna, such as her family, job, or neighbors. We were strangers who had been united by her struggle.

At first, I didn't recognize anyone and felt self-consciously alone. Then a tall woman wearing a black wool coat and a hat with a black lace veil over her face walked up to me and put her hand on my shoulder. It was Olga, Naum's daughter. She told me she had been shocked to hear that Inna died. "I had just spoken to her the day before and told her I was making plans to visit her the next week. We had such a nice conversation. It is such a shame I never met her," she said sadly.

Joan and Mark invited me to sit in the front row with them and Sister Ann Gillen. While I hadn't met Sister Ann before, we had spoken on the telephone about a year earlier after her return from visiting Inna in Moscow with Rabbi Mittleman. She hugged me and told me how sorry she was for my loss. Olga and her husband Misha walked down the aisle with us and sat behind our pew.

We received word at the synagogue that Lev was granted a visa at the last minute and was expected to arrive shortly, so a decision was made to delay the service for him. People took turns at the podium reading psalms in Hebrew to fill the time.

Finally, after almost thirty minutes, those in charge decided we could not delay the service any longer. A rabbi from the congregation and another from the Washington Board of Rabbis officiated. After an opening prayer, Anne was introduced, and her words about Inna were very heartfelt and spirited. She mentioned me as one of Inna's closest friends and that I had suggested she tell the story about the little fish. Anne made the point that Inna had been swimming freely in the daylight long before she left the Soviet Union and that it was her great triumph to be free in America before she died.

When the service ended, I, as an honorary pallbearer, followed behind the casket. To my right a bright television camera light shone in my eyes. Then there was commotion at the doorway of the synagogue and a cameraman turned his lens in that direction, where a man who appeared to be about thirty years old was walking toward the casket. He looked as if he had just emerged from a Moscow subway. A brown Russian fur hat covered his head, and an unbuttoned tan jacket fell comfortably over a brown cotton dress shirt and brown corduroy pants. The expression on his face was serene as he walked up to the casket and touched it. Then this man, Inna's son, took his rightful place in the front of her casket and, in the most natural and dignified way, helped carry it out of the synagogue.[1]

As I walked outside behind the casket, Joan approached me and invited me to ride with her and Mark to the cemetery. We joined a

---

[1] Lev had received a Soviet travel visa the morning of February 16. He went directly to the OVIR, to the American embassy, and then to the airport, where he was met by his wife and his aunt, Olga, who gave him some money and a travel bag. He managed to get on a flight to London, spent the night there, and then flew on a Concorde jet to D.C. the morning of February 17. His childhood friend, Boris Yousen, who had immigrated to the States the year before and lived in New York, was instrumental in helping Lev get to D.C. Boris met Lev at Dulles airport when he arrived the next morning and drove him to the synagogue.

crowd that was gathered near the hearse. I saw Lev, who was standing about five feet away from me talking in Russian with a group of people. He caught my glance and walked over, extending his hand to shake mine. I wanted to hug him and cry, but we had only met once, briefly, so I did not feel it would be appropriate.

"Lisa, thank you. You did so much for my mother," Lev said softly to me in Russian.

"I was so lucky to know her," I responded, also in Russian. I was not in the habit of speaking Russian, so I stumbled as told him that I saw his mother often the last few weeks and that she was comfortable. Then a man, who seemed to know Lev very well, interrupted us. Lev confirmed that I would be at the cemetery and said he would see me there.

I was standing alone when a woman approached me. It was Joy Weber, who I had met briefly in the hospital. She told me she had been thinking about me since she heard the news about Inna and handed me a card.

"How are you holding up?" She asked compassionately.

"I'm doing fine," I answered, caught off guard by her apparent concern for me.

"It must be so difficult for you." All seemed to become quiet and still as Joy shed her kindness on me.

I noticed Joan and Mark motioning me to their car.

"Will you be at the cemetery?"

"Yes."

"Good, I will talk to you there," I said, and she patted me on the shoulder as I walked away.

Once I got in the car, I opened Joy's card and read it:

February 15, 1987
Dear Lisa:
We have not officially met, other than a moment in the hospital, but I offer you my deepest sympathy on Inna's death.

I think about you often, and while I can't fully understand the depth of your grief, I feel for you very much.

I met Inna and Naum in the Soviet Union in September. As I also am ill, we had a great deal to discuss. On my second visit, Inna showed me one of your letters and told me all about you. Since then I have often thought of you and your extraordinary dedication, especially on the day Inna arrived in D.C. While your relationship with Inna was unique, I hope that you do not feel too isolated in your sorrow, and that you have good friends who support and understand you.

While I was in Russia, Inna and Naum were married according to Jewish tradition in a Jewish ceremony. She used my wedding ring, but I needed it back to leave the country. My husband and I would be happy for you to have the ring; if you would like it, let me know.

Again, my heartfelt sympathy. I hope that you don't feel I am writing too personally, but I feel too connected to you through Inna's words to just sign a sympathy card. I'm returning to the Soviet Union in October and will visit Naum. If there's anything I can carry for you, I'd be happy to.

Warm regards,
Joy Weber

Joy's tender expression of sympathy released all the emotions that had been churning just below my surface all day: my love for Inna and immense sadness that she was gone, but most of all, a great joy that she had died with the dignity she had fought so long and hard for—that she had died living free.

The procession of twenty cars or so traveled through a Maryland suburb and then onto the Washington Beltway. It seemed that we had been driving for miles before we turned off in the southeast part of D.C. Three cars behind the hearse, we crept along a narrow street as if without direction. Finally we turned a corner and stopped at the gate of Chesed Shel Emes Cemetery, which was locked.

A fat man in a soiled white T-shirt and blue jeans with a hole in one knee walked out of a small, dilapidated house across the street and talked to the driver of the hearse. The man then opened the gate and the cars drove into the cemetery and came to a stop in a horseshoe formation along a circular road. People got out of their cars and walked to the south end of the cemetery, where the grave was located. It was then that I noticed the same man run up a hill ahead of us with two shovels and two other men; the grave had not yet been dug. I heard Lev comment, "That is okay. My mother was not ready to die anyway."

The crowd formed around Lev, and he took the opportunity to say a few words. In soft, broken English, he gave a beautiful tribute to his mother. He spoke about how strong she was all of her life, how she raised him alone from when he was a boy, and how she worked hard to be both parents to him. He talked about her struggle to leave the Soviet Union, for her right, as she said, to fight for her life and for human dignity. He also noted the gratitude she felt toward all the people who tried to help her. "Ambassador Zimmerman and his wife Teeny fought at the highest levels for my mother," he said, "Teeny was a good friend to my mother. And Lisa Paul went on a hunger strike for my mother. She was so amazed by this."

The man on the hill signaled in our direction, then he and his two helpers walked back to the house. A few minutes later the service began next to the gravesite. Lev stood front and center, next to a rabbi who led the group in beautiful and melodic Hebrew prayers. When the prayers stopped, Lev picked up a handful of frozen, clumpy dirt and tossed it in the grave on top of the casket. All of us who had gathered there with him took a turn doing the same, including me.

It was a cold and dreary gray day, and it all seemed utterly surreal to me.

I started walking down the hill with the crowd as it was disbanding when Joy approached me.

"Your card was so nice, thank you," I told her, my eyes blurred with tears.

"I hope you didn't think I was too personal in my note to you," she responded, "but Inna spoke so dearly about you when I visited her in Moscow. I feel like I know you."

"No, you weren't too personal," I assured her. "It was very kind of you." Then, in an attempt to make conversation, I asked her to tell me about Inna and Naum's Jewish wedding ceremony.

"An American rabbi whom I was traveling with performed the ceremony. The whole idea was suggested by good friends of Inna and Naum's in Moscow and they were there too. Naum was less enthused about it than Inna. She was very cheery and was enjoying it all very much.

"Before the ceremony, I learned that Inna and Naum never took the time to get a wedding ring for her because she did not consider it important. I thought it would be nice for them to have a ring for the Jewish ceremony, so I gave my wedding ring to Naum and told him he should give it to Inna to keep, and I would buy another one for me when I returned to the States. A week later, before I was to leave Moscow, I remembered I had declared that ring on my customs form when I entered the country and that I would have to account for it on my way through customs when I left. So, to my regret, I had to ask Inna to give me the ring back. Since that time, I have felt like the ring is Inna's and that I have been holding it for her. I had planned to give it to her when I visited her in the hospital, but she was distracted so that I never even thought about it. Lisa, my husband and I both want you to have the ring." Joy showed me the gold band on her finger.

"I don't know how I could possibly take it from you."

"Just please take it. I am certain Inna would want you to have it. It was hers, and now it's yours—so it's as simple as that," Joy said as she took the ring off her finger and put it in my hand. I felt Inna's presence so close, as if she was standing right beside me. I put the ring on my finger. As I looked at it on my hand, I remembered the words Inna wrote to me after my hunger strike: "Leeza, if I survive, we will be together; if not, then we will also be together—I will always be with you, believe me."

And in my soul, I know that to be true.

Epilogue

Within a few weeks of Inna's death, Lev was called into the visa office and asked if he still wanted to emigrate. He responded affirmatively, and, on May 6, 1987, he, his wife, Marina, and their three children, Leah, Elisheva, and Yosef, arrived in Israel. Shortly after, Lev changed his name to "Levi," and his wife Marina changed her name to "Miriam" in recognition of their Jewish origin. They had four more children: Inna-Shifra, Dina-Hasya, Gedalia, and Nechemia. The entire family continues to live in Israel, where four of the adult children have served in the Israeli army.[1]

Seven thousand seven hundred and seventy-six Jews were allowed to leave the Soviet Union in 1987—eight times more than in the few previous years combined.[2] A few were long-term and well-known refuseniks, such as Alexander Lerner, Vladimir Slepak, Josef Begun, and Ida Nudel, who was Inna's good friend.

In the first letter I received from Naum after Inna died, dated April 9, 1987, he wrote that he saw a photograph of her taken a few days before her death and was "amazed her face was so happy and calm and relaxed." He also noted he was very much aware of how much I did for Inna, how much I loved her, and that it "was a mutual feeling."

He was grim about his own situation, describing his health as poor and his life in Moscow since Inna's death as "absolutely intolerable." I was tormented by his continued confinement in the

---

[1] I established contact with Levi in January 2002 via an Internet search, and he immediately put me in touch with Inna's sister, Olga Fookson. She, her husband, Alex "Shura" Kister, and their two children, Ilusha and Emilia, emigrated from the Soviet Union in 1989 and ultimately settled in Highland Park, New Jersey. Within two weeks of my initial correspondence with Olga, she came to Milwaukee to see me, and we have been good friends ever since.
[2] Source: www.jewishvirtuallibrary.org/jsource/Judaism/fsuemig.html.

Soviet Union and remained active on his behalf. I wrote letters to U.S. officials and, on December 7, 1987, I marched on his behalf at the "Freedom Sunday for Soviet Jews," when approximately 250,000 people gathered on the National Mall in D.C. to demand that the Soviet Union open its gates for Jewish emigration.

Almost 20,000 Jews were permitted to leave the Soviet Union in 1988.[3] One of those, finally, was Naum.

On January 22, 1988, Simone Veil, a member of the European Parliament who had long been an advocate for the Meimans, called Naum from Paris to give him the good news that his visa was going to be issued. A *Washington Post* article, dated January 27, 1988, reported that, while elated by the news, Naum could not call it pure joy as it came too late: "If it had come on time, I believe Inna would be alive today."

He arrived in Tel Aviv just over a month later, on February 28, at the age of seventy-seven. His daughter Olga, whom he had not seen for over twelve years, was there to embrace him at Ben Gurion Airport. He accepted a position of professor emeritus at Tel Aviv University, where he continued his work in theoretical mathematics.

In April 1989, Naum came to the United States to lecture at various colleges and, fortunately, visited Washington, D.C., where I spent time with him. He was in good spirits, looked physically well, and was tan from his travels. Our conversation was generally lighthearted and mostly in English as it was his preference not to speak Russian. He told me when his plane was landing in New York he thought about his life and years of struggle in Moscow and concluded that it took more effort to get him out of the Soviet Union than it had for Americans to send a man to the moon.

---

[3] By the time of the collapse of the Soviet Union in 1991, over almost a half million Jews emigrated, an amount that would double by 1997. Source: www.jewishvirtuallibrary.org/jsource/Judaism/fsuemig.html.

He enthusiastically described his travels to Texas, Boston, and Montreal, remarking that "God must have been in a favorable mood when he created Northern California." The highlight of his trip was Boulder, Colorado, where he saw his daughter, Olga, son-in-law, Misha, and, for the first time, his grandson, Yegor.

He did not ask me questions about Inna's time in D.C., so I did not approach the subject. When he mentioned that he had been to her grave he spoke in Russian and his voice became quiet.

My letters to him when he returned to Tel Aviv went unanswered. Nancy Traver, with whom he stayed in D.C., told me he regretted not immigrating to the United States where he could be close to his family, but he accepted his decision and would not change it.

Naum died in Tel Aviv on March 31, 2001, at the age of eighty-nine. A five-page obituary published in the journal *Uspekhi Mat. Nauk* summarized the final years of his life:

> [Meiman's] long fight for permission to leave was supported by many prominent Western scientists and ended only in 1988, when democratic perestroika and the disintegration of the USSR solved the problem automatically. Unfortunately, age and the years of exhausting struggle had taken their toll. In Israel, Meiman felt quite lonely, despite the warm reception that was given him and his post of honorary professor. To his final days he had a lively interest in science and events in Russia, to which he reacted with great emotion. . . . In the memory of those who knew Naum, he remains a brilliant, encyclopedically educated person, ready to help at a difficult moment, and firm in his convictions.[4]

[4]   D. V. Anosov,   V. L. Ginzburg,   A. B. Zhizhchenko,   M. I. Monastyrskii,   S. P. Novikov, Ya. G. Sinai, M. A. Soloviev, "Naum Natanovich Meiman (obituary)," *Uspekhi Mat. Nauk*, 57:2(344) (2002), 179–184.

Naum's daughter, Olga, and her husband, Misha, continue to live in Boulder. Their son Yegor and his wife, Annie Zhu, have two sons: five-year-old David and six-month-old Aaron. Olga is a successful artist in a style that integrates Russian artistic heritage with American freedom in classical still life.

꧁꧂

I have remained close to the Smiths over the years. In 1990, after five more years abroad—two in Geneva, Switzerland, and three in Dubai in the United Arab Emirates—the family moved to Morton, Illinois, near the international headquarters for Caterpillar Inc. Paul retired from Caterpillar in 1999 and, after twenty-six years away, he and Joan returned to their home state of Minnesota, where they live in a suburb of Minneapolis.

Kjirsten and her husband, Scott Wallace, live near Denver, Colorado, and have two children, Zachary and Olivia. Laura and her husband, Chris Lesinski, live in Minneapolis and also have two children, Kacie and Cameron. It was a special thrill for me when my daughter, Catherine, was a flower girl in Laura's wedding in 2003.

꧁꧂

On May 9, 1987, I started to dial the international operator in order to call Natasha on her birthday only to realize a call from me would cause her trouble. I put the phone down and cried. At that time, I had no remaining American contacts in Moscow who could hand deliver my letters to my Russian friends, so this marked the end of my communication with them.

When the Soviet Union collapsed at the end of 1991 and the coast was clear to call Moscow, I had forgotten the code in which I wrote my Russian friends' telephone numbers in my pocket-size Russian dictionary. The code was a protective measure in the event my dictionary was ever confiscated by Soviet authorities. Unfortunately, by 1992, I couldn't remember whether I had written the numbers with each digit higher or lower. I tried several variations, but each unfamiliar voice answered, "*Vy ne tyda papali.*" I had the wrong number. (Because corresponding by mail was not an option when I left Moscow, I did not have any of their mailing addresses either.) Defeated and heartbroken, I gave up trying to contact them and do not know what has become of them.

In 1992, when I was looking through one of my journals from Moscow, I discovered a piece of paper on which Vera had written her mother's address in Germany. I immediately wrote to Vera, in care of that address, and in July of that same year I received a letter from her full of news. She emigrated to Germany in 1986, had not married, and was training to be an artist. The information she provided about Galya was much more detailed:

> About six years ago she met a very nice man, she fell in love with him, and they married, and they had a son. But after two years, her husband died by a tragic death. She then lived with her mother, Vicka Chalikova, and they brought up the child. The death of Galya's husband was a terrible blow for them.
>
> Vicka became quite well known as a writer; she wrote many articles and delivered lectures. I think you will remember that Vicka was an energetic woman despite her stomach trouble. She soon got stomach cancer, but the doctors did not diagnose the disease in time and it was too late for an operation.
>
> Vicka was able to travel to Hamburg for a second opinion, but the doctors agreed that it was too late to operate. Soon after, Vicka passed away.

Vera went to Hamburg for the burial and described Galya as "brave and quiet, with her son standing by her side." Today, Vera lives in Munich, and Galya and her son live in Moscow.

When Larisa Bogoraz died on April 6, 2004, at the age of seventy-four, several international newspapers carried her obituary. *The New York Times* acknowledged her as a "legend of the Soviet dissident movement," and quoted Lyudmila Alekseyeva, her friend and Moscow Helsinki Group colleague, as saying she was "a moral influence since the beginning of the human rights movement and her influence defined the course of this whole movement." Her son, Daniel, from her first marriage to Yuli Daniel, described her as "an inexhaustible source of liberty."[5]

Perhaps the most significant tribute to her was an article, "Larisa Bogoraz's Cause Has to Be Kept Alive," which appeared in the *Moscow Times* the day after she died. It was written by Yevgenia Ablast, who was then the host of a political talk show. He described her as "from the cohort of dissidents who lived by the principle 'I cannot remain silent,' one of those stoics of the Soviet and post-Soviet period, for whom the rights of the individual came before all else—even her own freedom."

Tragically, Larisa's husband, Anatoly Marchenko, died on December 8, 1986, at the age of forty-eight in the hospital prison in Chistopol, five hundred miles away from Moscow. His death was the result of a three-month-long hunger strike, the goal of which was the release of all Soviet prisoners of conscience. Larisa was not allowed to bring his body back to Moscow for burial, so she, with their son Pavel and a few friends, traveled to Chistopol. His grave was marked by a simple pine cross on which Larisa wrote his name in ballpoint pen.

Marchenko had spent a total of twenty of his forty-eight years in prison, ultimately sacrificing his life for the cause of human rights in the Soviet Union. The international outcry over his death was the major catalyst of General Secretary Mikhail Gorbachev's decision to finally release Andrei Sakharov from seven years' inter-

---

[5] Source: www.kdhpg.org/en; April 27, 2004, quoting *The Kharkov Group for Human Rights biography of Larisa Bogoraz*, April 7, 2004, written by Aleksandr Daniel, her son from her first marriage.

nal exile in Gorky on December 20, 1986, and the large-scale release of political prisoners in 1987.[6]

I hope the echo of Marchenko's dissent reverberates through generations of Russians to come.

_⸰⸰_

Irina Grivnina, her husband, Voldja, and their daughters, Masha and Jana, continue to live in Amsterdam, where they were welcomed in October 1985 after being expelled from the Soviet Union. They became Dutch citizens in 1989. Irina is the author of several books, a journalist, and freelance translator (Dutch into Russian). Masha, a successful photographer, is married and has two young sons. Jana is a student at the University of Amsterdam.

_⸰⸰_

Each of Inna's four original fellow members of The International Cancer Patients Solidarity Committee made it to North America for medical treatment. Much of the information that follows was provided by Dr. Gerald Batist, Chief of Oncology at McGill University in Montreal. He helped establish the committee, knew each member personally, and played indispensible roles as the committee's medical adviser, devoted advocate, and liaison to family members in the West.

Rimma Bravve, who suffered from ovarian cancer, was the first to be granted permission to leave the Soviet Union, arriving in December of 1985 in Rochester, New York, where her mother, Khanna Anbinder, and sister, Larisa Shapiro, lived. She received treatment at Strong Memorial Hospital in Rochester for several months. Unfortunately, it came too late, and she died on June 23, 1987, at the young age of thirty-two.

Tatyana Bogomolny arrived on November 11, 1986, in San Francisco, where her father and sister lived. She was forty-seven

---

[6] The source for this biographical information on Marchenko is: http://en.wikipedia.org/wiki/Anatoly_Marchenko (September 2011).

years old. Her husband, Vinyamin, was allowed to emigrate with her, thus ending his record-setting twenty-year wait—the longest of any Jewish refusenik. When Tatyana arrived in the United States, her cancer was in remission, and her prognosis for recovery was positive. My attempts to find out her fate, via research and contacting several people with the last name of Bogomolny, were unsuccessful. I like to believe she is alive and well today.

Leah Maryasin was sixty-one when she arrived in Toronto with her husband, Alexander, in February 1987. She received treatment at Toronto General Hospital for malignant tumors, but as was the case for Inna and Rimma, the treatment was too late. She died within six months of her arrival.

Benjamin Charny was the last member of the committee to receive permission to emigrate. After a nine-year struggle to leave the Soviet Union, he arrived in Boston on July 17, 1988, with his wife, Yadviga. They joined their daughter, Anna Charny-Blank, and Benjamin's younger brother, Leon, who had been very active on his behalf. Benjamin, who suffered from malignant melanoma and heart disease, underwent three operations in Boston. He moved to San Diego in 1994 and became a U.S. citizen a year later. He died from both health conditions at age fifty-nine on January 31, 1997.

As Dr. Batist so poignantly stated in one letter to me: "All that was done to bring the plight of Soviet cancer patients to the world's attention helped point out the absolute moral corruption of the Soviet government—if it could treat cancer patients in the manner it did, it simply had no moral or compassionate legitimacy."

⁓

I first wrote this story down in 1988, when it was all so fresh in my mind and my heart. My journals, correspondence, and newspaper articles provided a contemporaneous account of all that I had experienced during the previous four years. My purpose in doing so was personal and, over the years, I infrequently—but never seriously—entertained the notion that I should try to publish the story.

I returned to Wisconsin in 1990 to attend Marquette University Law School, from which I graduated in 1993. I got married in 1995 to Ross Puppe. Our first daughter, Catherine, was born in 1999 and our second daughter, Jamie, in 2003.

Then, in April 2007, I saw the German movie *The Lives of Others* and it changed everything for me. As the film credits rolled, I realized that if a story about the omniscient power of the East German police could so effectively demonstrate why countries that have gained their freedom from communist rule must preserve it, then the story of Inna could surely do the same.

My initial surge of ambition to publish the manuscript I had written almost twenty years earlier was, however, derailed by challenges in my own life, especially the decline of my parents' health. My father died in June 2006, just six weeks after being diagnosed with lung cancer. Only six months earlier, we moved my mother—who was in the final stages of Alzheimer's—to a nursing home.

As witnessing the gradual yet complete destruction of my mother became unbearable to me, all that I had learned from Inna about courage, perseverance, and, most of all, hope gave me the strength I needed to get through that seemingly impossible time. And when my mother finally died in November 2008, those lessons helped me emerge from the darkness of my grief into the daylight of my life. Born from that daylight was the determination to write Inna's story in the way in which it needed to be told and to do everything possible to get it published. My hope is that the indelible lessons Inna taught me about optimism, courage, and the unbreakable human spirit will inspire others to stay in the daylight of their lives even during the darkest times.

Inna

Wasn't it yesterday
you were here
real in my life
you are gone now
leaving my heart
full of memory
will never forget
the way you lived
your life
how strong your fight
bravely you dared
an inspiration
you will be
unending
inspiration
to me.

Lisa C. Paul
February 27, 1987

Acknowledgments

My gratitute to the many people who made this book possible is great and will never diminish.

For their early and important endorsements, I thank Anne Garrels, Nancy Traver, Judith Kalb, Gary Hart, Barbara Frey, Alan Mittleman, and Micah Naftalin.

I am grateful for the support and encouragement I have received along the way: Paul and Jo Ellen Abbott, Tom and Carrie Abbott, Janet Brown, Catherine Zeppa, Vivian Fusllio, Jenny Kopetsky, Mary Jo Williams, Dotti Piotrowski, Julie Van Kirk, Amy Scovil, Teresa Conboy, Michelle Zook, Steve Feinstein, Mort Ryweck, Joy Weber, Jim Hammons, Rhonda Frederick, Mary McLean, Amy Bayer, Julie Rausch, Geri Pitroski, Janet Heins, Brenda Lewison, Sandy Radtke, Jeralyn Wendelberger, Larraine McNamara McGraw, John Weigelt, Dawn Capilupo, Julie Coenen, Debbie Dougherty, Pat Hackel, Lisa Hansen, Lisa Schmitting, Kim Peters, Mary Ann Renz, Joy Puppe, my colleagues at the Greg Cook and Will Techmeier law firms, and my friends in Shorewood.

For contributing crucial facts to this book, thank you to Leonid Stonov, Gerald Batist, Inna Grivnina, Levi and Miriam Kitrossky, Misha Plam, and to Joe Peschio for his transliteration work.

My special thanks to Monessa Overby, for giving me wings; Ann Wittman and Carolyn Kott Washburne for their confidence in my ability to write this story and their skilled editing work; Olga Fookson, for her insight and compassion; Judy Lauwasser Bruett, who never let me lose sight of the daylight; Greg and Kathie Guroff, who have been friends, mentors, and family to me both then and now; to Ellen Kort, for always believing with me in miracles; Jane Cliff for going the extra mile for me; and to Marguerite Wapneski for being there for me when my mother no longer could be.

I am indebted to Kathryn Mennone for recommending my book to Skyhorse, and to Jerry Benjamin for the essential role he played in bringing this story to light.

Thank you, Julie Matysik, my dedicated and talented editor, who worked so hard for and with me, and to Tony Lyons for giving me the opportunity of a lifetime.

I can't even find the words to thank the Smiths—Joan and Paul, Kjirsten (Wallace), and Laura (Lesinski).

Whether nearby or far away, I have always felt the love and support of my entire family, especially my sisters, Therese Barry-Tanner and Julie Marten; my brothers, Tom Paul and Jerry Paul; and of my parents, Helen and Jerry Paul, who were with me every step of the way.

It is pure joy to thank my daughters, Jamie and Catherine Puppe, for inspiring me—on a daily basis—with their energy and love; and my husband, Ross Puppe, without whom I would not have realized this dream.

And, finally, I thank God from whom all these blessings flow.